Trust and Power

Trust and Power

Niklas Luhmann

Edited, with a revised translation and new introduction,
by Christian Morgner and Michael King

Original translation by Howard Davis, John Raffan
and Kathryn Rooney

polity

First published in German as N. Luhmann, *Vertrauen* (1973, Ferdinand Enke Verlag, Stuttgart) and N. Luhmann, *Macht* (1975, Ferdinand Enke Verlag, Stuttgart)

Current German copyright: © 2012/2014, UVK Verlagsgesellschaft mbH, Konstanz/Germany

First English edition published as N. Luhmann, *Trust and Power* © 1979, John Wiley and Sons Limited (Translated by Howard Davis, John Raffan and Kathryn Rooney. Edited by Tom Burns and Gianfranco Poggi)

Polity Press
65 Bridge Street
Cambridge CB2 1UR, UK

Polity Press
101 Station Landing, Suite 300
Medford, MA 02155, USA

ISBN-13: 978-1-5095-1945-3

A catalogue record for this book is available from the British Library.

Library of Congress Cataloging-in-Publication Data

Names: Luhmann, Niklas, 1927-1998, author.
Title: Trust and power / Niklas Luhmann, Michael King, Christian Morgner.
Other titles: Vertrauen. English
Description: English edition. | Malden, MA : Polity, 2017. | Includes
    bibliographical references and index.
Identifiers: LCCN 2017006403 (print) | LCCN 2017037391 (ebook) | ISBN
    9781509519477 (Mobi) | ISBN 9781509519484 (Epub) | ISBN 9781509519453
    (pbk.)
Subjects: LCSH: Social interaction. | Trust. | Power (Social sciences)
Classification: LCC HM1111 (ebook) | LCC HM1111 .L84 2017 (print) | DDC
    302--dc23
LC record available at https://lccn.loc.gov/2017006403

Typeset in 10 on 11.5 pt Palatino by
Servis Filmsetting Ltd, Stockport, Cheshire
Printed and bound in the United States by LSC Communications

For further information on Polity, visit our website: politybooks.com

Contents

Niklas Luhmann's Sociological Enlightenment and its Realization in *Trust* and *Power*

Christian Morgner and Michael King

Sociological Enlightenment

Those engaged in the discipline of sociology, as it has evolved in English-speaking countries, may be forgiven if they have had some difficulty in recognizing these two books as bearing any close resemblance to what they have come to know as sociological research. After all, they make no attempt to apply established and respected empirical research methods to uncover facts about the ways in which people trust or exercise power, and to provide causal explanations for such facts. On the theoretical level, Luhmann's account may also appear strangely lacking in explanations of human social behaviour that would be amenable to testing through research in the way that Karl Popper recommended as marking the difference between science and non-science. Luhmann offers no explanations as such, but presents descriptive accounts of processes, using a conceptual framework that he himself has created. Yet, despite all this, Luhmann insists that the task he has undertaken is well and truly sociological, and rightly so, as this introduction will explain.

For Luhmann, the serious problems of fragmentation and credibility faced by the social sciences today can be traced back to the European Enlightenment of the seventeenth and eighteenth centuries. The old certainties – the belief in the capacity of human intelligence to develop a transcendental rationality, and the idea of infinite progress through this increased knowledge – seemed to work well for a time as a self-description of intellectual human endeavour. Where sociology was concerned, however, Luhmann saw this quest for truth and progress as an unfortunate starting point. It did not lead, as it was expected to do, to increased knowledge opening the way to a better world. Instead what has emerged is a multitude of coexisting theories and hypotheses which give the impression of employing reliable scientific methods, but which depend ultimately for their validity on the particular belief

about human nature that the particular sociological observer subscribes
to.

If sociology is to achieve its potential as a science, what is needed,
according to Luhmann, is a new kind of enlightenment – a sociological
enlightenment – one that rejects the unsustainable beliefs of 'old Europe'
by devising a totally new way of understanding what society consists of
and how it could be studied. This is the *Soziologische Aufklärung* (sociological enlightenment). Moreover, for Luhmann, sociology is uniquely
placed to enlighten society about itself. 'Sociology is enlightenment',
he explained, 'when it observes society in a manner different from the
way society in its different milieux observes itself.'[1] This is also meant to
enlighten sociology itself by establishing a theoretical vocabulary that is
on the one hand much more capable of grasping the complexity, eventful-
ness and ambiguities of social life, but on the other hand much more rigorous and encompassing in its approach. This puts emphasis on probing
and challenging established patterns of thinking by comparing and
relating them to, and contrasting them with, one another. Society is not
seen as a natural outcome of human action, but as an improbable result of
contingent events. Luhmann is here particularly interested in how these
improbabilities are transformed into systems of meaning-generating
communications. These are the generalized media of communication, of
which trust and power are but two examples. The next stage, the embryos
of which are visible in *Trust* and *Power*, but which is not fully developed
until his later works on different social systems, is to observe how, within
each system itself, the capacity evolves for constructing its own unique
version of its environment, so that one is left with not just one overriding version of what society accepts as truth and reality, but with several
versions, which coexist uneasily and which continually re-establish their
own identity through developing new ways of accommodating the versions of reality produced by other systems. This, for Luhmann, is what
both typifies modern society and makes classical, Enlightenment-based
sociology so ill-equipped to capture the complexity of that society.

However, Luhmann would not have been Luhmann had he not added
an ironic twist to the notion of circularity or self-reference, whereby within
each system events are explained in terms of pre-existing assumptions of
what constitutes truth and reality. 'Of course, sociology', he writes, 'is
nothing but a milieu of its own.'[2] So, as a result of this new sociological
enlightenment, the uniquely sociological way of observing society necessarily and inevitably becomes yet another 'milieu', another system which
observes society observing society itself. But at least this time the starting
point is exclusively sociological, rather than based on moral beliefs or,
as Luhmann puts it, ethical concerns, and at least this time the language,
concepts and methods that it deploys are rigorous and sociological.
Luhmann further explains that if sociology wants to see itself as a 'critical'
science it cannot simply interpret itself as an opposition science that takes

sides in the dispute between progressive and conservative ideologies.[3] This can only lead to a failure to reflect upon the unity of the difference. A 'critical' project would mean that sociology is in a position to distinguish and is able to reflect upon the use of its distinctions. In his short, enigmatic Preface to *Trust*, Luhmann takes a little further his explanation of the nature of this project. He provides an account of how one should distinguish his new approach to societal analysis from what he sees as the ideologically committed sociological thinkers whose work was influential in Germany at the time he was writing his book.[4] He identifies what he sees as 'the disadvantages' that can arise from importing into sociology 'terms and concepts from daily usage concerning the traditional world of ethical ideas'. These disadvantages predominate where this 'introduction of the moral into sociological concepts' takes the form of a 'critical demolition and surprising presentation of the familiar in unfamiliar ways or of unmasking ideological beliefs'. Clearly this is a mild but direct attack on members of the Frankfurt School who were indeed engaged in producing a version of sociology which involved investigations of what Luhmann regarded as moral issues and, in many instances, a commitment to one particular side in the moral debate. In the aftermath of the overthrow of National Socialism in the Second World War, this, for Luhmann, was indeed 'an easy trick to perform'. Luhmann ends his Preface by telling his readers a new kind of sociology, one that does not rely on moral implants but instead seeks 'to establish its intellectual position in positive terms by *formulating a theory of its own*'.[5] Only once this has been established, he remarks, might it be advantageous to enter into a dialogue with those morality-based understandings of the world.

As we have already noted, Luhmann made it clear in the *Soziologische Aufklärung* essays that he wrote at around this time that the task of his systems approach to functional analysis would be to offer a theory which would allow sociology to identify the concepts and processes that increase the likelihood of people acting together in communal ways and of these interactions repeating themselves in a way that provides stability for the participants. As Luhmann explains, 'Functional analysis is not a matter of establishing connections between established reasons or reliable knowledge in order to generate secondary knowledge.' Rather, 'Problems are posed in terms of the maintenance of stability of action systems.'[6] What then are these 'systems' and what is their role in Luhmann's theory?

The Meaning of Systems

Luhmann uses the term 'systems' in a very specific way – a fact that is very often missed by those who wish to classify him as a systems theorist in the traditional sense.[7] Early anthropological and previous functionalist theories understood systems through the existence of networks of people and describe the ways that individuals or groups of individuals, who are seen as belonging to the same organization or institution, relate to one another. The identification of a system and its description rely for their validity on the assumption of naturalism in the social world. Social systems exist naturally in society just as physical systems exist in the natural world. This makes it possible for observers of social systems to capture reality through unproblematic descriptions of what they are and what they do. In a similar way, people can be seen as belonging to a system. Judges, therefore, are part of the legal system, for example, and psychiatrists part of the medical system. Yet these predominantly naturalistic principles fail to capture the idea of the system as developed by Luhmann. Within his theory, systems are not simply parts of the natural world or extensions of physical entities. They are not subject to laws and logic governing their operations, the discovery of which increases the possibilities for control and improvement.

In contrast to these naturalistic accounts of systems, modern systems theory, as represented by, for example, Ludwig von Bertalanffy, Ralph Gerard, Kenneth Boulding and Anatol Rapoport, advances the idea that systems are open because they have external interactions.[8] In sociology, the most prominent author associated with this systems theory thinking is Talcott Parsons. Parsons presents a theory that attempts to understand system structures in terms of the functions they serve in the maintenance of structural patterns and how this persistence of the system could be explained through different variables. This systems theory received considerable criticism. According to the critics, human beings are seen as being reduced to mere tokens within a structure over which they have no control. Impersonal systems appear to be more powerful than individuals. Moreover, systems are not open to change, because their maintenance is necessary for the maintenance of society and social institutions and they are not open to deviant behaviour or fringe groups. It is clear that these criticisms were based not purely on scientific principles, but to a substantial degree on ideological grounds. This is something that we shall take up later in our introduction.

Although Luhmann calls his theory a systems theory, it is conceptually far removed from the sociological Anglo-American tradition of systems theories. His notion of systems, one cannot over-emphasize, is 1) anything but metaphysical or analytical, and 2) not concerned with structural maintenance, but with highly dynamic meaning-making. Firstly, Luhmann's conception of the system is not an analytical construct; systems are real-world empirical phenomena. His often quoted statement from the first chapter of his book *Social Systems*, 'The following considerations assume that there are systems',[9] does not mean that systems have an essence-like existence making them readily amenable to identification, description and research. Rather, as he states, '*the concept of systems refers to something that is in reality a system* and thereby incurs the responsibility of testing its statement against reality'.[10] In other words, Luhmann assumes that the reproduction and redundant formation of systems is an empirical reality. He therefore wants to devise sociological concepts whose validity ultimately depends on there being a reality against which they can be tested. He is seeking a close connection with empirical research that can be directed by those concepts. For instance, it is well known that Luhmann refers in his systems theory not to people, but to networks of communications. This does not mean that social systems could exist without people (or psychic systems), but that the meaningful reproduction and determination of meaning is a self-referential process determined by subsequent sequences of communication rather than by the will of individual human beings, the concerted efforts of groups of human beings, or some external force. Luhmann's notion of meaning has often been overlooked or misinterpreted, with the result that his insistence on systems of communication rather than people has been seen as anti-humanist or as evidence that he simply and wilfully ignored the importance of people. This is a fundamental misreading of Luhmann's intentions.

Secondly, Luhmann's systems theory is concerned with highly dynamic meaning-making in a complex world. Meaning-making cannot be grasped through the older models of systems theory that relied on presuppositions that defined in advance what the world is, as, for instance, in Parsons' assumption of an a priori integration through values and norms. Luhmann suggests that such an external position of an observer is not possible, because every observer is already part of this process of meaning-making. Luhmann's opening statement, citing Spinoza, to his *Theory of Society* acknowledges this direction: 'That which cannot be conceived through anything else must be conceived through itself.'[11] Meaning is not determined through an external structure (values or people), but meaning determines meaning. It is this self-referential dynamic of the term 'system' that Luhmann is interested in, or what he called 'a system that unfolded an intellectual dynamic all of its own, which is among the most fascinating phenomena that we are able to witness today'.[12] It is this new paradigm of the system that has led to a '"meaningful" revolutionization of the theory of society'.[13] This means that systems and communications relate to, and only to, the organization of meaning. They should not be understood as objects but *as observations and only as observations*. These observations in turn should not be understood as facts or objects 'but as boundaries, as markings of differences'.[14] An observation can be defined as both a distinction and an indication: something is distinguished, as an object or a subject, from something else and, through this distinction, it is indicated. For instance, the government can be distinguished *through observation* from its opposition, what is lawful can be distinguished from what is unlawful *only through observations*, and these observations, once made, allow for subsequent operations to make distinctions based on the distinctions government/opposition and lawful/unlawful. Observations, then, are not vehicles but the very operations that constitute a system. 'The system can constitute operations of its own only further to operations of its own and in anticipation of further operations of the same system.'[15]

At the level of society, these then are Luhmann's function systems. They are functional systems because they cope with the generation of specific meanings over time. These concepts of systems and function are quite unlike the notions inherent in traditional systems theory, including that of Talcott Parsons. The 'functional analysis' Luhmann undertakes in *Trust* and *Power* is not a matter of making connections either between systems of people or between bodies of existing knowledge, but of examining how precarious meaning-making and its identity, which allows the formation of society, emerges from the relation between system and environment in a complex world.

In *Trust*, and to a lesser extent in *Power*, Luhmann describes the way that social systems are able to solve a very specific problem for society – that of stabilizing communications over time. As he writes in Chapter 2 of *Trust*, '[a] theory of trust presupposes a theory of time'. There follows a fascinating discussion concerning the two ways of identifying time – either as a series of events or as a constancy, 'a continuously actual present, with the future always in prospect and the past flowing away'. Since trust can only be secured and maintained in the present, 'the basis of all trust is an enduring continuum of changing events, as the totality of constancies where events can occur'. For Luhmann, the problem of trust (as for all social systems) lies in the fact that 'the future contains far more possibilities than could ever be realized in the present and transferred to the past'.[16] This places an excessive burden on people, who risk being frozen into immobility or indecisiveness by the prospect of a wholly uncertain future or, as Luhmann puts it, 'this everlastingly over-complex future'. Nothing could be planned or calculated in advance. If one distinguishes *future present* (the future that will become the present) from *present future* (the future as seen in the present), one can understand how the discrepancy between them – a discrepancy brought about by unanticipated future events which change the *present future* – needs to be resolved for decisions to be made and projects put in motion. Trust, therefore, 'is one of the ways of bringing this about'. It does so by reducing complexity in a way that allows people to 'prune the future so as to measure up to the present … [i]t is an attempt to envisage the future but not to bring about future presents'.[17]

Where power is concerned, the problem of time takes on a somewhat different form. If it were not for the communicative system of power, it would be necessary for the threat of immediate violence to be continually present in order to bring about the 'avoidance alternative' that would keep the violence at bay and so achieve the desired result. The way that power is organized within the political system replaces and makes unnecessary the 'omnipresence of physical force'. This Luhmann refers to as 'temporalizing violence'. As he explains, '[p]hysical force is put in place as the *beginning* of the system, which leads to the selection of rules, whose function, rationality and legitimacy render them independent of past, initial conditions'.[18] Simultaneously it is portrayed as a '*future* event' which can be avoided, if one stays on the right side of those rules. Both time horizons – the initial threat of physical force and the future event that will trigger that force – are transformed into effective regulation through secondary coding by means of law. The system of power allows for a regulated present which is no longer dependent upon the immediate threat of violence and, perhaps even more importantly, cannot be controlled through violence.

The Historical and Sociological Context of *Trust* and *Power*

Trust and *Power* were originally published separately. The first edition of *Vertrauen* (*Trust*) appeared in 1968, followed by an extended edition in 1973. The book on *Macht* (*Power*) was published in 1975. Professor Tom Burns (d. 2001), at the University of Edinburgh, organized and arranged for the first translation of both books combined into one volume. The translation was undertaken by three Edinburgh postgraduate students with some knowledge of German. Both *Trust* and *Power* come from the pre-autopoietic period in Luhmann's work. Although Luhmann had already begun to elaborate his vision for a theory of society, his main theoretical terms gravitated around concepts like system, meaning (in the phenomenological sense), action, generalized symbolic media, and functionalism.

When Luhmann published the book on *Vertrauen*, the topic of trust was not much discussed within the wider social sciences.[19] The first edition of the book was written while Luhmann was working at the University of Münster Institute for Social Research, based in Dortmund. Founded in 1946 and focused on the economic restructuring of the Ruhr valley, it was seen as one of the key empirical and sociological institutes at that time in Germany. In the context of an empirical research environment and his growing theoretical ambition, Luhmann was struck by the 'statements about trust [that] are today still very far removed from being substantiated by methodologically valid means.'[20] The intention of the *Trust* book was therefore to progress with his theoretical project, but with an applied and empirical direction in mind.[21] The reader will notice that the book contains frequent references that point to further empirical research. Luhmann extended the book for the 1973 edition, which was the basis for the English translation in 1979. Luhmann's identification of trust in relation to complexity as being a social not just a psychological coping mechanism had an impact on several other influential sociologists in the Anglophone world.[22] As a sociological topic, trust has attracted increasing interest since the 1980s, but in that decade there were already signs of Luhmann's declining interest in the subject, despite a minor essay,[23] as well as a chapter in the book *Social Systems*.[24] In Luhmann's late work of the 1990s the issue has almost completely vanished, beyond sporadic remarks and footnotes. However, despite this visible attenuation, it seems that Luhmann did not regard the topic as irrelevant; rather, the shift can be attributed to more general changes in his theory. In the early writings, trust was strongly bound to the problem of reduction of complexity within an action-theoretical framework. These two elements (action and reduction of complexity) subsequently faded into the background or were displaced by later theoretical developments – as, for instance, in the transition to an emphasis on communication and observation – and the term *trust* was never fully reworked to reflect these later developments. Luhmann's *Social Systems* (1984/1995), which set the benchmark for terms like communication and autopoiesis, sought to combine trust with the problem of double contingency, but no integration of the concept of trust can be found in his subsequent works.

The book on power had a different origin. At the time it was published, Luhmann was already being appointed professor at the University of Bielefeld. Since the early 1960s, a number of studies in the wider field of systems theory that analysed the political system and related phenomena had been published.[25] These publications had received considerable criticism, however, for their neglect of the role of power. It seemed that the control abilities associated with the term system would define power out of existence. Luhmann was well aware of this debate and referred to it in the posthumously published *Macht im System* (Power in the System).[26] It seemed quite clear to him that this direction of systems theory would ignore empirical research and would not fit with his knowledge of the political milieu. He was therefore actively looking for a way to remedy this deficit of systems theory, and attempted to address the problem in a second book published posthumously, called *Politische Soziologie* (*Political Sociology*).[27] The original outline for this account of the political system included a planned chapter on power, but it was never written, nor did Luhmann attempt to integrate the smaller book on the subject into the final manuscript of nearly 500 pages. It seems that both posthumous publications, while written during Luhmann's pre-autopoietic period, remained unpublished during his lifetime because he was unhappy with their theoretical conclusions and their inability to account adequately for this aspect of social reality.

Published in 1975, the German text on *Macht* represents a first culmination of these enormous efforts. The book can be seen as the first application of the newly developed or developing theory of symbolic generalized communication media; in particular, it reflects Luhmann's growing interest in social communication as the unit of social systems. He notes that this theoretical change represents the most severe break with older theories of power. Power should simply be seen as a personal property or ability, but needs to be integrated into a theory that can account for a specific and meaningful steering of communication. The wealth of empirical research that informs this small publication is quite outstanding, covering topics including violence, conflict, the state, political parties, democracy, leadership, authority, terrorism and much more. In Luhmann's later writings communication became the defining paradigm of social systems, with power being one of the central topics that informed a range of later publications and culminating in the posthumous publication of *Politik der Gesellschaft* (*Politics as a Social System*),[28] in which power, communication, medium and social system are the central theoretical terms.

Functional Analysis and its Semantics

Luhmann's approach to empirical research bears little relation to the ethnographic studies, social surveys or observational reports that fill the pages of today's sociology journals. Both Luhmann's methods and the technical vocabulary he employs all flowed from the theoretical problems he set himself. While his eclectic research methods may not comply with the conventional, contemporary requirements for social science research, with its insistence on replication, testability and compliance with a recognized methodology, they are nevertheless empirical in that they rely on observations in the broadest sense of the term – both his observations and those derived from secondary sources. As we have mentioned, Luhmann does not subscribe to the view that sociological observers are in the business of capturing truth or reality. They rely, like all other observers of their environment, on a version of external reality that has been made possible through reduced complexity. Their observations will inevitably depend upon the presuppositions they bring with them about the nature of the phenomenon being observed. This will influence what they select to research and how they interpret their findings. The fact that other empirical sociologists accept these findings as valid does not mean that they correspond to some universal truth, just that they are true for those empirical sociologists. As Luhmann writes in *Power*, 'there are no independent foundations for empirical certainty'.[29] Reality is accessible only in a partial form through the selections of each observer, be they individuals or social systems. Scientifically validated research methods operate, like all prescriptive modes of observation, as filters which make selective aspects of reality accessible. As a general rule, the more rigorous the methods the narrower the aspect of reality that becomes accessible to the observer.

It is for this reason that Luhmann himself employs research methods that, as we have noted, are eclectic and multi-faceted, to say the very least. In these two books, he draws upon his own empirical research (with Renate Mayntz), his informal ethnographic observations obtained through his travels throughout the world, and his extensive knowledge of both classical Greek and Roman works as well as European and American literature across a wide range of disciplines, both historical and contemporary. As regards empirical scientific work, he refers throughout the two books to studies by sociologists, political scientists, criminologists, anthropologists and social and developmental psychologists. When he is not engaging with the ideas of other theorists and contrasting them with his own theses, he is constantly using the evidence provided by other people's work as an assurance that what he is describing is not just a figment of his own speculations.

Turning to Luhmann's semantics, we have already noted how important it was in his eyes to generate terms and concepts relating to society that were essentially sociological, rather than using those already in existence in daily usage with their moral overtones. His objective was not to produce an esoteric language shared only by social theorists, but to develop a language which was able to manage the new ideas created by the dynamism of his new enlightenment and its unique way of observing the world. The hope was that these terms, once created, would eventually provide a common vocabulary to enable communication to take place between different understandings of the social world. If one takes the physical sciences as a model, this is not too outrageous an ambition. For example, genetics has successfully created around the concept of 'the gene' a whole new theoretical language to describe the process of evolution, a language that has found its way into the legal and political spheres, allowing laws to be drawn up and policies to be formulated. The same is true of the concepts generated by quantum physics. New scientific discoveries have brought about the need to generate new terms, to find a new theoretical language in order that these new ideas can be communicated and discussed. Many of them have subsequently found their way into common parlance to the extent that the new reality that they create is treated by the communications media as factual knowledge. In seeking to develop a new conceptual language fit for the purpose of describing how society operates, Luhmann was not, in scientific terms at least, preaching revolution. Yet in relation to mainstream sociology, this was combined with his rejection of the prevailing narrative tradition, derived for the most part from anthropology – the 'telling of stories' to account for the way that people think about and act towards one another in social situations. This narrative technique, of course, had the added advantage of creating the expectation that anyone who had acquired a high level of literacy should be able to understand sociological texts. Luhmann's writings tended to confound this expectation.

Luhmann turns his back on the narrative form conceived as a way of making life easy for the reader. In *Trust* and *Power*, as in his many other books and essays, the way he develops his solutions to the problems he himself poses, and defends those solutions against criticisms that he himself deploys, is much more in keeping with the philosophical tradition, and in particular the Greek rhetorical tradition of argument and persuasion. He devotes each chapter of these books to his ideas around a particular topic. The chapters thus take the form of a series of linked essays. The books themselves are structured as a progression culminating in a final analysis which could not have been achieved if the arguments set out in the earlier chapters had not been fully discussed. Although each chapter may appear to the reader to be self-contained, only by reading the chapters in sequence is one able to grasp the full impact of Luhmann's theoretical position.

The Reception of Luhmann's Sociology in English-speaking Countries

The publication of the English versions of *Trust* and *Power* in 1979 was the very first time that any of Luhmann's books had appeared in English. *A Sociological Theory of Law* was to follow five years later, and *Love as Passion* in 1986. His major theoretical work *Social Systems* was published in the 1990s, as well as several other of his many books and articles. These publications reflect an initial burst of interest among English-speaking sociologists in Luhmann's new scientific, ideology-free sociology. This may even have given him some hope that the day of his sociological enlightenment was about to dawn. It is difficult to know in retrospect whether this early interest was driven by the novelty of Luhmann's ideas, contrasting sharply as they did with the critical stance taken by the Frankfurt School and the more naturalistic approach to social inquiry adopted by many American sociologists, or whether it was inspired by an admiration for Luhmann's apparent attempt to revive the nineteenth-century vision of a 'grand theory' of society. In any event, the years that followed saw a decline of interest in Anglo-Saxon countries, at least among sociologists. The result was that, in sharp contrast to, say, Habermas, Foucault or Bourdieu, only a fraction of his vast output was translated into English. Today, sociology, as it is taught and studied in English-speaking countries, appears either to ignore Luhmann entirely or is actively hostile to his theory. In both the UK and the US any reference to his works in the sociological literature is a rarity, and accounts of his theory are almost totally absent from the syllabuses and textbooks of academic undergraduate and postgraduate sociology courses.

Within these countries and Anglophone academia generally, Luhmann is much more likely to be included in law, political science, German literature, art, media and cultural studies or business management programmes than studied as a social theorist in sociology departments. Not surprisingly, there is a tendency among these non-sociological disciplines to treat Luhmann's writings selectively, in ways that throw light on their specific intellectual concerns, paying little or no attention to his vision of a sociological enlightenment or even to the general theory of communicative function systems that underpins all his accounts of the operations of different communications media and different social systems. There is little doubt that Luhmann was pleased to see his ideas influencing so many different academic fields. Yet the pay-off for such success has undoubtedly been a substantial decline of interest in his work within sociology, and in Anglophone countries an almost complete neglect of – and in some instances marked hostility towards – his general social theory. Significantly, in the five years before his death in 1998 he was much more likely to be invited overseas to speak at law conferences and seminars than at sociological or social theory events.

Various reasons have been put forward for the apparent failure of Luhmann's original and creative approach to the study of society to make any headway within Anglophone sociology. These include:

- The sheer abstractness and complex nature of the theory, which requires a considerable devotion of time and effort before it can be properly understood and applied. This makes it difficult both to study and to teach.
- The way that the theory describes how society exists and operates is entirely counter-intuitive. It runs contrary not only to all the self-descriptions of the roles played in social events and social evolution by all the main social systems, including politics, law, the mass media and science, but also to the accounts of reality that human beings have acquired through socialization concerning the world around them, their place in that world and their ability to change their environment and their own destiny. This applies to versions of society and social change offered by religions as well those inherent in secular beliefs about humanity and human destiny.
- The perception that, underlying Luhmann's theoretical notion of closed systems, there is a normative agenda for promoting the ideal of minimal state intervention. This plays into the hands of liberal conservative factions and antagonizes those academic thinkers who advocate the expansion of the welfare state as a means of promoting social justice and equality.[30]
- The portrayal of Luhmann among American theorists as 'a fully committed systems theorist', with all the naturalistic tendencies associated with that label. This leads to the view that Luhmann supports the view that systems are more important than the individual, with the reduction of complexity that systems achieve being seen as a restriction of the horizon of human possibilities.[31]
- The view that Luhmann's theory is anti-humanist in that it reduces human beings to mere objects within or semantic artefacts of social systems. We have already discussed how this misrepresents Luhmann's ideas, but the misinterpretation has not prevented some extreme ver-

sions of this criticism emerging and gaining credence among social theorists.[32]

• The difficulties in reconciling Luhmann's theory with the growing demand within sociology for empirical testing using accepted and accredited research methods.[33] We have already discussed this issue at some length in our section on 'Functional Analysis and its Semantics'.

• Luhmann's detachment throughout his academic career from any direct involvement in ongoing political or moral debates. No doubt he saw this lack of commitment to any policy agenda and unwillingness to make pronouncements on matters of public interest as necessary to protect his position as a social scientist. His trenchant warnings against ideologically motivated sociology were, after all, sustainable only to the extent that he himself remained aloof from all ideological concerns. Nevertheless, this aloofness appeared to have prevented him from gaining the popularity that was accorded to some other philosophers and social theorists, both European and Anglo-American, during the turbulent period immediately before and after the social upheavals of 1968. Choosing not to come out in support of radical social change was to risk being seen as someone who defended the existing social order. For example, Luhmann's theoretical observations on the relative impotence of 'New Social Movements' (*Ecological Communication* (1989)) and 'Protest Movements' (*Risk* (1993)) in changing the world tended to be interpreted as direct criticisms of these movements.

As one would expect, the factors that have been identified as accounting for the indifference of Anglophone sociology towards Luhmann's general theory of society are varied and complex. Those that can be attributed to his intricate style of writing or the form or nature of the theory itself do not on their own provide a sufficient explanation for the neglect or hostility that has led to its absence from sociology syllabuses in English-speaking countries. Many social theories are abstract and difficult to understand, but if they had been rejected on this basis, only the simplest, easiest to grasp, ideas about the social world would have gained any credence among sociologists. This is clearly not the case. Similarly, philosophers from Plato onwards have produced counter-intuitive ideas about society, the nature of reality, and the capacity of human beings to change the world around them, but this has not resulted in their rejection or prevented them from being studied and assessed on the basis of their contribution to understanding. To explain why Luhmann's ideas have had such little influence within Anglophone sociology, therefore, one needs to go beyond the features inherent in the theory or its elucidation and examine the interaction between those features, the perception of the theory among sociological scholars, the self-description of society, and the trajectory that sociology as an academic discipline has taken since the 1970s in English-speaking countries.

Much of that sociology is split along ideological lines. Peter Berger, the eminent American sociologist and author of *Invitation to Sociology*, calls this 'the ideologization of sociology'. 'The ideologues', who have been in the ascendancy for the last thirty years, he wrote in 2002:

> have deformed science into an instrument of agitation and propaganda, ... invariably for causes on the left of the ideological spectrum. The core scientific principle of objectivity has been ignored in practice and denied validity in theory. Thus a large number of sociologists have become active combatants in the 'culture wars,' almost always on one side of the battle lines.[34]

Berger sees this 'marxisant' antagonism to capitalism and bourgeois culture, and its combatant role for intellectuals, as evolving into a version of sociology that paved the way for divisions within the discipline which reflected the different identities of oppressed groups – feminist, ethnic, racial and gay – each with their own theories and research agendas and, eventually, their own sub-discipline within sociology.[35]

This combination of identity- and issue-driven sociology with a trend towards specialization within all academic disciplines has contributed in the present century to the fragmentation of sociology into many different 'sociologies'. Because of sociology's uncertain theoretical foundations – built on often conflicting ideological beliefs about the nature of society and the causes of social change – this trend towards fragmentation has been far more marked than in other scientific disciplines. The lack within the discipline of a common theoretical paradigm with a shared theoretical language – which, of course, Luhmann sought to promote – has made it impossible to prevent sociology's fragmentation.

Within the US and the UK the one unifying factor which allows those working from different presuppositions and within different fields of interest all to claim that what they are doing is 'sociological' has been that of empirical research methods. In addition to providing a common body of knowledge which unites all or almost all social scientists, sound methodology has been elevated to the status of a gold standard by which the validity of any piece of research should be measured. While the intention is clearly to align the social sciences with the natural sciences and avoid the kind of subjective, value-laden studies that have dogged sociology's reputation in the past, some would argue that this preoccupation with methods has gone too far. Peter Berger, for example, labels it 'methodological fetishism – the dominance of method over content'.[36] We would argue that it has also led to the dominance of method over theory and to unsustainable beliefs concerning the ability of methodologically sound research to capture reliable facts. Once again, Luhmann's theory, with its assertion that truth or reality are accessible only through the medium of social communication systems and its emphasis on the relative and limited nature of any one system's ability (even that of science) to provide incontrovertible knowledge, simply does not fit with the assumptions that lie behind this over-concern with methodology. By the same token, Luhmann's own eclectic approach fails to meet the standards required today by the guardians of social science research orthodoxy, making his own research at worst poor scholarship and at best an irrelevance for academic sociology as it is currently practised.

Today, the most complex modules in sociology courses tend to be those on research methods, with their emphasis on statistical testing and validation. After all, it is on the soundness of methodology and not on the grasp of theory that research grant applications are assessed and funds awarded. Social theory, by contrast, has been downgraded, because of the need to make it accessible to students as well as to grant-givers and policy-makers and relate it directly to current social issues. For this reason many social theories in recent years have tended to take on a narrative form, embracing ideas about social events and the nature of society that are prevalent within the mass media and popular culture. This notion of theory enhances a view of sociology as a body of knowledge that any reasonably intelligent and socially aware person can readily understand.

In short, for many different reasons, the sociological enlightenment that Luhmann offers simply does not fit the version of sociology that has evolved in the English-speaking world. Those, like us, who admire his work might argue that the decline in sociology from its heyday in the 1970s is due, at least in part, to its failure to pay sufficient attention to Luhmann's ideas for a general social theory. If sociologists had heeded the warnings set out in his Preface to *Trust*, to which we drew the reader's attention earlier in this introduction, perhaps things could have been different. Although we would not claim that Luhmann was prescient in identifying the intrusion of morality into sociological endeavours and the continued reliance by mainstream sociology on 'concepts taken from daily usage', or 'the everyday understandings of the world', the extension and acceleration of these trends, already apparent in the 1970s, have undoubtedly contributed to the decline of sociology.

Luhmann's general theory of society represents the road that sociology did not take back in the twentieth century. We would suggest that the road it did in fact take has not led to any fulfilment of its Enlightenment-inspired claims to 'understand society' and, through the generation of scientific knowledge, to make the world a better place. The vast majority of the predictions made through the acquisition of sociological knowledge have failed to materialize, and the social world in the year 2017 appears more unruly, out-of-control and precarious than has been the case for many generations. Perhaps the time has come for sociologists to abandon their misguided ideologization and their trust in methodology and to spend the time and effort required in studying Luhmann's complex ideas about the nature of society. If they do so there may be some hope that sociology can recover from its long decline and become once again a discipline that offers perspectives leading to understandings of the world that are not available elsewhere. It is just possible that by providing what we believe to be an accessible translation of Luhmann's books on *Trust* and *Power* we will have helped to begin this new search for enlightenment.

Notes

1 Cited in Baecker (1999), p. 9.
2 Cited in Baecker (1999), p. 9.
3 Luhmann (2013), p. 322. See also *Power*, chapter 3, section 11.
4 Particularly Husserl's with its 'worship of reason ... and a socially responsive human being'. Baecker (1999), p. 5.
5 *Trust*, p. 3, emphasis added.
6 *Trust*, p. 6.
7 See Murphy (1982).
8 See Weinberg (1975).
9 Luhmann (1995), p. 12.
10 Luhmann (1995), p. 12, emphasis added.
11 Luhmann (2012b), n.p.
12 Luhmann (2013), p. 43.
13 Luhmann (2012b), p. 28.
14 Luhmann (2012b), p. 29.
15 Luhmann (2012b), p. 33.
16 *Trust*, p. 15.
17 *Trust*, p. 15.
18 *Power*, p. 173.
19 See Arnott (2007); Ebert (2007); Bachmann and Zaheer (2006, 2008).
20 *Trust*, p. 3.
21 Franz-Xaver Kaufmann, one of Luhmann's colleagues at that time, mentioned to us that he had inherited a research project that dealt with the motivations and reactions of the German public towards newly introduced social welfare policies. The study included a newly developed trust and distrust measurement scale. Luhmann had shown an early draft of *Trust* to Kaufmann.
22 Barber (1983); Gambetta (1988); Giddens (1990).
23 Luhmann (1988).
24 Luhmann (1995).
25 Deutsch (1963); Easton (1965); Wiseman (1966); Young (1964).
26 Luhmann (2012a).
27 Luhmann (2010).
28 Luhmann (2002).
29 *Power*, p. 215.
30 Borch (2011), pp. 17–18; Thornhill (2006).
31 Murphy (1982).
32 Bankowski (1994).

33 Besio and Pronzi (2010).
34 Berger (2002), n.p.
35 Summers (2003).
36 Berger (2002): 'Methodological fetishism has resulted in many sociologists using increasingly sophisticated methods to study increasingly trivial topics. It has also meant that sociological studies have become increasingly expensive.'

References

Arnott, D. C. (2007) Research on trust: a bibliography and brief bibliometric analysis of the Special Issue submissions, *European Journal of Marketing* 41, 1203–40.

Bachmann, R. and Zaheer, A. (eds) (2006) *The Handbook of Trust Research.* Cheltenham.

Bachmann, R. and Zaheer, A. (eds) (2008) *Landmark Papers on Trust*. 2 Volumes. Cheltenham.

Baecker, D. (1999) Gypsy reason: Niklas Luhmann's sociological enlightenment. *Cybernetics & Human Knowing* 6:3, 5–19.

Bankowski, Z. (1994) How does it feel to be on your own? The person in the sight of autopoiesis, *Ratio Juris* 7:2, 254–66.

Barber, B. (1983) *The Logic and Limits of Trust*. New Brunswick, NJ.

Berger, P. (2002) Whatever happened to sociology? *First Things* (October), https://www.firstthings.com/article/2002/10/whatever-happened-to-sociology (accessed 29 December 2016).

Besio, C. and Pronzi, A. (2010) Inside organizations and out: methodological tenets for empirical research inspired by systems theory, *Forum: Qualitative Social Research* 11:3, http://www.qualitative-research.net/index.php/fqs/article/view/1539/3043 (accessed 29 December 2016).

Borch, C. (2011) *Niklas Luhmann*. Routledge.

Deutsch, K. W. (1963) *The Nerves of the Government: Models of Political Communication and Control*. New York.

Easton, D. (1965) *A Framework for Political Analysis*. Englewood Cliffs, NJ.

Ebert, T. A. E. (2007) *Interdisciplinary Trust Meta-Analysis: Analysis of High Rank Trust Articles between 1966 and 2006*. Discussion Paper 2007–18. Munich School of Management.

Gambetta, D. (ed.) (1988) *Trust: Making and Breaking Cooperative Relations*. Oxford.

Giddens, A. (1990) *Consequences of Modernity*. Cambridge.

Luhmann, N. (1967) Soziologische Aufklärung [Sociological Enlightenment]. *Soziale Welt* 18, 97–123 (reprinted in N. Luhmann, *Soziologische Aufklärung: Aufsätze zur Theorie sozialer Systeme, Volume 1*. Opladen, 1970, 66–91).

Luhmann, N. (1981) Erleben und Handeln [Experience and Action]. In *Soziologische Aufklärung, Volume 3: Soziales System, Gesellschaft, Organisation*. Opladen, 67–80.

Luhmann, N. (1988) Familiarity, confidence, trust: problems and alternatives. In D. Gambetta (ed.), *Trust: Making and Breaking Cooperative Relations*. Oxford, 94–107.

Luhmann, N. (1989) *Ecological Communication*. Cambridge.

Luhmann, N. (1993) *Risk: A Sociological Theory*. Berlin.

Luhmann, N. (1995) *Social Systems* [German edition 1984]. Stanford.

Luhmann, N. (2002) *Politik der Gesellschaft* [Politics as a Social System]. Frankfurt.

Luhmann, N. (2010) *Politische Soziologie* [Political Sociology]. Frankfurt.

Luhmann, N. (2012a) *Macht im System* [Power in the System]. Frankfurt.

Luhmann, N. (2012b) *Theory of Society*. 2 volumes. Stanford.

Luhmann, N. (2013) *Introduction to Systems Theory*. Cambridge.

Murphy, J. W. (1982) Review of *Trust and Power*, *Studies in Soviet Thought* 23:3, 266–70.

Summers, J. H. (2003) The end of sociology? *Boston Review* 28:6, at http://boston-review.net/archives/BR28.6/summers.html (accessed 29 December 2016).

Thornhill, C. (2006) Niklas Luhmann: a sociological transformation of political legitimacy? *Distinktion* 13, 33–53.

Weinberg, G. M. (1975) *An Introduction to General Systems Thinking*. New York.

Wiseman, H. V. (1966) *Political Systems: Some Sociological Approaches*. New York.

Young, R. O. (1964) A survey of general systems theory, *General Systems* 9, 239–53.

Editors' Note on the Revised Translation

We cannot overstate the enormous difficulties in translating Luhmann's works into English. Anyone who has read them in the original German will know about his idiosyncratic style with its long, complex sentences and eccentric punctuation. Communicating complex, abstract ideas is always a difficult task in any language, but the well-established German tradition of philosophical writing allowed Luhmann to assume that his readers would be sufficiently well-read and intellectually trained to follow his detailed, intricate arguments. If one adds to this Luhmann's propensity for inventing new words or combinations of words and giving familiar words new meanings, together with his propensity for irony, one can begin to see just how enormous are the problems in rendering an English version which captures not only the meaning of the German text, but also something of the richness and originality of Luhmann's style.

Given that these two works were the first of Luhmann's books to be translated into English, the three translators of the first edition did a remarkable job. However, as we compared the English and German texts, it became increasingly clear that there were some significant deficiencies in the translation and that to leave them uncorrected would have been irresponsible on our part. Apart from obvious mistranslations, there were also passages which either did not make good sense in English or were based on a misunderstanding of the theoretical concepts.

Any translation always involves a balance between a literal rendition of the original and producing something which both reads well in the target language and at the same time conveys the ideas and intentions of the author. We took the early decision that our prime task was to publish a text that was readily understandable by English-speaking readers, even if that meant failing to give every German word its literal translation. Even so, these two books present as formidable a challenge to readers in English as they do in German, and there is nothing that translators can or should do to reduce that challenge by trying to simplify the text. The only major concession we have made in this direction has been to modify

Luhmann's original punctuation by making the translation comply with English rules and conventions. We find it strange that so many translations of Luhmann do not make these changes, but insist rather on sticking rigidly to the original German punctuation, which, we believe, unnecessarily increases the difficulties of comprehension for English readers.

Fortunately, we have enjoyed some considerable advantages over the original translators. Firstly, we have both been students of Luhmann's social theory for many years and have followed it through its various stages of development. Unlike the original translators, we have been able to benefit from reading Luhmann's expressly theoretical works, notably *Social Systems* (*Soziale Systeme*) and *Introduction to Systems Theory* (*Einführung in dem Systemtheorie*), published some years after *Trust and Power* and which are now available in both languages. We have the added advantage of combining a native German speaker, who now teaches and writes in English, with a native English speaker, who has been involved in several previous translations of Luhmann's books. Most of our discussions together have been devoted to working out how best to capture in accessible English some of the more complex ideas that Luhmann sets out in these books.

Finally there is the major difficulty of vocabulary where Luhmann uses a German word or phrase in a very particular, theoretical way. We have listed these below. There will no doubt be those who disagree with our choice of English to translate the German, so we have explained wherever appropriate the thought processes behind our choices, always giving the German word or phrase so that the readers may consult their own dictionaries and find alternatives which might, in their eyes, be preferable.

Below are some notes on specific points.

Trust

Chapter 1
p. 6: Luhmann refers to 'problems' in the sense of analytical or mathematical problems rather than social problems.

Chapter 2
p. 12: Luhmann uses the words 'Bestand' and 'Bestände' to explain that the continuity of social activities is based on constantly changing events, and events are only made possible because they are provided with a continuity that secures the constant reoccurrence of events. Luhmann is likely to have been influenced by A. N. Whitehead, who developed a very similar conception, but who uses the term 'permanence', without any plural. Luhmann presents a much more self-referential understanding by adding a plural. In order to express this notion, we have decided to use the terms constancy and constancies.
p. 13: It is common to translate the German word 'Sinn' as meaning.

However, the reader should be aware that the German word does not directly include the notion of meaning and signification. In this context, one could say that Sinn precedes meaning or that meaning results from Sinn. For Luhmann Sinn refers to the phenomenal conception of the horizon of possibilities.

Chapter 5
p. 36: In the title, as elsewhere, 'exceeding information' conveys the idea that having a mass of information is not necessarily helpful or necessary in trust situations. The underlying notion is that trust always involves an extrapolation from the information available on the object of trust.
p. 39: 'trust protection' is a provision in the German civil code which provides for legal action in cases where a fiduciary relationship has been abused.

Chapter 8
p. 68: Throughout the text Luhmann uses the word 'schenken' – to give something as a present. There is no direct equivalent in English to translate this. One can talk of 'gifting', as a verb, meaning 'to endow with gifts' or 'make a present of'. However, Luhmann's use of this word in this context is a deliberate attempt to convey the liberal dimension of giving trust, which cannot be demanded (just as one cannot really demand presents if they are to remain presents, one cannot demand trust without raising suspicions). We have translated 'schenken' as to give, bestow, confer, according to the context.
p. 68: The term 'ontification' is used by Husserl to describe the sense of being as temporally constituted. Luhmann seems to suggest in this context that trust as a virtue or moral standard can be gained or applied in social contexts that have an emphasis on temporal endurance and stability; for instance, the patron/client relationship in Ancient Rome was based on such a concept of trust – known as *fiducia*.

Power

Chapter 2
p. 132: Luhmann uses in his writings the two words 'Erfahrung' and 'Erleben', which both translate as 'experience' in English. There is a semantic overlap between the two German words, but 'Erleben' is closer to the English 'to experience something', or 'to go through some experience', while 'Erfahrung' is closer to the notion of experience in the sense of 'to be experienced in something', that is, to learn something or to obtain knowledge about something by having gone through the experience. The same kind of translation problem presents itself in deciding the closest English equivalent to the German 'Handlung' and 'handeln', which can mean either action or act or acting (in the sense of carrying out an action).

An elaboration of this difference can be found in Luhmann's 1981 essay 'Erleben und Handeln'.

Chapter 3
p. 143: In the German original Luhmann uses the word 'archaic', which was an accepted term at that time, but contemporary ethnologists would, perhaps, speak of early ethnic groups or societies.
p. 150: Luhmann uses the term 'Neben-Code', which has the meaning of being an extra or supplementary code. Such codes do not always substitute for the primary code of the system, but if they do Luhmann often calls them secondary codes.
p. 153: 'Rules of evasion': Luhmann uses this English term in the German original, which we have not changed, although the meaning in English may not be as clear as Luhmann appears to believe.
p. 156: The words 'conditional' or 'conditioning' have a different meaning in Luhmann's writings than in behavioural psychology. Conditioning refers for Luhmann to the selective temporal arrangement of relationships between elements. Systems are not simply relationships between elements, since these relationships have to be regulated, and this is where he uses the term conditioning.

Chapter 4
p. 169: The German word 'Gewalt' has a broad meaning and can be translated as force or violence. In most cases, the word force seems the most suitable translation. However, depending on the context, we have also made use of the word violence.
p. 178: The words 'lifeworld' and 'technique' are inspired by phenomenological philosophy. Luhmann was a keen reader of Edmund Husserl. Technique is here used in a much broader sense than skill, referring to a way of carrying out a particular task or procedure. Technique means that this becomes more autonomous and calculable without considering all the needs and references that might be implicit in the task or procedure.

Christian Morgner and Michael King
December 2016

Part I
TRUST

Preface

There is a question worth serious consideration of whether it is advisable for sociologists to employ terms and concepts taken from daily usage of the traditional world of ethical ideas. The advantages and disadvantages of such a moral intrusion into sociological concepts appear to balance each other, but they can be presented as appearing almost separate from one another. If one remains at the level of critical demolition and surprising presentation of the familiar in unfamiliar ways or of unmasking ideological beliefs through providing causal explanation or evidence of hidden side-effects, then the disadvantages predominate. The identity of terms so employed is misused in order to discredit their invoked meaning horizon. In the current intellectual climate, this is an easy trick to perform – perhaps too easy, in that sociology could learn something from this, and construct some theoretical application out of it. If, on the other hand, sociology could go beyond this level and seek to establish its intellectual position in positive terms by formulating a theory of its own, and then enter a dialogue with the everyday understanding of the social world and its formation of this understanding through ethics, then the advantages of a certain common vocabulary might well outweigh its disadvantages. It is in this sense that the following reflections on the notion of trust are aimed at a contribution to sociological theory.

Work on this manuscript was undertaken at the Institute for Social Research, University of Münster in Dortmund, when it struck me rather forcibly that statements about trust are today still very far removed from being substantiated by methodologically valid means. Detailed discussions with Dr H.-J. Knebel and Dr F. X. Kaufmann have been most stimulating and have strengthened me in the view that this gulf between theory and empirical work is inevitable but not unbridgeable.

Niklas Luhmann
Dortmund, Winter 1967/8

1

Defining the Problem:
Social Complexity

Trust, in the broadest sense of confidence (*Zutrauen*) in one's expectations, is a basic fact of social life. In many situations, of course, a person can choose in certain respects whether or not to bestow trust. But a complete absence of trust would prevent him or her from even getting up in the morning. He would be prey to a vague sense of dread, to paralyzing fears. He would not even be capable of formulating definite distrust and making that a basis for precautionary measures, since this would presuppose that he trusts in other ways. Anything and everything would be possible. Such abrupt confrontation with the complexity of the world at its most extreme is beyond human endurance.

This point of departure can be regarded as a datum, an incontrovertibly true statement. We put our trust in the self-evident matter-of-fact 'nature' of the world and of human nature[1] every day. At this most basic level, confidence is a natural feature of the world, part and parcel of the horizon of our daily lives, but it is not an intentional (and hence variable) component of experience.

Secondly, the necessity of trust can be regarded as the correct and appropriate starting point for the derivation of rules for proper conduct. If chaos and paralyzing fear are the only alternatives to trust, it follows that man by nature has to bestow trust, even though this is not done blindly and only in certain situations.[2] By this method one arrives at ethical maxims or natural-law principles which are inherently reversible and of questionable value.

A third possibility is to think about and use one's imagination to portray the anxieties of an existence without trust. By this means one can transcend the everyday world, and provide a distanced interpretation of it through the philosophical tradition. The prospect of this borderline situation has held great fascination for psychologists and doctors,[3] not to mention eminent thinkers of the present day. In fact, although spurious conceptions have their uses and can be instructive, they nonetheless remain spurious.

Functionalism in psychology, and in the social sciences generally, approximates to this kind of existential philosophical approach in a number of different ways – particularly through its rejection of substantive principles. This is why it has to be so careful about keeping clear of such approaches,[4] for functionalism is characterized by distinctive presuppositions and theoretical perspectives. Since such distinctiveness is controversial[5] we must attend to its basic features[6] before looking at the function of trust.

Functional analysis is not a matter of establishing connections between established reasons or reliable knowledge in order to generate secondary knowledge; it is concerned ultimately with identifying problems and their solution. The method is therefore neither deductive nor inductive but heuristic in a rather special sense. Problems are posed in terms of the maintenance of stability of action systems – or, more abstractly, of identity in the real world. Moreover, continuity, and likewise identity, are no longer seen as a matter of essence or invariance but instead as a relation between variable orders, namely between system and environment. From this perspective, problems, as well as their solutions, take on their meaning not from some assumed invariable, essential, property but from particular positions in a framework of alternative possibilities. The 'nature' of this or that identity is defined by the conditions under which it might be replaced by another. Given this approach, the process of research in functional analysis is open to all kinds of possibilities. Its potential for envisaging complexity appears boundless, and a number of different features point to the very great capacity for dealing with complexity from all aspects, a capacity not to be found in the everyday and traditional understanding of the functional method.[7]

Complexity, and the capacity for dealing with it, however, is not just the hidden motive, the unifying purpose behind the whole conceptual orientation of the functional method; it is at the same time the most fundamental substantive problem for functional research. It is only from the standpoint of its uttermost complexity that it is worthwhile attacking the problem of the world as a whole, the universal horizon of all human experience.[8] Since it has no boundaries, the world is not a system. There being nothing external to it, it cannot be threatened. Even radical changes in its form of energy can be interpreted only as events within the world. The world poses a problem only in relation to the existence of true and consistent identities, due to its spatial and temporal complexity and due to its superabundance of realities and possibilities, which make it virtually impossible for stable expectations to emerge. This inhibits successful adaptation to the world by the individual. From its interior the world appears as unmanageable complexity, and this is the aspect of the problem that it presents for systems which seek to maintain themselves in the world.

A second advantage of taking complexity as a fundamental problem is that its high degree of abstraction and universality blurs the categorical distinction between psychic and social systems and thus the difference between psychological and sociological theory. We know, from our own experience as well as from scientific research, that readiness to show trust is dependent on the systemic structure of psychic systems as measured, for example, on the F-Scale.[9]

But we can be equally sure that a purely psychological explanation will be inadequate. Far from the psychological point of view, completely different grounds can motivate the offering or refusal of trust.[10] And, in any case, trust is a social relationship which is subject as such to its own rules. Trust occurs within a framework of interaction which is influenced by both psychic and social systems, and cannot be exclusively associated with either. This is why we must take refuge in a more general theoretical language, where concepts such as system, environment, function and complexity are formulated at such a high level of abstraction as to lend themselves to psychological as well as sociological interpretation. Talcott Parsons sought a similar way out, although in the direction of a very different, more definitely structural, theory of a general 'action system'.[11]

The concept of complexity has therefore to be defined in very abstract terms. This can be done straightforwardly in terms of a distinction between system and environment and in terms of a system's potential for actualization. The concept then signifies a number of possibilities which are opened up through system formation.[12] It implies that the conditions (and hence boundaries) of possibility can be specified, that the world becomes constituted after this fashion and also that it contains more possibilities than can be realized, so that in this sense it has an 'open' structure. From one angle this relationship between world and system can be seen as a problem of overload and of a constantly threatened stability. This, in fact, is the approach of functionalist systems theory. From the opposite perspective, the same situation appears as a 'higher' order, constructed by reducing complexity through system building, which renders the problem one of selection. This latter approach is that of cybernetic systems theory.

The world is overwhelmingly complex for every kind of real system, whether it consists of physical or biological units, of rocks, plants or animals. Its possibilities exceed those to which the receiving system has the capacity to respond. A system locates itself in a selectively constituted 'environment' and will disintegrate in the case of disjunction between environment and 'world'. Human beings, however, and they alone in this, are conscious of the world's complexity and therefore of the possibility of selecting their environment – something which poses fundamental questions of self-preservation. Humankind has the capacity to comprehend the world, can see possibilities, can realize its own ignorance, and can perceive itself as one who must make decisions. Both this outline plot of the world and individual awareness are integral to the structure of the individual's own system and a basis of conduct, for he comes to experience other human beings, who, for their part, are simultaneously experiencing what for him is merely a possibility, are mediating the world for him, and are treating him as an object. This makes it possible for him to identify himself – by assuming their point of view.

Opening up the world in this way, and identifying meaning and self-hood in the world, are possible, therefore, only because we invoke a whole new dimension of complexity – the subjective 'I-ness' of other human beings which we experience (perceive) and understand. Since other people have their own first-hand access to the world and can experience things differently, they may consequently be a source of profound insecurity for me. Over and above the plenitude of real objects of various kinds and the amplification of their variety in the course of time, the complexity of the world is further enhanced through the social dimension in which man appears not simply as another object but as an *alter ego*. This is why further increases in complexity call for new mechanisms for the reduction of complexity – above all, of course, for language and for reflexive self-consciousness which act as mechanisms of generalization and selectivity.

No convincing philosophical account of that fact of *alter ego* within an always intersubjectively constituted world (which cannot be imagined differently) has yet been given – not even within the framework of Husserl's transcendental phenomenology, which basically revolved around that problem.[13] Different kinds of human unpredictability are dealt with by positivist science in various ways (in so far as humans are not simply ignored); it is seen as a problem accounting for the functions of a variety of ordering arrangements. Thomas Hobbes' endeavour to establish the necessity of absolute political domination has its roots in this problem, although by interpreting the problem of complexity through the narrow perspective of law and order he arrives at a solution in terms of absolute rule which makes him blind to any alternative. Husserl's theory, elaborated by Alfred Schütz, of intersubjectively adjusted typifications of the possibilities of experience has this background of incalculable complexity which is rooted in the presence of an *alter ego* in the world, and which must be reduced to common types. Similarly, Parsons' theory of the social system is built upon this same fundamental idea. It can be perceived in his concept of the 'double contingency' of all interactions, which makes necessary the formation of norms to ensure the complementarity of role expectations.[14] Recent organization theory inspired by economics seeks to take the same consideration into account and seeks thereby to go beyond the utilitarian attempt merely to aggregate individual utility functions.[15] All these ideas can be compressed into a single formula: in conditions of increasing social complexity humankind can and must develop more effective ways of reducing complexity.

It would be wrong to regard this as the emergence of first one (increased complexity) and then the other (reduction of complexity) in some historical sense, as though one were a cause or energizer of the other.[16] Causality is to be seen in both, in a mutual cause and effect relationship. The functional compartmentalization of this unity into a problem (increase of complexity) on the one hand, and a solution (reduction of complexity) on the other, serves simply as a means to compare different kinds of solutions. In the final analysis, the increase and reduction of complexity belong together as complementary aspects of the structure of human response to the world. By a simple inversion of the concepts it can also be said that the social dimension of human experience in both its aspects – added complexity and new possibilities for the absorption of complexity – increases the potential for complexity and thus extends the human world. Through the existence of an *alter ego* a person's environment becomes the world for all humankind.[17]

It is beyond the scope of this study to do more than trace a few of the most important consequences of this point of departure. It does, however, define the problem of reference in terms of which trust can be analysed functionally and compared with other, functionally equivalent, social mechanisms. Where there is trust there are increased possibilities for experience and action, there is an increase in the complexity of the social system and also in the number of possibilities which can be reconciled with its structure, because trust constitutes a more effective form of complexity reduction. In the pages which follow we will attempt to analyse trust on this basis. A comparison would presuppose appropriate preliminary work on other mechanisms, such as law and formal organization, but this cannot be dealt with in a single monograph. Except for passing references we shall have to be satisfied with working through those facts concerning trust which are amenable to comparison.

Notes

1 This constantly recurs in the regrettably sparse literature which has trust as its main theme. See, for example, Diesel (1947), pp. 21ff.
2 See, for example, Hartmann (1962), pp. 468ff.; Bauch (1938), pp. 67–74; Darmstaedter (1948), cols. 430–6 (433); Eichler (1950), pp. 111ff.; Stratenwerth (1958), pp. 78ff. As Stratenwerth points out in his discussion, this kind of 'Yes/But' argument is only meaningful if one can assume a prevailing set of values which specifies where the 'Yes' changes into 'But'.
3 See for example Nitschke (1952), pp. 175–80.
4 A preliminary, though inadequate, orientation is provided by Marcel's dichotomy of 'problème' and 'mystère'. See especially Marcel (1935), pp. 162ff. It is made unserviceable for the purposes both of transcendental phenomenology and of functional analysis by the fact that it anchors the conception of the problem to the questions of producing and possessing. In this case 'producing' and 'possessing' basically act as ciphers for a highly abstract fundamental relationship between the self and the world, for relationships of independent variation and of relative invariance respectively.

5 See, for example, the attempt by Davis (1959), pp. 757–72, to blend functional and causal analysis, which gives the impression of widespread conviction.

6 For a detailed discussion: Luhmann (1971), pp. 9ff., pp. 31ff.

7 Such different features include the following:
   (a) all functional expressions are only valid in relation to particular action systems; and the number of systems is vast;
   (b) a single action can be attributed to several systems, so that systems may be interconnected in a very complex way;
   (c) the functional analysis of systems not only seeks to disclose manifest functions (conscious action goals), but places special emphasis on latent functions as well;
   (d) it takes into consideration the dysfunctional as well as functional consequences of action and makes the former the point of departure for further analyses;
   (e) it is a comparative method, whose prerequisite is the rejection of *a priori* similarities and comparisons in everyday life, and which, by transferring the judgement of similarity from the object to the function, shows the most heterogeneous phenomena to be functionally equivalent from the point of view of specific outcomes.

   Taken as a whole, these features show that the functional method in principle transcends the limitations of the action perspective and attains to greater complexity by studying what lies beyond, or beneath, mere interest and purpose.

8 Concerning this phenomenological world view, see especially Husserl (1948), pp. 23ff.; and (1954), pp. 105ff.; and comments by Landgrebe (1940); Brand (1955), pp. 13ff.; Fink (1958); Bednarski (1957), pp. 419ff.; and Hohl (1962).

9 See Deutsch (1960b). For a discussion of reliability and other methodological problems of this research, with its questionable choice of almost tautological personality variables, see especially Wrightsman (1966).

10 'A trusting choice may be based upon "despair", "conformity", "impulsivity", "innocence", "virtue", "faith", "masochism", or "confidence"', according to Deutsch (1962), p. 303, although the notion of such multiplicity is rather unsophisticated. Social psychology in fact constantly attempts to reduce the social sphere to individual psychological variables (see also Deutsch (1962), pp. 306ff.), which is why it is in no position to account for these facts very clearly. One of the first lessons of a theory of social systems is that very different personality systems can be functionally equivalent in social systems, so that social systems may to a certain extent be free from the personality processes of individuals.

11 For the most recent presentation and critical discussion of the way social psychology uses individual psychology in a reductionist manner, see Parsons (1970).

12 The notion of complexity can therefore be compared with the notion of substance in classical European philosophy. But 'substance' was then conceptually related to 'form', whereas the notion of complexity presupposes systems which reduce by means of selection.

13 See, especially, Husserl (1952), pp. 190ff.; (1954), pp. 185ff., pp. 415ff. and

passim. Characteristics of Husserl's limitations are that he asserts the priority of I-subjectivity in the sense of transcendental subjectivism and seeks on this basis to understand the constitution of others, the intersubjective community of experience and the world as contained within the horizon of this subject. This basis for thinking in the world can only be reached through a step by step methodological process of abstraction, which Husserl terms 'reductions'. To this extent Husserl himself becomes involved in the same dilemma as an absolutely static functionalism, and has to propose as fundamental perspectives which are artificially isolated. All the attempts to escape from this dilemma proceed straight from it back into the already constituted world and hence make no impression on the Husserlian problem. See especially Schütz (1932), especially pp. 186ff., and a number of later essays collected in Schütz (1962–6, 3 volumes); for further criticism of Husserl's efforts: Schütz (1957). See also Sartre (1950), pp. 273ff.; Merleau-Ponty (1945), p. 398ff.; Hocking (1953/4), pp. 451ff.; Landgrebe (1963), pp. 89ff.; and Theunissen (1965).

14 For a particularly clear formulation, see Parsons and Shils (1951), p. 16; also Parsons (1951), pp. 12ff.; and Gouldner (1959, 1960).

15 This is true on the one hand of Simon's idea of the inadequate capacity of human beings – and this is a mirror image of the problem of complexity to gain a functional grasp of the organization of decision-making: see especially Simon (1957a and 1957b); it is also true of the attempts at a theory of organizations inspired by game theory which attack the problem of the 'rational indeterminacy' of all human situations with concepts of strategy – see for example Neumann and Morgenstern (1944), especially pp. 9ff.; Marschak (1954, 1955), and also Gäfgen (1963), especially pp. 176ff., and (1961). Garfinkel (1963) also focuses on the game theory model to support the general thesis that trust is to be found behind every 'normal' experience, that other people share the same pattern of expectations.

16 The doctrine of social contract of early modern times makes use of the historical or utopian account, but only to conceal a functional statement.

17 See Plessner (1964), pp. 41ff., and by way of contrast, Cazeneuve (1958).

2

Constancies and Events

It needs no more than a cursory inspection to show that the theme of trust involves a problematic relationship with time. To show trust is to anticipate the future. It is to behave as though the future were certain. One might say that through trust time is superseded or at least differences in time are. This is perhaps the reason why ethics, out of concealed antipathy towards time, recommends trust as an attitude which seeks to make itself independent of the passage of time and so come close to eternity. But both the proposition itself and the underlying conception of time are inadequate. Time cannot be thought of as a flow, as motion, nor even as a measure of movement. The idea of movement in fact tacitly presupposes the idea of time.

There is even less help to be found in the distinction which is commonly made in sociology between structure and process. Even apart from the distinction's notorious failure to grasp either the changeable nature of structures or the structured nature of processes, it makes use of the reified notions of something fixed and of something flowing, the mutual opposition of which conceals the nature of time. We would be reluctant to identify trust in terms of either structure or process, which illustrates the inadequacy of this distinction as well as the inadequacy of current sociological theory when it comes to the theme of trust. It also shows the proximity of this theme to an idea of time which has yet to be fully understood.

A theory of trust presupposes a theory of time, and so leads us into territory so difficult and obscure that we cannot map it out here. Nevertheless, recent discussions in systems theory provide some clues. They have to do with the relationship between temporality and the differentiation of system and environment.

As soon as systems differentiate from their environment by formulating boundaries, problems about time occur. In the first place through the dislocation of processes which maintain the differentiation by making them sequential, for not all relationships between system and environment can be instantaneous one-to-one correlations. Rather the maintenance of the difference, in more complex systems at least, necessitates detours, and these take time. This occurs partly because of the absence of any reaction to environmental events, partly because of late reactions, and partly because of anticipatory reactions. Immediate responses need occur only to a very small extent. Talcott Parsons' well-known four problem matrix for dealing with system problems is based on this, with the juxtaposition of the difference between system and environment and the difference between present and future fulfilment.[1] Parsons makes use of this idea only for a theory of system differentiation. It does, however, contain far-reaching implications for the constitution of temporality itself and for follow-up problems of structural generalization internal to systems.

If this inference is accepted, then the experience of time produces out of differentiation both change and non-change conjointly. This situation is to be found also in meaningful systems of human experience and action, and here too it determines the conditions of structural generalization.[2]

According to the latest findings, all human experience of time lies in the reflection achievable from an experience of duration in spite of change. These findings, whatever they may be,[3] lend themselves to interpretations from two opposite viewpoints; these are duration and change. From these findings, 'objective time' is formed, by a process of intersubjective construction as a continuum of chronological points in time, is the same for all human beings and, although it may contain that which is constant and that which changes, remains itself neutral towards this distinction. The paradox of this distinction, therefore, is, so to speak, suffused by the notion of time, but is sustained as the contrast between two mutually exclusive ways of identifying time.

Either, that is to say, something can be identified as an *event*, which is a fixed point in time, independent of every present experience which progresses on the scale of time constantly transferring point to point the future into the past. The event obtains its temporal identity independent of any qualification of future, present or past and the meaning of its identity is just this invariant quality in contrast to the changing qualities of time. An event, however, requires this change in order to become reality in the present, in order to occur.

Or, something can be identified as a *constancy*, which carries on regardless of changes of points in time. Duration in this sense is nothing more than the continuously actual present, with the future always in prospect and the past flowing away. Constancies, therefore, can be identified only to the extent that they exist in the present. In the future or in the past they can perhaps be understood as series of events, made into a constancy through the altered form of continuously present expectations or recollections.[4]

In Antiquity, therefore, there were good grounds for thinking of everlastingness only as the present, while the contemporary conception, which is based on the identity of points in time, and which consequently has to think of the present as continually on the move, comes closer to an understanding of eternity, just as the general event of the world can perhaps be seen as a continuous creation, and thus leads to an understanding of time as the history of events.

These two perspectives are mutually exclusive, since the identity principle, by which one is defined as constant, is precisely what has to be treated as varying in defining the other. They cannot therefore be employed simultaneously. But precisely because of this mutual exclusiveness, both forms of identification reinforce each other as complementary negatives. In other words, variation, as such, is inconceivable, if one cannot assume identities with respect to which something is changing. Both forms of identification negate (and thus make it possible to understand) what varies in the other. In this way each elucidates the meaning of time for the other kind of identity. The identity of events constitutes the aspect of time problematical for constancies, namely, the advance of the present as a moment of actuality which cannot simply carry its own constancies along, but which must always take care to preserve the past and absorb the new. The identity of constancies constitutes an aspect of time problematical for events, namely, the unstable flow of events out of the future into the past and their mere fortuitous, chance, combination with constancies.

The contradiction between these forms of identity allows no conclusion to be drawn concerning the alleged 'unreality' of time.[5] If such a conclusion were to involve a notion of reality which ignored temporality it would be particularly unproductive and misleading. Trust does not pose any problem of unreal propositions. Rather, the nature of time consists in that twofold possibility of negation, having reality as possibility as well as negation, having in other words actual, demonstrable, effective capacities.[6] This twofold negation in which each varies in terms of the other initially yields a complete model of time which actually eludes being captured as a complete schema. Neither the ancient notion of time, focusing on the present, nor the modern notion of time, focusing on points of time, is adequate. The perspective associated with these notions of time present only a scheme to question constancies and events, but one which would have to be corrected by a counter perspective in considering time.

These brief reflections will have been enough at least to show that trust cannot simply be regarded as 'superseding time'. Moreover, neither time perspective, in so far as it predominates in the processing of experience, precludes the development of trust. It would be highly questionable to maintain that time as experienced in Antiquity in fact afforded greater opportunities for the formation of trust than our experience of time, because it could grasp constancies as the continuously immediate present and not simply as succession of events. There is nevertheless one crucially important inference which can be made from our analysis, namely, that the security of a constancy – and that means security per se – is only possible in the present and therefore can only be achieved in the present.[7] The same is true of trust as a form of security. Trust can only be secured and maintained in the present. Neither the uncertain future nor even the past can arouse trust, since what has been does not eliminate the possibility of the future discovery of another past. This present-relatedness and its implications for trust cannot be understood and elaborated if the present is conceived in terms of an event fixed to a point in time, as a moment, as the instant at which the event occurs. Rather, the basis of all trust is the present as an enduring continuum of changing events, as the totality of constancies where events can occur.

The problem of trust therefore consists in the fact that the future contains far more possibilities than could ever be realized in the present and thus be transferred into the past. The uncertainty about what will happen is simply a consequence of the very elementary fact that not all futures can become the present and hence become the past. The future places an excessive burden on a person's ability to represent things to himself. People have to live in the present along with this everlastingly over-complex future. They must, therefore, prune the future so as to measure up with the present, that is, to reduce complexity.

This problem can be grasped more clearly if we distinguish between *the future present* and the *present future*.[8] Every present has its own future, as the open horizon of future possibilities. It envisages a future from which only one selection can become the present future. In progressing towards the future, these possibilities make way for the selection of new presents and thereby new future prospects for the present. In so far as the present and future presents remain identical in the present it brings about constancy; in so far as it generates discontinuities it gives rise to events. In so far as experience brings awareness of this difference between its present future and its future present, it creates, where the present future appears hazardous, the opportunity of a conscious selection in the light of both uncertainty and a need to secure connections between current and future presents.

These demands cannot be postponed. They involve, as a permanent requirement, corresponding performances by people in the continuous present. Trust is one of the ways of bringing this about. The formation and consolidation of trust is therefore concerned with the future horizon of the actual present. It is an attempt to envisage the future but not to bring about future presents. Every kind of planning and advance calculation of future presents, all indirect, long-lasting and circuitously conceived orientations, remain problematical from the point of view of trust. They have to be referred back to the present, in which they have to be anchored. The growing complexity of such plans calls for satisfaction and decision-making to be increasingly deferred and thus cause their forward planning and fixed deadlines to lose their certainty. So with increased complexity there is a corresponding growth in the need for assurances about the present, for example, trust. An instance of this is provided by research into small groups and the distinction between instrumental and expressive variables which has in recent years assumed such increased significance in sociological systems theory.[9]

In this distinction, the bases for which are still unclear,[10] the problem of time is inherent.[11] Whereas instrumental orientations have reference to goals, to effects anticipated for the future, the expressive content of experiences serves to stabilize the present in the security of its constancies rather than as a flickering presence of momentary events, but a present that constitutes itself – through its own particular horizon of the future and the past – as the enduring basis of changing events.[12]

The forward thrust of instrumental orientations at the expense of the present is a condition for an increase in performance through rationality. But this leads (and this may be seen in industrial sociology studies generally) to the present being emptied of meaning and thus increasing the pressure of a need for expressive variables. The conception dominant in theory and praxis treats such pressure as a problem, which calls for planning, for increased instrumentation, and for the organizational provision of suitable expressive conditions.[13] What is involved is a forceful attempt to break out of the unavoidable contemporaneity of common human existence and to project the presentness of other human beings into the future, thereby gaining time to plan this presentness and exert influence by selective manipulation of representations. But all people live and grow old together in a common and ever-present constancy.[14] Whoever wishes to manipulate the present of others must be able to escape from it into another time. The impossibility of this means that all manipulation runs the risk, evident also within its own present, of itself becoming open to expression and thereby betraying its goal. This can, of course, be obviated to a very large extent through social differentiation, role separation, barriers to communication and control of information – in short, by social organization. But the effect of this will simply be to arouse universal suspicion of manipulation, regardless of whether individual cases provide confirmation or not. Trust, therefore, can be maintained only if it finds a form which allows it to live with such suspicion and become immune to it.[15]

This dilemma between the instrumental and the expressive, as developed by Parsons and others (Note 9, above), between control of events with reference to the future and present security of things in so far as they are constancies (a dilemma which grows more acute with the increasing complexity of circumstances), can be more clearly discerned if we link it to the theme of the previous chapter, the problem of complexity. To this end the next task is to extend our analysis of time with some further considerations.

The constitution of objective time, the interpretation of the subjectively experienced opposition between duration and change through the objective opposition between identical constancies and identical events, serves to open up an area of variance. From the perspective of events, constancies are moved on as the present moves on. From the perspective of constancies, events are moved on as the future and the past move on. Both perspectives are thus opened up to alternative possibilities. The variability incorporates everything that is, without exception.[16] The duality of the mutually exclusive perspectives guarantees this completeness and saves people from the unimaginable idea that everything could vary simultaneously with everything else. In other words, time is constituted as unlimited yet reducible complexity. The temporal dimension is therefore, like the social dimension, an interpretation of the world in terms of extreme complexity. It points to the fact that everything could become something other than what it is. But the foundation of this model of the world, which enables time itself, which enables the world itself and even extreme complexity to become a constancy, is the actual enduring presentness of immediate experience. The complexity of all other possibilities is reduced through this presentness to a level that can actually be experienced, and the world itself is, for instance, reduced so that it can witness the 'horizon' of experiences. The constancies which form part of the actual present are the means by which this extreme complexity can be grasped and reduced, by which the undefinable can be defined or – in the traditional, time-excluding language of metaphysics – matter can be given form. By interpreting, structuring and thereby simplifying the world, they allow events to adopt an informative value and blend with human action in a process of selective choice. In functioning as an aid to reduction in this way, the constancies of experience create assurance about the present.

Thus, time may also be understood as reduction of complexity – whether the present is regarded as the standpoint, continually advancing into the future, from which experience is subjectively selected, or whether it is seen as a stationary filter built into the 'river of time', transforming the possible into the actual. We now know that both images of motion are inadequate metaphors for that process of mediation between the complexity of the world and the actuality of experience to which we give the name reduction.

This discussion has helped to throw the function of trust into sharper relief. It strengthens the capacity of the present for understanding and reducing complexity: it strengthens constancies as opposed to events and thus makes it possible to *live and to act with greater complexity in relation to events*. In terms of a well-known psychological theory, trust increases the 'tolerance of ambiguity'.[17] This effect is not to be confused with instrumental mastery over events. Where such mastery can be assured (i.e. 'actualized'), trust is not necessary. But trust is required for the reduction of a future characterized by more or less indeterminate complexity.

Making a distinction between mastery over events and trust is not only necessary for conceptual clarity, but is also necessary in order to gain

certain insights into how the two are related. The indeterminate complexity of possible events is, in other words, not simply a consequence of defi-
cient forward planning, but is in other senses a consequence of the extent
of instrumental planning.[18] Future possibilities in fact do not contract but
rather expand with planning projections, which incorporate long and
complicated chains of cause and effect involving many parameters and
the many actions by different people. Moreover, as far as the individual
is concerned, it is precisely this planned complexity which gives rise to
a new form of insecurity. Furthermore, such planning contains a high
proportion of *technically significant indeterminacy*. It makes sense to postpone decisions until more events have occurred in the course of time and
there has been further reduction of complexity. Money, power and truth
(to which we shall be returning in detail) are social mechanisms which
permit decisions to be postponed and yet guarantee assurance in the face
of a future of greater uncertainty and complexity of events. The stabilization of these and other mechanisms in the present presupposes trust.
Mastery over events and trust are thus not merely functional equivalents,
mutually exchangeable mechanisms of complexity reduction. Given an
increase in the complexity of possible events both mastery and trust find
themselves, separately and jointly, the objects of increasing claims.

So it is not to be expected that scientific and technological development of civilization will bring events under control, substituting mastery
over things for trust as a social mechanism and thus making it unnecessary. Instead, one should expect trust to be increasingly in demand as a
means of enduring the complexity of the future which technology will
generate. Talcott Parsons was right in regarding the expressive solidar-
ity of the small group as the basis of political trust precisely in relation
to the unavoidable indeterminacy of complex political processes.[19] The
same circumstance points to the fact that subsystems of society such as
the political, and perhaps the economic system, which are not adequate
for present-day requirements, remain dependent on other fields of action
where the orientation to the present, required for the formation of trust,
has been preserved.

Notes

1 The clearest formulation to date is Parsons (1970), pp. 30ff. Similarly, Piaget
(1955), especially pp. 275ff., for personality systems.
2 Bergson and Husserl, in particular, have carried their investigations into a
more fundamental notion of time than the everyday and scientific notions. See
Bergson (1889) and Husserl (1928).
3 Bergson and Husserl refer to this finding itself as 'time'. Husserl, however,
later acknowledges: 'The original time [Urzeit] which is not yet truly time.'
(Manuscript Ch. 7, p. 17, cited in Brand (1955), p. 96.)

4 The necessary presentness of all constancies is beyond the grasp of current objectivist modes of scientific thought. It is no coincidence that thinkers of some consequence are able to conceive of constancies only as the sum of similar events. Hence, for example, the notion of event structure. For an application of this see Dewey (1926), p. 72, or Allport (1955), pp. 614ff., or Nadel (1957), pp. 127ff. As far as the theory of trust is concerned, the unavoidable present relatedness of all security of constancies is an insight of the greatest importance, without which the time problem involved in trust cannot be solved.

5 Following McTaggart (1908), this view has been much discussed. For a more recent interpretation see Gale (1968), and the references cited. In fact, this discussion is predicated upon a looser conception of the problem, which distinguishes only between a conception of time which considers the movement of positions from the past through the present to the future, and one which is simply concerned with irreversibility. However, subsequent discussion has failed to overcome the difficulties of interpreting this distinction.

6 There are a number of observations on the functions of negations in Habermas and Luhmann (1971), pp. 35ff.

7 On this briefly, but to the point, see Mead (1938), p. 175.

8 The fact that these two determinations of time are not synchronized is, logically speaking, a prerequisite for the possibility of selection, although it is rarely taken into consideration in the experience of time and is explicitly denied in the recent logic of temporal statements. See, for example, Prior (1957), p. 10; (1968), p. 8; Rescher (1968), p. 214.

9 See Bales (1951); Parsons et al. (1953); Parsons and Bales (1955); Slater (1959), pp. 300–10; Thibaut and Kelley (1959), pp. 278ff.; Marcus (1960), pp. 54–9; Etzioni (1961), especially pp. 91ff., and *passim*, (1965), pp. 688–98. See also the distinction, borrowed from Durkheim, between instrumental and consummatory variables, which Parsons employs to construct the time axis of his theory of action systems, for example in Parsons (1959a), pp. 3–38.

10 A source of particular difficulty in small group research is the view that the satisfaction of the socio-emotional needs of group members through expressive action is an *internal* problem (goal fulfilment and so on) as opposed to an *external* one; hence the antithesis between expressive and instrumental variables becomes confused with the system-defining categories of internal and external. The implication is that a group comprises people with all their concrete personal needs and not simply roles, a conception which has long since been abandoned as untenable. If sociological systems theory is taken as a basis, one cannot but regard the satisfaction of the socio-emotional needs of group members as an external systems problem; in which case the distinction and separation of expressive and instrumental aspects, actions or simply roles becomes a meaningful differentiation in the manner in which a system deals with different environments, i.e. with its members on the one hand, and non-members on the other.

11 This view is also basically Parsons'; see for example (1961a), p. 324; (1970), pp. 31ff.

12 It is characteristic of the prevailing theory of time that Parsons is able to

articulate only the relation of expressive conduct to the present in terms of 'consumption', that is to say as event, which is why he uses the instrumental-expressive and instrumental-consumption dichotomies in the same sense.

13 The theories of dual leadership, which are treated in the above-mentioned literature (Note 9), and more generally, every attempt of the human relations movement to subordinate affective group processes to organizational goals, are illustrative of this. Characteristic of the general theory of the presentation of social identities are the writings of Erving Goffman; see especially Goffman (1959). For the realm of politics, see Edelman (1964).

14 This common ageing is a condition of the intersubjective constitution of time, as Alfred Schütz in particular emphasized time and again. See Schütz (1932), pp. 111ff., and further elaboration in the later papers collected in Schütz (1962–6), *passim.*

15 We will come back to possibilities for such a symbiosis of trust and suspicion in Chapter 9, 'Trust in Trust'.

16 From the perspective of the history of ideas, this concept replaces the ontological location of being in time in the idea of motion, where the universality of temporality had to be combined with the idea that everything is in motion.

17 See, for example, Frenkel-Brunswik (1949); Hofstätter (1959), pp. 160ff. Also closely related: Atkinson (1957).

18 See Tenbruck (1972).

19 See Parsons (1959b), especially pp. 96ff.

3

Familiarity and Trust

The limits of the human capacity for experience are set and characterized by their intentional structure. Every intention captures something meant – and thereby presupposes the world. The boundaries of what is meant at any given time can, and indeed must, be continually surpassed. It is impossible to halt experience, to stick to one and the same subject area all the time. This self-mobilizing of experience is crucial for achieving this, in order that the complexity of the world can be confronted and reduced to meaningful directives for conduct. But experience can transcend its boundaries only at any given time in so far as it shifts them, and accepts other boundaries. In this movement of experience factual identities are constituted, which lead from one experience to another, which hold out the prospect of future experience and preserve the past. The world is therefore constituted as the universal horizon of experience, which must be presupposed in every movement and can never be broken through.

The manner in which experience is constituted through meaning and world so as to make the complex conditions of existence comprehensible is an *intersubjective achievement*.[1] A transcendental-phenomenological elucidation of the world and its complexity has been aware of the transintentional intersubjectivity of this constitution. Because of the different forms that acquaintanceship takes, the capacity for truth, and the extent of the comprehensible complexity of what exists in the world, vary according to the manner in which meaning and world are intersubjectively constituted.

Meaning and world are, in the main, constituted *anonymously*.[2] Everybody is presupposed and co-experienced as sharing the same formal, empty entity of another ego, as being another 'I', an impersonal 'one'.[3] This constitution remains undifferentiated and is, in a diffuse way, shared by everybody. Up to this point, no special need for trust in one's fellow human being arises. Anyone who does not concur does not shatter the commonly held world view, but in fact cuts himself off from reasonable humanity. This anonymous form of constitution corresponds to the communication medium, truth, as the form of acquaintanceship to

familiarity and the self-evident quality of being. In interpersonal communication only part of this familiarity is verbalized; the rest is presupposed as the basis for understanding, being well and truly guaranteed as
self-evident by moral approval.[4] The genuine, familiar being does not as
such prompt any further questioning about 'who' experiences, about the
subject of meaning construction. Being itself appears to him as 'subjec-
tum', too. The constitutive process is thus hidden from view. The need to
pursue questions of 'who, and who not' does not, therefore, arise.

Of course, this indisputably self-evident manner of the world cannot,
in fact, be regarded as a fully consensual world. It includes differences
and varieties of opinion, enough and to spare. These will not, however,
be attributed to the world but rather to human beings as an object in the
world, to their irrationality, to their evil intentions, to their alien origins
or, nowadays, to their 'complexes'. As a result, differences lose significance. Since they are interpreted in this way, they do not cause misgivings
and create uncertainty in individual experience. They belong to special
circumstances in the world which can be dealt with by means of defin-
able acts of distrust, caution, readiness for conflict, or by psychologically
induced indifference.

Since the constitution of meaning and the world is consistently anonymous and latent, the full range of experiential possibilities which it allows
– the extreme complexity of the world – will be excluded from consciousness. Which means that the familiar world is relatively simple and also
that this simplicity is guaranteed down to fairly narrow limits. The complexity of its inherent possibilities does nevertheless make itself felt,[5] in
particular as a break, a schism, between the familiar and the unfamiliar,
the strange, the uncanny, something which has to be either fought against
or treated as mysterious. As soon as another person figures in consciousness, not simply as an object in the world but as *alter ego*, as freedom to
see things differently and to behave differently, the traditional taken-for-
granted character of the world is upset and its complexity manifest in a
quite new dimension, for which there are no appropriate ways for the
time being by which it can be grasped or absorbed.

Familiarity in this sense makes it possible to entertain relatively reliable
expectations and, as a consequence, to absorb the remaining elements
of risk as well. In itself, however, familiarity denotes neither favourable
nor unfavourable expectations, but the conditions under which both are
rendered possible. Familiarity is the precondition for trust as well as distrust, i.e. for every sort of commitment to a particular attitude towards
the future. Hazardous as well as propitious outlooks require a certain
familiarity, a socially constructed typicality, so as to make it possible to
accommodate oneself to the future in a trustful or distrustful manner.
This alternative reference to a favourable or unfavourable future does
not yet possess anticipatory ordering, which develops only in relation
to action intentions or system interests. Familiarity structures existence,

not action. And it applies to the world, whereas trust and distrust only ever apply to selected aspects of the world, giving shape to relatively tiny sectors of possible meaning.

In familiar worlds, the past prevails over the present and the future. The past does not contain any 'other possibilities'; complexity is reduced at the outset. Thus an orientation to things past can simplify the world and render it less harmful. One can assume that the familiar will remain, that the established will be repeated and that the familiar world will continue into the future. And this is by and large a plausible assumption, since all human beings depend on it and yet are not capable of suddenly doing anything differently. Humanity cannot consign its own lived experience to the past. The essentials of experience must be represented in history, since history is the most important way of reducing complexity. By this means, the time dimension, in respect of what is past, solves a problem which belongs strictly speaking to the social dimension, namely, the exclusion of unanticipated action. The socially contingent nature of the world is thereby obscured, so that in the familiar world, the unavoidable social construction of meaning remains anonymous.

As against this, there is the future orientation of trust. Trust is only possible in a familiar world; it needs history as a reliable background. One cannot confer trust without this essential basis and without all previous experiences. But rather than being just an inference from the past, trust goes beyond the information it derives from the past and takes the risk of defining the future. The complexity of the future world is reduced by the act of trust. In trusting, one engages in action as though there were only certain possibilities in the future. One fixes one's present future to a future present. In this way one offers other people a determinate future, a common future, which is not readily apparent from the past.

Familiarity and trust are therefore complementary ways of absorbing complexity and linked to each other, in the same way as past and future are linked. The unity of time, which presently separates past and future and yet constantly refers one to the other, allows this relationship between complementary performances, one of which – trust – presupposes the other – familiarity. It is to be expected, however, that this relationship will not be constant, but will allow for changes of emphasis, and also that the need for a social order, for familiarity and for trust will change according to the complexity of the social systems themselves and their relationship to time. As a social order becomes more complex and variable, it tends on the whole to lose its matter-of-fact character, its taken-for-granted familiarity, because daily experience can envisage or recall it only in a fragmentary way. Yet the very complexity of the social order creates a greater need for co-ordination and hence a need to determine the future – i.e. a need for trust, a need which is now decreasingly supported by familiarity. In these circumstances, familiarity and trust must seek a new mutually stabilizing relationship which is no longer grounded in a world which is immediately experienced, assured by tradition and close at hand. Assurance for such a relationship can no longer be provided by confining strangers, enemies and the unfamiliar to the other side of some boundary. History then ceases to be remembrance of things experienced and is instead simply a predetermined structure which is the basis for trust in social systems, trust which must refer itself to these systems.

This hypothesis has been put forward by reference to the structure of social systems and their increasingly complex character. It can be reiterated and elaborated at the transcendental level, where one is not so much concerned with the complexity of social systems as with the complexity of the world. In the modern world it was recognized quite early on that conceptions of the world were expanding to cope with increasing complexity, principally in two related sequences of events, namely, the trend in metaphysics towards the subjective and the confinement of the realm of truth proper to the positive sciences. But in neither case was the change in the style of intersubjectivity taken into account.

The Cartesian turning point in metaphysics substituted the conscious awareness of thought, which thinks about itself, for the previous conception of the being of entities. But self-consciousness of thought is regarded as an inner experience of the individual human being, and, on that basis simply, rendered into a generalization. It was not really studied as the intersubjective process of constituting meaning and the world. The positive sciences reduce truth-enabling knowledge to the function of ordering the relationship between perception and concept, on the assumption that perception, as well as concepts (particularly if they are congruent), can be brought to unequivocal intersubjective certainty and secured against the arbitrariness of the *alter ego*. So it is that the vast, booming enterprise of science is increasingly content to justify its methods by their success without admitting any question of what happens in those areas of knowledge in which intersubjective certainty cannot be attained and without questioning the overall significance of setting up this kind of intersubjective certainty in place of the old and familiar evidence by which truth used to be measured.

The questions which arise from these considerations cannot be articulated adequately, let alone answered here. However, if the problem of trust is to be distinguished from, and contrasted with, the general familiarity of the lifeworld, it is essential not to lose sight of this complex of problems of intersubjective constitution. The overall, anonymously generated, familiarity of the lifeworld, including nature and human relationships, which is constructed in generalized terms, is and will continue to be the self-evident ground of being, the practical basis for all intentional approaches to specific objectives. People live from day to day in this intermediate zone without specific problems of trust or distrust. Intersubjective constitution is the prerequisite for trust and distrust, but people do not see them as having this basis, nor do they perceive it as a problem unless they are in the position of having to turn this familiarity with the objective world into trust in the process of its intersubjective constitution.[6] They dwell in the cave of shadows described by Plato and have to be content with forms already reduced for them, unless they put themselves into a position in which the full complexity of the world can be encountered with more effective ways of reducing it. It is not a question, therefore, of their withstanding the evidence of ideas which are more illuminating than the power of their vision,[7] but more a question of creating stable systems out of processes of intersubjective communication – systems which better encompass and reduce the complexity of the world – and of putting their trust in the functioning of these systems. Only in this way is it possible to *realize* the *transcendental* process of the constitution of world and meaning[8] at a higher level of complexity.

From this general analysis, it appears that, as far as the particular problem of trust is concerned, a change of mode will occur on the way to greater and more consciously articulated complexity. In anticipation of the following chapter, what follows from this suggestion may now be outlined. On the basis of familiarity with the everyday world, trust is principally interpersonal trust (and is therefore limited). It serves to overcome an element of uncertainty in the behaviour of other people which is experienced as the unpredictability of change in an object. In so far as the need for complexity grows, and in so far as the other person enters the picture both as *alter ego* and as fellow-author of this complexity and of its reduction, trust has to be extended, and the original unquestionable familiarity of the world pushed back, although it cannot be eliminated completely. It becomes as a result a new form of system trust, which implies renouncing as a conscious risk some possible further information and implies as well a wary indifference to and a continuous control of results. System trust is not only applicable to social systems but also to other people as personal systems. This change, if one looks closely at the assumptions which lie within the mode of trusting, corresponds to a change from bases of trust which are defined in primarily emotional terms, to those which are primarily performance based.

Notes

1 On this thesis, developed from foundations laid by Husserl, see the several references in Chapter 1, Note 13; see also Gurwitsch (1962); Berger and Pullberg (1965), pp. 102f.; Berger and Luckmann (1966). Sartre's notion of 'totalization' also implies this intersubjectivity; see Sartre (1960).

2 Alfred Schütz in particular deserves credit for the elaboration of these ideas, see Schütz (1932), pp. 220ff. See also Husserl (1954), pp. 114ff.

3 Heidegger's (1949), pp. 114ff., devaluation of the social dimension as a mere 'being with' of the person follows from this basic assumption but wrongly gives

it the status of an 'inauthentic' as compared to an 'authentic' being. On the other hand, Berger and Kellner (1965) show that intimate contact especially also has significance for the articulation of the world.

4 See Garfinkel (1964); Berger and Luckmann (1966), pp. 140ff.

5 An outside is always accessible; Plessner (1964), p. 45, rightly sees a fundamental difference between the familiar world of the close-at-hand for humans and the environment of animals. See also corresponding observations on the notion of meaning and the notion of horizon in Hülsmann (1967), p. 4.

6 Adler (1936), p. 91, refers to trust in this transcendental sense – that is, to trust in the capacity of other human beings to experience reality correctly.

7 As is well known, even Husserl allowed himself to be influenced by this platonic idea and thereby blunted the full impact of his life's work.

8 See also Luhmann (1971), pp. 66ff. Hülsmann (1967) posits targets similar to those of sociology in his thesis that hermeneutics can lift the anonymity of the *alter ego* involved with us in the constitution of meaning. But he does not clarify how the specific result *accomplished* by anonymity, that of securing a background for all more specific experience of meaning, can be attained in any other way. Yet as long as we do not replace anonymity, and remain incapable of moving from transcendental familiarity to transcendental trust, we simply cannot dispense with it.

4

Trust as a Reduction of Complexity

We are now in a position to formulate the problem of trust as *an advance payment*.[1] The world is being dissipated into an uncontrollable complexity; so much so that at any given time people are able to choose freely between very different actions. Nevertheless, I have to act here and now. There is only a brief moment of time in which it is possible for me to see what others do, and reactively adapt myself to it. In just that moment only a little complexity can be envisaged and processed; thus only a little gain in rationality is possible. Additional chances of a more complex rationality would arise, if I were to place my trust in a given future course of action of others (or for that matter in a contemporary or past course of action, which I, however, can only establish in the future). If I can trust in sharing the proceeds, I can allow myself forms of co-operation which do not pay off immediately or directly.[2] If I depend on the fact that others are acting, or are failing to act, in accord with me, I can pursue my own interests more rationally – driving faster in traffic, for example.[3]

Trust is only involved when the trusting expectation makes a difference to a decision; otherwise what we have is a simple hope. If a mother leaves a child in the care of a babysitter, a number of hopes are associated with this. These are, that nothing untoward will happen, that the girl will be kind to the baby, will not disturb its sleep by turning up the radio, and so on. Her trust only extends to eventualities which, if they occur, would cause her to regret her decision to go out at all and to leave her child in the care of anybody. Trust therefore always bears upon a critical alternative, in which the harm resulting from a breach of trust may be greater than the benefit to be gained from the trust proving warranted. Hence one who trusts takes cognizance of the possibility of excessive harm arising from the selectivity of others' actions and adopts a position towards that possibility. One who simply hopes has confidence despite uncertainty. Trust reflects contingency. Hope ignores contingency.

This is not to assume, on the other hand, that risk and the grounds for trust will be weighed up rationally before doing anything. Trust can also be shown to be thoughtless, careless and routinized, and thus to require no unnecessary expenditure of consciousness especially if expectation approaches certainty. One who goes unarmed among his fellow human beings puts trust in them, and does not nowadays seriously weigh up the alternative of carrying a sword or pistol. Trust merges gradually into expectations of continuity, which are formed like firm guidelines by which to conduct our everyday lives. But not all expectations of this nature involve trust; only those concerning conduct do so, and among the latter only those in the light of which one commits one's own actions and which if unrealized will lead one to regret one's behaviour.

Whether action on the basis of trust has been right, therefore, in the final, retrospective reckoning, depends on whether the trust has been honoured or been broken. From the purely objective and timeless perspectives of the kind which obtain in economic theories of rational choice, it would seem that this is just a question of one out of many uncertainties, the probability of which may, to a large extent, be estimated and calculated. This view, however, does not take time sufficiently into account; time, as it were, charges for providing the expectation of certainty. The decision-maker at the moment of decision does not have that knowledge at his disposal or rarely has it in the form of calculable probability.[4] We have to conclude, therefore, that the appearance of a manageable rationality makes a crucial difference as to whether or not action is founded on trust.

In both the examples mentioned, co-operative action and co-ordinated individual action open up trust, by reducing complexity, so revealing possibilities for action which would have remained improbable and unattractive without trust – which would not, in other words, have been pursued. For this reason, the benefit and the rationale for action on the basis of trust are to be found – as is shown in particular in the examples of the 'Prisoners' Dilemma' and driving in traffic – less in the definite mastery of longer chains of action or more extended causal connections (although this can also be a result of trust) than, and above all, in a boost towards *indifference*. By introducing trust, certain possibilities of development can be excluded from consideration. Certain dangers which cannot be removed but which should not disrupt action are neutralized.

A further example of the reduction of complexity through trust becomes significant in an increasingly organized social structure. Despite every effort of organization and rational planning, it is impossible for all actions to be guided by means of reliable forecasts of their consequences. There remain uncertainties to be accommodated and there must exist roles whose special task this is. Roles such as the politician's or the managing director's, for example, are typically monitored in terms of successful outcomes rather than of measurable standards, precisely because the correct action cannot be identified in sufficient detail in advance. But success – if it appears at all – does not appear till after the action, while there must be commitment beforehand. This problem of time is bridged through the trust that is granted as an advance on success and on cancellation, for example, through the appointment of people to public office, through loans of capital, and such like.[5] In this way the problem of complexity is divided up and therefore diminished. Provisionally, one trusts that the other will successfully master ambiguous circumstances, will in other words reduce complexity, and indeed, on the basis of such trust, the other, in fact, has a better chance of being successful.

Reduction in this sense is not deduction. Rather, it resembles induction. In the last resort, no decisive grounds can be offered for trusting; trust results from exceeding existing information. It is, as Simmel pointed out,[6] a blending of knowledge and ignorance. Although the one who trusts is never at a loss for reasons and is quite capable of giving an account of why he shows trust in this or that case, the point of such reasons is really to uphold his self-respect and justify him socially. They prevent him from appearing to himself and others as a fool, as an inexperienced person ill-adapted to life, in the event of his trust being abused.[7] At most, they are brought into account for the placing of trust, but not for trust itself. Trust remains a risk.

Going beyond factual circumstances in this way achieves a relative independence from specific prior experience, from particular grounds for trust – something which has been termed 'generalization' in learning theory.[8] Judgements about trust generalize experiences, extend them to other 'similar' cases, and stabilize indifference to variation in so far as they stand up to test. This process of generalization of expectations possesses three aspects which are significant and worthy of further consideration. It involves *partial displacement of the problematic* from '*external*' to '*internal*', a process of *learning*, and *symbolic fixing* of outcomes in the world around.

Generalization in general, and the building of trust in particular, assume the existence of systems as supports to their operation – systems which are themselves complex enough to be able to replicate certain processes of their environment within themselves. Of course, no system is capable of repeating or duplicating in its representations the real world in all its unfathomable complexity. Kantian metaphysics was stubbornly attached to this assumption since it abstracted 'the subject', or 'consciousness', as a kind of partner with the world and so raised it to the same level of complexity. What was overlooked was the decrease in complexity between reality and image, between world and intention, between 'inner' and 'outer', and so it failed to grasp the function of the image as the creation of order through the reduction of complexity.

The fact is that all internal processes – and it is precisely here that the meaning of the difference between 'inner' and 'outer' is to be found – work at a lower level of complexity and hence exhibit fewer possibilities, or more order, than their environment. They work selectively; relationships between data in their environment are taken in and operated upon as information relevant to the system. Thus they substitute the internal ordering of data-processing for the original amorphous complexity of the environment, and the problems of this internal order are fed into the system as the normal working basis for adapting to the environment.

In the case of trust, reduction of complexity takes special forms through its subjectification. Such forms can be described as changes in the level at which uncertainty is absorbed, or made tolerable. The system substitutes inner certainty for external certainty[9] and in so doing raises its tolerance of uncertainty in external relationships. The problem of the complexity gap thereby shifts to some extent into the secondary problem of inner certainty. Inner certainty can come about in two different, indeed opposite, ways – and it is largely because of this that the development of trust can be pretty reliably anticipated time and again, despite very diverse system conditions. It may be based on the fact that the object of trust fulfils an indispensable function for the internal structure – the processing of experience. A weakening of trust, accordingly, would have very far-reaching consequences for self-assurance, and will not be countenanced as a possibility because it would lead to extensive changes in internal dispositions for which the system lacks time, energy or endorsement by the environment. In quite the reverse way, the certainty of trust may depend on a more strongly differentiated internal system, with the consequence that the failure of the object of trust can inflict only partial and isolated damage and the object of trust can be replaced by functional equivalents. In both cases the primary support of trust comes from the functions it plays in the ordering of information-processing internal to the system, rather than directly from guarantees originating in the environment. Thus the internal ordering of the processing experience comes to take the place of a foundation for the 'correctness' of complexity reduction located in the outside world.

This condition of trust as something internal increases the likelihood of a particular style of attitude of trust towards something, namely, as bearing on the problem of trust generally, since it is bound up with distrust as well as with trust. Translated into the conceptual language of Parsonian 'pattern variables',[10] trust and distrust would be considered to be *affective*[11] (nonneutral) and *diffuse* (non-specific) attitudes and, according to the way in which the object is presented, as *particular* (non-universal) and *ascribed* (not achieved). The relationship of trust to an object, therefore, is independent of specific individual interests and contexts of experience, and occurs regardless of the particular state of affairs to which it becomes relevant. As a typical example, trust in a particular person will be activated wherever the one who trusts encounters this actual person regardless of their respective role contexts. But even trust, in contrast to knowledge based on experience, in more abstract performance textures, such as, for instance, trust in the value of money, presupposes a similarly concrete reification. Only through the mediation of the reified objects does trust become controllable symbolically – in a way which will be clarified below. Trust is therefore an attitude which is neither objective nor subjective; nor can it be transferred to other objects or to other trusting people.

As an attitude of this kind, trust – and here too we see that it is not simply a mechanical consequence of influences from the environment – has to be *learned*, just like any other kind of generalization. The underlying assumptions of this learning process are laid down in infancy. In the family, trust in its earliest form finds its first confirmation in a world which is rendered less complex through social institutions and through the particular successes of trust between family members.[12] Of course, the learning process does not end there. New situations and new people are continually posing new problems of trust throughout life. The ways of preparing for relationships of love and friendship, or more generally for all kinds of personal ties and deepening acquaintanceship, can be interpreted as the testing and learning of relationships of trust. Differentiated and mobile social orders set a particularly high standard which can only be met if not only trust but learning how to trust can themselves be learned, which takes part of the socialization function away from the family. Nor would it be too misleading to assume that social systems have to learn trust as well.

Our understanding of this learning process is still quite incomplete. Presumably it is not simply a question of generalizing from isolated experiences of the world, of transferring and generalizing experiences of specific situations in which trust was not betrayed. For one thing, the idea that primary experiences are to be regarded as specific to particular situations is very questionable. This notion (like behaviouristic learning theory in general) is incapable of explaining how generalization is set in motion, how the child manages to transfer good experiences of trust from the mother to the father, to brothers and sisters, and eventually to strangers. Instead, one has to proceed from the starting point that the learning process is mediated by the experiences of the learner with himself and is steered by the self-developing (also learned) identity of the learner.

If the child establishes its own self by differentiating 'I' and 'You', the first thing it has to do is unlearn its first, practically unmotivated, act of trust and find a form of trust which takes account of this differentiation. The learning process will not force the separation of I and You into complete and absolute distinctions. On the contrary, the You stays as 'another I'. The learner reasons from himself to others and is thus in the position to generalize from his experiences with others.[13] Because he feels he is prepared to honour the trust of some unknown person, he is also able to show trust to others.[14]

Finally, the precarious nature of trust is evident in the manner in which it is projected back onto the environment. The persons and social arrangements in which one puts trust become *a complex of symbols*, which is especially sensitive to disturbance and which, as it were, registers every event in terms of the issue of trust. Everything that takes place within the boundary of this issue of trust consequently takes on symptomatic relevance. As in the case of random tests, single events assume overriding significance for the whole. One falsehood can entirely upset trust and, by their symbolic value, quite small mistakes and misrepresentations can unmask the 'true character' of somebody or something, often with unrelenting rigour. The compulsive character of generalization, the tension arising from the *inevitability* of a *simplified* image of the environment, finds expression in the fragility of trust.

A good illustration of this is to be found in the depiction of the relationships between Congressmen and members of the administration during the preparation of the Federal Budget.[15] The reality of public administration is far too complex for Congressmen to be able to comprehend it fully and evaluate it. They cannot act without trusting in the personal integrity of the members of the administration. Hence representatives do not in practice exercise control over the factual circumstances but rather over the extent to which they are prepared to trust, and only through this are they able to exercise indirect control over the factual situation. Under these rather constrained circumstances, they react with great emotional intensity to the slightest sign of dishonesty through withdrawing trust, and through other sanctions.

Whoever trusts has to keep control over his own preparedness to accept the risks involved. He must make it clear to himself, if only to reassure himself, that he is not trusting unconditionally but rather within limits and in proportion to specific, rational expectations. It is himself he must curb and control when he puts his trust in someone or something. This is an intrinsic part of the structure of motives which trust makes possible, and comes about by making the object of trust more attainable with the help of symbols of trustworthiness.

The form and direction of the sensitivity of trust towards disturbance which is mediated symbolically may of course vary from case to case. However, the principle remains the same. Because reality is too complex for actual control, trust is kept under control with the aid of the implications provided by symbols. This is supported by a crudely simplified framework of indices as a form of feedback loop carrying messages about whether or not the continuance of trust is justified.

Nevertheless, not every message threatens or disrupts trust. The trusted person enjoys a certain credit which allows even unfavourable experiences to be effectively reinterpreted or absorbed. As we shall argue, particularly in differentiating between trust and distrust (Chapter 10), control is exercised by means of thresholds which may not be crossed without the withdrawal of trust. Controls through thresholds differ essentially in style, technique and flexibility from control by means of definite goals, norms or values.[16] It is a simpler way of tolerating greater complexity but it does presuppose that the thresholds, or the modes of conduct which are critical for trust, can be recognized and defined with sufficient clarity.

The way in which symbolic controls operate, moreover, tends characteristically to be unquestioned and indeterminate. It proceeds for the most part by inferences which remain uncommunicated and which therefore do not even need to be defined or properly justified. This is why a very precise articulation of reasons and views is not in keeping with either the demonstration of trust or the withdrawal of trust.[17] Even for those who seek trust, it is not required; it can quite easily even become a disrupting factor or, even more, may arouse distrust. It would contradict the function and style of trust to request and offer detailed factual information and specialized arguments, although the possibility of such an explanation ought to be hinted at. The expert can become a threat to the politician and his reasons when he takes to arguing along those same lines. The more reasons the politician can offer, the less need there is to trust him and the less it will matter *who* puts the programme into effect. Alternatively, if the question of trust is still relevant, the massing of reasons betrays an uncertainty which can lead to the withdrawal of trust.

All three structural components of the trust relationship (firstly, the substitution of an internal order and its problematic for the more complex external order and its problematic; secondly, the need for learning; and thirdly, symbolic control) confirm our assumption that trust is associated with reduction of complexity, and, more specifically, of that complexity which enters the world in consequence of the freedom of other people. Trust functions so as to comprehend and reduce this complexity.

Functional propositions, according to the model 'A has a function for B', may look like findings and can easily mislead analytical study into stopping there. Nothing could be more dangerous. The value of the proposition for understanding comes mainly from its relationship to other, similarly constructed propositions. Thus it appears on closer inspection that the notion of trust is by no means a statement offering a ready-made solution to a problem, requiring only to be put into effect to rid the world of the problem. It is more a matter of a substitute formulation for the original problem of complexity. Trust is and still remains a problem. Complexity is an unavoidable risk. In view of the inevitability of risk, the form it takes will be decisive. In the majority of cases, systems can absorb it more easily as the risk inherent in trust. But the question remains – under what conditions, and with what further, follow-up, problems?

Notes

1 This is where we find the most important point of contact we are able to make with Rudolf Schottländer's ethical analysis of trust. Schottländer (1957), pp. 18ff., also emphasizes the moment of the 'pledge' in trust; see also Deutsch

(1958), pp. 265f., who likewise bases his concept of trust on the actual motivational value of a behavioural prediction. In psychology, on the other hand, one quite frequently sees a more generally inclusive and less well-defined concept of trust, the operationalization of which has still to be achieved. See, for example, the accounts given by Bruner, Goodnow and Austin (1956) in relation to the definition: '"Confidence" is essentially the degree of sureness a person feels in making a categorization' (pp. 225–6). As a result, no distinction is made either between familiarity and trust, or between trust and the calculation of probability.

2 See the experiment by Deutsch (1960a); also Zand (1972).

3 See also, for example, discussion of the 'Prisoners' Dilemma' in terms of game theory. In this, two prisoners are able by confessing to obtain mitigation of sentence at the expense of the other, and without confessing can only be convicted for an unimportant offence. In this case the rational course would be to keep silent, distrusting confession. On this, see Luce and Raiffa (1957), pp. 94ff.; Rapoport (1960), pp. 173ff.; Rapoport and Chammah (1965); and the experiment which replicates this case in Deutsch (1958). One implication of this example (and to that extent it exhibits some approach to reality) is that communication would be sufficient in itself to bring about trust. The significance of communication in the case of mutual interdependence is demonstrated in the experiment by Loomis (1959). For a more detailed exposition see below, pp. 46–7.

4 There are grounds for scepticism in other respects, in that a convincing method of calculation or subdivision of probability and utility values which is independent of individual preparedness for risk has yet to be found – a lack which is symptomatic and one which is cleverly concealed by current formulations in terms of the maximization of expected utilities; see Koch (1960). Besides, the calculation of a risk against high odds is a form of calculation akin to a wager or a game played against nature, in which context the problem of trust hardly applies in the strict sense. Hence also Deutsch (1960a), pp. 124f. and (1958), p. 226.

5 There are some pertinent observations on this interplay between trust and criteria of success in Braybrooke (1964), especially pp. 542ff. See also Vickers (1965), p. 180 and *passim*.

6 Simmel (1922), pp. 263f.

7 On the problem of self-presentation and the necessary social arrangements for assistance which are activated in such situations of disappointed trust, see pp. 90ff.

8 Extensive studies in behaviouristic psychology are based on this concept. For a review in German, see Stendenbach (1963), especially pp. 90ff., or Eyferth (1964a), pp. 103–10, or alternatively (1964b), especially pp. 357–60.

9 Claessens (1962), pp. 91f., makes some pertinent observations on the formation of trust in a process of generalized self-release through inner certainty. It is primarily this inner certainty which makes it possible to tolerate distance and absence in the confined social system of the family.

10 For the theoretical elaboration of this see especially Parsons et al. (1953), and Parsons (1960).

11 Parsonian theory leaves out the possibility of differentiating between feeling and volition. The term 'affective' must therefore be understood in such a way that it includes both and so comprehends not only emotional but also, and primarily, volitional forms of trust.

12 See especially Claessens (1962), pp. 88ff.

13 See Mead (1934), who emphasizes the reciprocal aspect of the learning of an individual self through experiences with others. It is a question here of complementary aspects of a unitary process.

14 See the hypothesis of a statistical correlation between preparedness for trust and trustworthiness in Deutsch (1958), pp. 278ff., which supports these interpretations of the learning process. See Roos (1966) for critique.

15 See Wildavsky (1964).

16 There is also a reference to this in Vickers (1965), p. 34.

17 This is also stressed by Hauke (1956), pp. 52f.

5

Exceeding Information and Possibilities for Sanctions

Trust rests on illusion. In actuality, there is less information available than would be required to give assurance of success. The actor willingly surmounts this deficit of information. In the last chapter we have outlined how this happens. Problematical aspects are partially shifted from the outside to the inside, and dealt with through internal modalities of learning and of symbolic control. This way of conceptualizing the matter can be rendered in abstract terms by making use of general cybernetic systems theory, which claims to be valid both for personal and social action systems (as well as for organisms and machines), and therefore developing the abstract formula: the objective world is more complex than any system.

This world comprises more possibilities than the system itself provides for and can realize. In this sense the system exhibits a greater degree of order (fewer possibilities, less variety) than the world. This discrepancy in the degree of order, as already indicated, is offset through the system developing a 'subjective' image of the world. That is, the system interprets the world selectively, covers the information which it receives, reduces the world's extreme complexity to an amount of complexity to which it can meaningfully orient itself, and so structures the possibilities of its own experience and action. If such reduction takes place through intersubjective agreement, it yields socially guaranteed knowledge, which is thus experienced as 'true'.[1] The reduction can also be guaranteed through certain internal processes, which will be dealt with in greater detail in Chapter 11, 'Readiness to Trust'. In this case the system replaces external information with internal information or with premises which it has learned for its own processing of experiences, and which impart structures. One may, with Karl Deutsch, call this replacement of external by internal bases of experience 'will' (in the sense of conation or making autonomous decisions).[2] In this sense trust is an operation of the will.

This is not to say that such an operation can take place without any connection with the environment, and thus in the same fashion can be brought about whatever the environment. Indeed, the structures of the environment, and particularly those of the social order, impinge most directly on the question if and in what form trust can prosper. We must now look rather more closely at the protective circumstances under which that self-assurance, or the making good of informational deficiency by means of 'will', can take place.

Such an operation can – in extreme but imaginable situations – result from purely internal conditions, and lead to a form of pathological trust regardless of partners, situations and circumstances. Generally speaking, however, the truster seeks in his subjective image of the world some objective clues about whether or not trust is justified. Without any previous information trust would be nearly impossible. Trust exceeds on information; it rests on the truster being already au fait with certain general features, being already informed, even if incompletely and unreliably.

The clues employed to form trust do not eliminate the risk; they simply make it less risky. They do not supply complete information about the expected behaviour of the person to be trusted. They simply serve as a springboard for the leap into a bounded and structured uncertainty. It should not be assumed, therefore, that empirical research will yield strong law-like relationships between bases for trust, treated as causes, and demonstrations of trust, treated as effects, but one may expect there to be statistical correlations,[3] since one may assume that on average trust is more likely to be conferred when certain preconditions are met. Such preconditions are the concern of this chapter.

What general direction should be pursued in the search for what may offer support for the formation of trust? Familiarity with the trusted person is undoubtedly a vital factor. One is more likely to trust a familiar person than a stranger. Yet this aspect should not be overrated. For the most part, closer familiarity keeps the problem of trust from even becoming a matter for reflection. And when reflection does occur in such circumstances, the taken-for-granted nature of familiarity will be lifted. A gulf of obscurity opens up even with respect to things and people nearest to one, which doubt removes into a surprising impression of foreignness. And so one looks for other bases of trust which will stand up to scrutiny. Whoever is confronted with the question of trust, and does not know the future actions of the other party, can focus his attention instead on motivational structures. On the one hand, he will find it worthwhile to ask himself with what prospects for gain and loss his partner can reckon if he is trusted. Could there be especially large rewards for him if he broke trust? On the other hand, significance attaches to the possibility he (i.e. the potential truster) possesses of exercising influence (at a cost to be taken into account) upon the fate of his partner.[4] In fact, such potential influence may be taken into account in the partner's calculation of his gains and losses, and to this extent this set of considerations carries most weight.

Through his future influence the truster can sanction a breach of trust; he can also, when such a possibility is to be envisaged, reckon on his partner also reckoning with it, while he ponders a breach of trust, and thereby being restrained. Legal arrangements which lend special assurance to particular expectations, and make them sanctionable, are an indispensable basis for any long-term considerations of this nature; thus, they lessen the risk of conferring trust.[5]

However, trust and law can remain closely congruent with one another only in very simple social systems, those which have barely any structural problems, and are small enough for all members to be familiar with one another. In such systems trust is expected and distrust becomes an affront, an offence against the rules of collective life and thus against the laws of the system, and vice versa, any breach of trust claimed and proven is sanctioned as wrongdoing. Under such circumstances anyone who distrusts cannot give expression to his feelings and fears without becoming a social isolate. As a consequence, the basic laws of the system steer him in the direction of a socially typified trust. Perhaps trust of this nature lies at the root of the development of law in general, and, for example, of contract as a juridical phenomenon. At any rate in such simple social systems the mechanisms of law and trust cannot be separated from one another.

In all more sharply differentiated, more complex social orders, on the contrary, it is inevitable for law and trust to become separate in this way. Risks are individualized; showing trust is no longer so strongly socially required and controlled; he who is in breach of trust is entitled to put forward excuses, to lay claim to extenuating circumstances. Above all, at the societal level, legal situations and norms have become too differentiated, and trust is too general and diffuse a social claim, for them to overlap widely. Finally, law and trust stand apart from one another also in their motivational bases. Conformity with law can be motivated by society only indirectly and impersonally, and can be guaranteed only with the aid of an 'ultimate means', namely, physical force. Trust, on the contrary, rests on motivational sources of a different nature, such as personal readiness to take risks, or concrete proof. As the social order itself becomes more differentiated and complex, the number of possibilities it opens up for experience and action increases. As a consequence, also, the mechanisms for the reduction of complexity must become differentiated, assume a more specific configuration, and operate more effectively. In view of the sociological and theoretical problems which now demand solution, it would no longer be rational for law and trust to coincide fully.

In particular, the legal institution of the contract formed purely through the concurrence of the parties' declared intentions entails a juridical reformulation of the principle of trust in terms of law which makes it too independent for trust to play a role either as a factual condition or as a ground for the validity of contracts. Claims are based directly on contract, and it does not matter who, if anyone, has made an investment advance in a given case. In fact, if contracts are to be trusted it is necessary that their performance be made independent of the question of who, if anyone, has in fact trusted.

Legal doctrine well conveys this differentiation between law and trust. Law no longer gives any indication of the extent to which it developed out of conditions of trust, and at any rate juridical terms give no indication of that. It is true that various legal regulations can be subsumed under the notion of 'trust protection'. But in fact they are very disparate, have developed each independently of the others, and particular doctrinal constructions have been placed upon them only much later: firstly, trust based on the factual condition of formal legal certification, such as possession of documents; secondly, trust in the authenticity and completeness of a statement in the course of the preparation of an ordinary contract; thirdly, trust that legal powers delegated, for instance, through a power of attorney, will not be misused, and conversely trust that a proxy is actually covered by a corresponding power of attorney; fourthly, trust in the correctness of information and conversely in the avoidance of indiscretions; and fifthly, trust in the further granting of financial assistance from public funds or permissions which have been granted by administrative act, and others besides.[6] Such legal notions are gathered under the concept of 'trust protection', but there is something inconclusive, accidental and therefore unsatisfactory about this. These juridical terms which refer exclusively to trust as their own foundation are partly the product of the later elaboration of earlier legal notions, partly late arrivals into a juridical sphere previously consolidated, which now seek to assert themselves vis-à-vis existing concepts and principles by making appeal to a new, ethically grounded argument, that of the 'safeguard of trust'. Hence the legal system must place restrictions upon itself in its application of the principle of trust, lest it make legal constructions by more appropriate paths untenable. Otherwise there would be a disorderly, undisciplined development of concepts involving superfluous parallel constructs, undifferentiated grounds of argument, and above all, erosion of the division of powers by the judiciary through the protection offered by trust in situations which have come about through violation of the law. This differentiation of trust, law and legally actionable trust protection is the result of a long development, which obscures its origins. Ultimately, the notion of trust, as total reliance upon other people, lies at the foundation of law, in the same way that, conversely, the modalities of trust can only come about thanks to the risk-mitigation afforded by the law.

All the same, it is not an historical accident that the doctrinal constructions of law are what they are; rather, it shows how, over time, law has distanced itself from the notion of trust, and the two mechanisms have become differentiated. Hence, trust and law must largely operate *independently* of one another, be connected only through the *general* conditions which make them possible and, when the *need* arises, be capable of mutual co-ordination with reference to individual problems of some significance. It is possible to establish this not only for law, but for trust as well. Here again, a closer look reveals that trust cannot be reduced to trust in the law and in the sanctions which the law makes possible.

We had in fact already noticed that the legal situation and the possibility of sanctions in the event of a breach of trust offer some support to someone considering whether to trust. They allow the circumstances to be foreseen under which the trusted person will have the good sense to make decisions. It is not decisive, in this regard, whether or not the partner will in the end actually make a complete calculation with reference to law and sanctions to suit himself. The argument does not directly rest upon this calculation, but upon the truster's ability to anticipate it. In this context it operates tacitly, without poisoning the relationship with the threat of sanctions and thus putting paid to emergent trust. It is possible that with such a supposition the truster does not do justice to a partner who either has not yet considered a breach of trust or indeed would never consider it. The truster may also go astray in assuming that the prospect of sanctions would intimidate the partner. It is on this account that the calculation is not carried out jointly, and does not become the object of communications between the partners. The structure of the trust relationship requires that such calculation should remain latent, evolving in its generalizing fashion covertly, purely as a reassuring consideration. In his overt behaviour the truster must show himself 'utterly trustworthy', lest he himself sow the seed from which later reciprocal distrust may grow, thereby producing exactly the result which he is trying to avoid. For this reason the calculation of eventualities is also largely independent of the actual structure of motivation, and especially through this simplified form, through a reduction of the 'just in case', it offers security and activates the further reduction of complexity through the show of trust.

This delicacy in human relations, this tact in presentation or performance, this subtlety of conduct – indeed, enthusiastic devotees of the ethics of trust might well speak of delusion or deception – constitute the background against which one may go on to ask how objective structures which open up possibilities for mutual sanctioning are thereby transformed to produce trust. By giving notice of sanctions it is possible to bring about an interdependence of needs which previously did not exist, or was not perceived. This applies especially to the threat of negative sanctions, but also to the possible advent of gratuitous benefits or forms of support which the partner could not have taken into account. Because contrived interdependencies of this nature are not expected, to bring them about requires open communication about them between the people concerned, and this, as we have suggested, may introduce a climate unfavourable to trust into the relationship.

The situation is different when such interdependencies already exist and can be presumed to be known, when the participants are living in a system which is familiar to both of them, so no further information about it is required, since it tacitly provides an everyday basis for mutual understanding. In such circumstances the participants know that they are bound to encounter one another again, and that they are bound to become dependent on one another in situations which cannot be exactly foreseeable, and which sometimes favour one of them, and sometimes the other. They also know, each of them, that their partner assesses the situation in those terms.

Trust relationships find a favourable soil in social contexts with the same kind of structure, i.e. characterized by the relative persistence of the relationship, by reciprocal dependencies, and a certain quality of the unforeseen. The overriding consideration is the law of meeting again. The participants will have to go on seeing each other. This makes it more difficult for trust to be breached, at any rate when any breach could not be hidden from the partner or acceptable excuses offered. It appears, therefore, that social systems which are thrown upon mutual trust to an exceptional extent by the very structure of their internal interdependencies at the same time also generate more favourable conditions for the emergence of trust. That is, possibilities of sanction produce a generalizing effect in the context not only of hierarchical relations, but also of those between equals. They stabilize interaction through the anticipation of extreme possibilities.

The possibilities of sanction possess not only this manifest aspect, whereby they structure motivations and diminish uncertainties, but also a latent function, essential for the foundation of trust, for by the same token they structure the attribution of guilt, and thus the risk of social disgrace and condemnation. How socially approved possibilities of sanction are distributed has a bearing also on the side third parties would take if a breach of trust should occur, or whether – and to what extent – they would hold whoever commits a breach of trust responsible, or whether they would charge the truster with naivety or foolishness. If the truster unthinkingly waives his right to apply sanctions, he may lose thereby the possibility of slanting the attribution of guilt in his own favour, and find himself the object of reproach. If I ask a stranger to bring my gold watch to a watchmaker who is to repair it, and he violates my trust, I lose thereby not just my watch, but my social standing. It is quite a different matter if I ask strangers to help me clear my house which is on fire, and they make away with some objects. In general, it is possible to see in operation in the attribution of guilt a morality which goes well beyond official law, has a considerable capacity for fine discriminations, is at the same time predictable, and whose verdict primarily depends on whether control over the situation has been renounced out of necessity or by carelessness. The fact that such attributions of guilt are typified and predictable assists the formation of trust, allowing the truster to foresee whether he is risking damage only or derision as well.

If we reconsider these hypotheses in the light of the information problem raised at the beginning of this chapter, it appears further that a problem of this kind, on which the need for trust is grounded, cannot be solved by tackling it directly. It is not possible to acquire information on the future behaviour of others except in an incomplete and unreliable fashion. But one can shift this problem into a realm where it can be mastered more effectively. One can inform oneself instead about certain structural properties of the system which one shares with others, acquire thereby the supports necessary for building trust, and so overcome the need for information which is lacking. As in many other functional contexts, structure reduces the need for information.

Notes

1 The methodological standards which guarantee the objectivity of positive science, and in particular the reduction to simple perceptions and to findings, which can be attained through precisely replicable operations are, at bottom, intended to secure the intersubjective transmissibility of knowledge. They serve to keep social complexity, the diversity of the individual subjects with their respective perspectives on the world, out of the realm of verifiable knowledge. In this they serve the same function as does trust – the reduction of complexity.

2 See Deutsch (1963), pp. 105ff. Also the similar concept of 'autonomy' in Kidd (1962).

3 For an attempt in this direction see Deutsch (1958). Compare the general statement in Kahn et al. (1964), p. 90, to the effect that unclear and ambiguous situations imperil trust. See also below, Chapter 11, Note 14.

4 For experimental evidence see Deutsch (1958); Solomon (1960); and (with special reference to the possibility of sanction) Evans (1964).

5 This relief is the only plausible meaning one can attach to the notion occasionally advanced that law is a substitute for trust, thus for instance Darmstaedter (1948), pp. 433f.

6 A comprehensive review of the question in the field of private law is offered in Canaris (1971), where the peculiarity of the guarantee of trust is primarily set against the responsibility deriving from legal transactions. See also Eichler (1950); Lenz (1968); Craushaar (1969); and, with special reference to public law, Mainka (1963); Ossenbühl (1972).

6

Personal Trust

One cannot trust chaos. If nothing connects with anything else or everything with everything else, it becomes impossible to build generalizations. In other words, a single system cannot, by itself, generate higher generalization or trust. Their accomplishment presupposes an environment which already possesses structure, though not the same degree of order, and the same limitations on what is possible, as the system itself. But what structures the environment is none other than the existence of other systems in the environment.

It is through systems of a special kind, namely human beings, that there comes into the world that enlargement of complexity on which trust is focused – this is freedom of action. It is not surprising, therefore, that trust is extended first and foremost to another human being, in that he is assumed to possess a personality, to constitute an ordered, not arbitrary, centre of a system of action, with which one can come to terms. Trust, then, is the generalized expectation that the other will handle his freedom, his uncanny potential for diverse action, in keeping with his personality – or, rather, in keeping with the personality which he has presented and made socially visible.[1] He who stands by what he has allowed to be known about himself, whether consciously or unconsciously, is trustworthy.

For, in addition to its immediate significance as regards situation and purpose, every socially comprehensible action also involves the actor's presenting himself in terms of his trustworthiness. Whether or not the actor has this implication in mind – whether he is aiming at it, or consciously disclaiming it – the question of trust hovers around every interaction, and one's self-presentation is the medium by which decisions about it are attained. Every actor is experienced by the others, not only as a causal process, by which causes are transformed into effects, but simultaneously (so as to extend some generalizing control over this process) as a complex of symbols. And he senses this, knows the symbolic implications and expressive value of his every action and inaction, for the most part, much better than he knows their effects and so, more or less consciously, gauges his behaviour accordingly.[2] His motives may be of widely different kinds – he may be concerned to appear trustworthy; he may make an effort to remain true to himself and to live in a way which affords him self-respect; he may act spontaneously, according to the facts of the situation and, to that extent, in a socially naive way, by allowing his personality to function as an unconscious selection mechanism.[3] In every case, despite the variety of possible structures of motivation, a similar result is forthcoming – a selective presentation of self, which provides other criteria on which to build up trust and to establish norms of anticipated continuity. To some extent, therefore, foundations of trust in the social order can be formed largely independent of the fluctuations in, and differences between, individual motives.

Since all communication, indeed every perceivable form of behaviour, says something about the person who is behaving, communication – even merely being seen by others – is a risky undertaking which requires some kind of safeguard. An individual's behaviour always gives away more information about himself than he can reconcile with his ideal self and more than he consciously wants to communicate. Thus, his mere appearance presumes some minimum trust, trust that he will not be misinterpreted, but that he will be accepted by and large in the guise he wishes to appear. There are people who experience this prerequisite site of trust to such an extreme degree that they have difficulty merely being – let along doing anything – in the presence of other people. Their sphere of action is limited in proportion to their lack of trust and, furthermore, inability to show trust limits their chances of winning trust. The possibilities for action increase proportionately to the increase in trust – trust in one's own self-presentation and in other people's interpretation of it. When such trust has been established, new ways of behaving become possible – jokes, unconventional initiatives,[4] bluntness, verbal short cuts, well-timed silences, the choice of delicate subjects etc. When trust is tested and proven in this way, it can be accumulated by way of capital.

So far as personal trust is concerned, therefore, the foundations of trust in a society are adjusted according to the prospects and conditions for self-presentation and the tactical problems and dangers involved in it. This mechanism transforms societal-structured conditions into sources of trust, which means that it is not to be viewed and understood merely in terms of personal strategies, as it is by Goffman. The individual personality's system of reference is only one possible area of interest for functional analysis. On the other hand, strategic consistency is one indispensable element in the total context and the extent of the functionalization of self-presentation, the extent of psychological sensitivity, and the extent to which people are prepared to cooperate tactfully in delicate areas of self-presentation. These aspects are important variables regarding the conditions of trust in society. This determines the style in which personal trust can be created and maintained.

We cannot go here into the varied manifestations relevant to this context. We cannot even produce a classification or survey. A few short examples of analysis are all that is possible. Limiting ourselves to the question of learning, and leaving aside the extensively researched problems of infant socialization, we will consider a few of the social conditions which make it easier to bring about relationships of trust.

The question of the formation and consolidation of personal trust enables us to transfer our abstractly formulated problem of the reduction of complexity to the dimension of time, and to show that the problem of forming trust relationships must be solved gradually, step by step. The 'principle of small steps'[5] replaces simpler forms of adaptation to the environment when the environment also operates in a contingent fashion or is too complex for adaptation at one stroke. For these, systems need time.

It is a necessary precondition that the situation permits selective steps, meaning behavioural choices, and that behaviour is not already determined either institutionally or historically. Thus the first basic prerequisite for building up personal trust is that human actions are perceived in general as personally determined.[6] Trust is founded on the motivation attributed to behaviours. Conduct on the experience of which trust depends must appear as an expression and reaffirmation of personality. However, only such actions as are treated institutionally as 'free' are imputed to personality.[7] Firstly, there is freedom, in the, as it were, pre-social sense of other people's uncontrollable potency to act – the source of the need for trust. Secondly, there is institutionalized freedom, namely freedom bound up with and moderated through the social order, freedom as a complex of actions or aspects of actions for which one is personally responsible, which is the source of the ability to learn trust. In order for trust to emerge and fulfil its function, freedom must be transferred from one form into the other.

The question of which actions or aspects of actions are considered significant as expressing personality is less a matter of pure causality than of what clarifies, normalizes or delimits the causal social context. Social expectation determines whether or not actions are attributed to personality. The institutionalization of such expectation, however, is a selective, simplifying process which reinforces what is selected. A few examples will serve to clarify this.

An action will not be reckoned as attributable to personality if it is recognized as the result of a direct instruction from a superior (even if the instruction amounts to putting a signature to a proposal made by the subordinate). Therefore, subordinates who want to show themselves to be trustworthy must strive to exhibit the utmost industriousness, conscientiousness and readiness to carry out tasks loyally, well beyond what is customary practice. And, on the other hand, the same reason gives rise to the opposite strategy, namely, of rising to higher positions in order to reach a status in which, according to accepted opinion, one is regarded as personality-visible and can make free decisions (even if structure and circumstances virtually predetermine those decisions).[8] In general, roles, not causal laws, serve in social life as the basis for judging any behaviour to be voluntary, i.e. intentional, or involuntary, i.e. unintentional.[9] Further to this, the outcome of any complex technological process – and this includes what results from actions by superiors – appears to be relatively impersonal. The greater the combination of recognizable causes, the more difficult it becomes to isolate who originated the action. Who was responsible for Hiroshima? Appraising the behaviour of motorists clearly reveals a combination of complex mediate effects, the visible demands of circumstances, and personally attributable behaviour. A mechanically generated high speed, although responsible for everything, is not a matter of personal choice but 'normal' practice. On the other hand, unexpected reactions are attributed to the person because of the considerable demands made on concentration and skill. Acting according to the norm is usually inconspicuous and weak in expression, and therefore is not a suitable base from which love and trust can be generated.[10] What proof of being deserving of trust can anyone give by saying that he has never been in prison? Against this, deviant behaviour, initiative or criticism are attributed personally. They can only occur if the social order can at the same time offer security, for such behaviour assumes the existence of relationships of trust and strengthens them by utilizing them. In market exchange, where deals can be concluded immediately because of the guarantees afforded by financial and credit systems which bridge differences in time, it is true that personal interests are reflected in the choice of goods, but such deals do not reflect character traits relevant to the question of trust. The same does not apply to presents and favours, which call for expressions of thanks; they arise spontaneously, and run the risk of not being reciprocated.

In a situation which is relatively open-ended, double contingent, and where both parties can operate selective choices which influence one another, it is possible to set in motion a process which forms trust by tackling the problem of the reduction of complexity over several discrete steps, i.e. sequentially.[11] The process itself has, on the one hand, a framework of conditions by which it is made possible and, on the other, requirements for steps to be taken to strengthen the process of mutual selection which brings trust into being. We must maintain the distinction between conditions of possibility and conditions of realization, at least for purposes of analysis.

First of all there has to be some cause for displaying trust. Some situation has to be defined in which the person trusting is dependent on his partner, otherwise the problem does not arise. His behaviour must then commit him to this situation and make him run the risk of his trust being betrayed. In other words he must invest in what we called earlier a 'risky advance'. One fundamental condition is that it must be possible for the partner to abuse the trust; indeed, it must not merely be possible for him to do so but he must also have a considerable interest in doing so.[12] It must not be that he will be likely to toe the line on his own account – in the light of his own interests.[13] In his subsequent behaviour the trust put in him must be honoured and his own interests put to one side. For this shelving of interests to serve as confirmation of trust, it must attain a certain level – it must present itself as a sort of missed opportunity, and not merely as the temporary postponement of a betrayal of trust. All these elements in combination might constitute the first sequence in building up trust. From this we can already draw one important conclusion – that the process demands *mutual commitment* and can only be put to the test by both sides becoming involved in it, in a fixed order, first the trusting and then the trusted person.

However, we have as yet only covered one initial possibility, and, even then, only the course it outwardly follows. There are, in addition, cognitive and normative aspects which cannot be arranged at will into some arbitrary sequence but must follow a definite order. It does not suffice for the process simply to take some particular course. The participants must know the exact situation and they must know from one another that each knows it. The building up of trust therefore depends on easily interpretable situations and not least, for that reason, on the possibility of communication.[14] In some cases a *post hoc* inference will suffice; it might even be that ignorance of particular aspects does no harm, i.e. does not obstruct progress towards trust, but this can hardly be decided without empirical research. However, the process may become more liable to break down where relevant circumstances are not known, even if the requisite behaviour has been followed in the initial phases. It can also become more liable to break down through an excess of knowledge, such as when the participants mutually infer that the process is being employed in order to build up trust. For in such instances, motives are unavoidably put in question, and such questioning can easily turn into distrust.

Finally, we must add normative requirements to the cognitive ones we were able to deal with only in rather vague terms. Questions of the ethics of trust will not be dealt with until Chapter 12. Here we are only concerned with the questions whether and how the process whereby trust is generated can become the object of norms. This brings us up against a difficulty of a rather special kind. As we have seen, at the start of the process lies a risky advance, which because of its wagerlike nature does not lend itself easily to being disciplined by norms, corresponding in this sense to heroic or saintly acts. The same thing can be said of the act whereby trust demonstrated by one individual evokes a corresponding response on the part of another. In both cases the formulation of norms would simply shift the problem to another level, with no serious guarantee that trust would actually ensue. It is not possible to demand the trust of others; trust can only be offered and accepted. It is for this reason that demands to trust cannot start trust relationships off. This can only be done by what we have called an advance. The initiator may confer trust, or perhaps utilize an opportunity arisen by chance, to show himself trustworthy (for instance by returning a lost object which he has found). The truster sees in his own vulnerability the instrument whereby a trust relationship may be created. Only his own original trust offers him the possibility of putting it forward as a norm that his trust is not to be disappointed, and thus bringing the other over to his side. However, the impossibility of formulating trust in a normative sense does not totally exclude it altogether from the normative sphere.

We can use an old concept and qualify this peculiar advance with normative consequences we have been talking about as a *supererogatory performance*. One may call supererogatory a performance which does not flow from some previously assumed duty but manifests itself as meritorious, and attracts respect. In spite of recent attempts,[15] the relationship between such a performance and duty remains logically and analytically obscure. However, what is of interest to us here is purely its function in the genesis of trust. It entails somehow an excess on the normative which has some parallels with the excess on the information discussed previously; it constitutes a surplus performance, which nobody can require, but which (for the self-same reason) engenders claims – as benefactions for instance engender a claim to gratitude. Trust relationships are not imposed, but are normalized subsequently. Thus, the function of this supererogative can be seen in the fact that *it transforms conditions for emergence into conditions for maintenance*. And this is exactly what is required if trust is to emerge.

If supererogatory qualities function as a rule for generating claims which can become the object of norms, they cannot, of course, be brought into play arbitrarily, but rather only where such claims are acceptable. Help and gratitude are one case; trust another. Obviously such limitations cannot entirely exclude abuse. One can create a bond by showing trust, as one can by giving a present.[16] The only way to counteract this is at the beginning, when the relationship is still at the voluntary stage, by refusing more or less tactfully to participate in the process.

We are, however, still at the beginning. We have described one typical basic unit in the process of building up trust. Usually several are involved. For in the first round no one plays for high stakes – neither with great personal commitment nor against powerful interests. Deception and deviant behaviour on both sides are instances which illustrate very aptly the sequential character of the general process, its problems and its tactics.

A personal relationship on the basis of mutual favours usually opens with small-scale activities. Kindnesses, offers of help, and small gifts which cost nothing are proffered in a form which leaves room for tactful rejection. The relationship can only be deepened when acts of friendship have been reciprocated, when there is a spark of grateful recognition, and when the relationship has stood the test of everyday coming and going. It can then involve larger gifts, and, because each person trusts the other, can sustain a long, drawn-out imbalance. At this stage of development, immediate and exactly gauged reciprocation becomes a sign of distrust, because the person acting in this way presents himself as someone wanting to extricate himself as soon as possible from the bonds of gratitude. Such behaviour makes it impossible for the donor to display trust and for the recipient to prove himself when burdened by trust in the manner suggested.

A similar deepening of trust, demanding even greater delicacy, sensitivity and tact, can be observed when illegal – or semi-legal – matters are concerned.[17] Where involvement in espionage, in homosexual relationships or in drug traffic is concerned, or even in the case of far less extreme instances – such as when secretaries exchange indiscretions, or newcomers are being initiated into the usages common in workplaces[18] – a series of tests has first to be gone through without those involved being betrayed, allowing them to retreat indignantly behind the screen which behavioural norms provide, or to explain it away as some harmless misunderstanding. The true character of the relationship only unfolds slowly when the candidate appears to pass the tests – and for this he must himself carry out counter-tests or even involve himself to such an extent in the situation where he too would then be guilty. Once mutual trust has been safely established, it would be blatantly tactless – if not a quite disastrous lapse – if one of the participants wanted to return to the learning stage and to use the cautious strategies which were sensible at that early juncture.

If we may now generalize, it is clear that such learning processes are only complete when the person to be trusted has had opportunities to betray that trust and has not used them.[19] It is impossible to eliminate this risk during the process of learning. It can, however, be divided up into small stages and thereby minimized. But there are two qualifications to be added to this rule.

One must not infer that during the learning process trust can grow steadily and expand uninterruptedly into more important and consequential matters. To that extent experimental research in social psychology, which is concerned solely with minimal and trifling risks, affords a misleading basis for generalization.[20] Changes in what is at stake and shifts in the balance between anticipated advantage and possible loss build into the learning process thresholds which make for qualitative differences – for instance, when the person who trusts is risking not only himself but also others, his family, his work, or his country. In so far as this happens to be the case, there are additional conditions for consensus formation and responsibility adjustment. A second example concerns the opposite of the conditions necessary to build up trust. In completely risk-free role relationships (for example, if the participants are shielded from all personal consequences by their membership of an organization) there are hardly any available starting points for the development and stabilization of personal trust. In this regard even establishing acquaintanceship is severely limited.[21] Although trust is even then an inescapable basis for the conduct of existence, it is not primarily in the form of personal trust. It seems that personal trust is only formed where it is needed. This is the case – even today – if the individual personality takes on a social-structural relevance, if the configuration of interaction relationships is arranged in the social system in such a way that it can only be arranged thus and now has to be restructured after that individual ceases to be involved. Equally characteristic of modern society are those borderline cases of personal trust which occur not at the level of large organized systems but within simple, everyday interaction systems. Such instances are frequently short, involve different participants, are impersonal and are unlikely to be repeated, but they nevertheless not infrequently involve considerable risk. A clear example is the problem of risks and trust involved in a taxi ride.[22] Due to lack of time and lack of background knowledge the participants have to depend on highly standardized 'tests' of the normality of the situation – and on a sufficiently normalized environment which makes the risk, although serious, appear unlikely. In this context it is particularly worth noting that a breakdown in the environmental premises cannot be cushioned by building up trust within a small system, but at best involves reorganizing the way one approaches the taxi.

Questions of how far personal trust is still needed today, in which social systems, and in which functions, would make a subject for extensive empirical research. Such research would, I suppose, indicate very quickly that the need to orientate oneself to other people's individual characteristics is as strong now as ever it was in all areas of social life where repeated contact takes place,[23] and that the myth of mass society has its origins in some kind of optical illusion. On the other hand there is no doubt that modern differentiated social orders are much too complex for the social trust essential to ordinary living to be created solely by this type of orientation towards persons. It is all too obvious that the social order does not stand and fall by the few people one knows and trusts. There must be other ways of building up trust which do not depend on the personal element. But what are they?

Notes

1 As I have tried to show in another context, conscience serves as a control centre for the reduction of the potential for action to the scale of the individual personality. See Luhmann (1965a). It could also be said that trust is placed fundamentally in the functioning of conscience. This would explain the sense in which conscience at once individualizes and socializes.

2 See particularly Goffman (1959, 1955).

3 Such socially naive spontaneity, of course, assumes a high degree of trust by the actor in his audience – trust in their trust, if you like; this is only possible in a tightly structured social consensus. For remarks along this line see Burns (1953), especially p. 661; Blau (1964), pp. 60ff. (especially p. 75); Luhmann (1965c), especially pp. 169ff.; and on the particular dangers of unconsidered surrender to the situation, see Goffman (1957). Sociometric research also works from this basic idea and attempts to promote spontaneity by means of groupings strong in consensus and trust. For example see Jennings (1950), especially pp. 320f.

4 An example of this is given in the remarks of Guest (1962), pp. 82ff., to the effect that initiatives from below also increased when the climate of trust in a factory improved. See also Zand (1972).

5 For a general discussion of this point, see Claessens (1970), pp. 122ff. For its application to the formation of trust, see Pilisuk and Skolnick (1968).

6 See Strickland (1958). Deutsch (1962), pp. 304ff., refers to 'perceived intentions'.

7 For an interpretation of freedom as the institutionalization of a sphere of personally attributable action (and not as lack of determinacy), see Luhmann (1965b), pp. 63ff.

8 For the significance of hierarchies in distorting perceptions and guiding the attribution of responsibility, see Thibaut and Riecken (1955); Jones, Davis and Gergen (1961); Jones, Gergen and Jones (1963); Friedeburg (1963), pp. 113ff.

9 See Turner (1962), especially p. 28. For a fundamental analysis see Heider (1944, 1958).

10 See also Weigert (1949), pp. 304f.

11 Swinth (1967) contains theoretical statements on this theme, and an experimental test. See also Pilisuk and Skolnick (1968). For the case of deception see also Blau (1964), pp. 91ff., pp. 107f., and for further illustrations Goffman (1969), pp. 130ff.

12 Swinth (1967), pp. 336f., shows that this condition (the existence of a contrary interest) can be replaced by another. Trust can also arise where there is no interest in violating it, but on condition that both parties mutually show trust, i.e. duplicate the other conditions.

13 For such cases of 'untrusted credibility' see Goffman (1969), pp. 105ff.

14 One of the more definite findings from the 'Prisoner's Dilemma' experiments is that the formation of trust is hindered by the exclusion of communication. See Goffman (1969), p. 24, Note 3. See also Loomis (1959); Wichman (1970).

15 See Feinberg (1961); Stocker (1968).

16 We may conclude from this that in some situations it is advisable, if possible, to escape the trust offered by a stranger if one is in no position to live up to it. Tirpitz must have experienced this when, in his memoirs, he singled out 'slight disfavour' as the most satisfactory relationship with a monarch. Tirpitz (1920), p. 133. See also the rules for avoiding acquaintanceship assembled by Goffman (1963a), pp. 112ff.

17 See also remarks by Simmel (1922), pp. 284ff., on learning trust in secret societies. Simmel very rightly points out that it is the continual problem of always having to renew trust which becomes a strong social binding force. The same can be said of our previous example, the free exchange of favours.

18 The literature of organizational sociology shows many incidental examples of this. For somewhat greater detail see, for example, Blau (1960); Long (1962); Evan (1963). The case of the new recruit is also especially suitable for the institutionalizing of 'thresholds' of trust (see also Chapter 10), which can be indicated, for example, by an initiation ritual. For one example see Janowitz (1960), pp. 128ff., on 'initiation techniques' in the American army, particularly at West Point.

19 For this reason distrust is a bad basis for learning trust, as the experiment carried out by Strickland (1958) showed in the case of strict supervision. The distrustful person structures what he perceives in such a way that he attributes acts which could make the actor appear trustworthy not to the actor himself but to other causes (for example, his own distrustful precautions).

20 Epstein makes the same point in his remarks on Deutsch (1962), pp. 319f. See also Wrightsman (1966).

21 For more detail see Luhmann (1964), pp. 355ff.

22 See Henslin (1968).

23 This even applies to the supposedly extremely impersonal workings of large bureaucracies. See Luhmann (1962).

7

Communications Media and System Trust

In simple social systems a secure mode of living which went beyond trust in specific other people was established – in so far as it was at all – by means of religiously based assumptions about true being, nature and the supernatural, by means of myth, language and natural law. This meant that the right ordering of things was taken as normative and assumed to be trustworthy. In this sense the world was removed from human disposition and its complexity assumed to be already reduced. No impersonal forms of trust were required. Whenever it was necessary to communicate, or to explain, this order of things, this was achieved via the authority of gods, saints or knowledgeable interpreters, who were trusted in the same way as one trusts a person. In contrast to this, differentiated social orders have an increased capacity for processing problems and can therefore view the world as more complex.[1] A very complex world, which is rich in possibilities but is nevertheless determined or determinable, can only be formed and held in view if, and in so far as, the consequential tasks of selecting experience and action can be regulated and divided within social systems. The individual's capacity, which is limited, can only be increased marginally. Thus a high degree of complexity in the world assumes a multiplicity of selective processes – means by which selections are connected one with the other. And it can only guarantee a simultaneous and present world if selection can be presented not only as the result of one's own actions but also as a simultaneous and present, or currently memorizable or expected, selectivity of others. In this sense there are intrinsic *connections between the complexity of the world on the one hand and the socially regulated processes for differentiating and connecting multiple selections on the other*.

We employ the concept of generalized media of communication in order to tackle this problem, and to designate devices additional to everyday language, devices which are symbolically generalized codes of selection, the function of which is to provide the capacity for intersubjective transmission of acts of selection over shorter or longer chains. Truth, love, power, money[2] are outstanding examples of this kind of device which have evolved successfully.[3] Through the generalizing capacity of such media, structures of expectation and patterns of motivation are formed which make it possible for selections made by one individual to be relevant to another, in the sense that he is aware of them and also does not treat them as an open question but performs his own selections as consequences of them.

The increasing differentiation and working out of such media, the cultural legitimation of increasingly complex forms and their support in differentiated social systems, such as the political state, science or the economy, acquire a wide-ranging significance for the evolution of the societal system, above all for the emergence of modern society and the particularly wide world horizon. This is something which cannot be elaborated with detailed evidence in this present essay. Our special interest is the fact that there is concurrently a perceptible alteration in the conditions under which trust comes to be the basic assumption of a normal and rational way of life. In so far as the world becomes more complex and, at the same time, more capable of being determined by contingent processes, so that conscious acceptance of this change increases its effectiveness, the old unity of nature as a source of norms disintegrates, or is forced back to extremely formal decision-making premises. The jump from general and common assumptions of belief to personal trust can no longer bridge the ever-growing gap and the increasing length of the chains of selective processes. Trusting other people no longer readily includes accepting their view of the world as authoritative. One has to learn to put up with different interpretations of the world, linking one's own behaviour nevertheless to the selections of others. Trust then becomes, so to say, privatized, psychologized and thereby individual-tolerant; or else its function is narrowed down to certain types of communication in which the other person is demonstrably competent.

In these circumstances, the need for the social capacity for selection to be connected with the scale of the individual's ability to take decisions and to act becomes a more complex and differentiated affair. The differentiated media of communication, their language and their symbols, bring new sorts of risk and thus pose a new type of problem in regard to trust. It has now become apparent that communication is made by people and affects people, but it no longer rests on an unchanging view of what is right or on close personal acquaintance. How is it that, in spite of this, such communications are reliable, and their reduction of complexity can be trusted? How is the intersubjective transfer of selection processes, already accomplished, made possible? We hope to clarify these questions by using the examples of money, truth and legitimate political power.

To summarize the known facts briefly, money is transferable freedom against a limited choice of goods. It guarantees this freedom abstractly, by means of an opportunity for exchange, on a quantitatively limited basis, leaving open questions of when, with whom, for which object and under what conditions the person possessing the money will carry out the exchange. Money is acquired by means of communication without the value of the money changing during the process of communication, or, in other words, without forfeiting the complexity of which it is a manifestation. When acquired, the money symbol expresses a certain uncertainty in the available possibilities of gain, and makes possible reduction of this complexity according to individual wishes. The decision about how this complexity will be reduced, how, when, and with whom, and for what purpose the individual spends his money has, in principle, no consequences for the social system – and that is one of the prerequisites for the institutionalization of general, individual freedom.[4]

A cross-section of the whole economic system in all its complexity can therefore be placed literally in the individual's hand by means of money. We do not need here to go into detail about the indispensability of such a decentralizing mechanism for the formation of a complex economic system. However, there has to be a presumption that money itself enjoys trust for the mechanism to be workable. The individual must be able to work on the basis that, when he holds the money symbol in his hand, he also really possesses the possibilities which it promises, so that he can confidently put off his decision about the final use of the money and can enjoy or make best use of the complexity of the possibilities it represents in abstract form. This is where at the junction of the temporal and social dimensions the contours of the general problem of trust are clearly displayed. A rational search for advantage by indirect means, renouncing gratification, deferments or advances which may be implied, can only be capable of motivation if the disturbing interference of other people's free and incalculable actions can be excluded by trust. The question is how such trust, which is quite independent of whatever material value serves as support to the money symbol, can be built up and maintained.

Anyone who trusts in the stability of the value of money, and the continuity of a multiplicity of opportunities for spending it, basically assumes that a system is functioning and places his trust in that function and not in known people. Such system trust is virtually automatically built up through continual affirmative experience in utilizing money. It needs constant 'feedback' but does not require specific built-in guarantees and is therefore incomparably easier to acquire than personal trust in new and different people all the time. On the other hand, it is incomparably more difficult to control. It is true that there are numerous events relating specifically to money which have symptomatic significance for the question of trust. They serve as warnings for those in the know and are suggestive of specific defensive or adaptive reactions. But to retain mastery over such events places very great demands on attention, time, the acquisition of knowledge, and intelligence, so only a few people manage it. By converting personal trust into system trust, the process of learning is rendered easier, but control is made more difficult. Thus, typically, trust in money arises in, as it were, an automatically learned fashion, whereby the person trusting realizes his dependence on the functioning of a highly complex system which he cannot see through, although in principle it can be seen through. The person trusting knows he is unable to make corrections; he thus feels himself exposed to unforeseeable circumstances, but nevertheless has to continue trusting as though under compulsion to do so. Whenever such trust in money is institutionalized, and, generally speaking, sustained, a sort of *equivalent-certainty* is created. Anyone who has money has at his disposal a *generalized* means of solving problems and within that context is able to do without anticipating *specific* problem situations. Liquidity reduces the need for information.[5] At this stage every financial investment, every abandonment of liquidity, becomes a problem. The disposal of money involves a sacrifice of freedom and of certainty. Thus it requires a specific guarantee, to be found on the one hand in exact planning and anticipation of the results of investment, and on the other in maintaining an exactly calculated balance.[6] Besides, this is how the possibility of sacrificing liquidity and still maintaining it – for example by converting money into marketable securities – gains a key position both for the individual and for the economic system. This logical marvel of the simultaneous sacrifice and maintenance of liquidity is achieved by means of increasing the money supply,[7] and thus implies an increase in, and thereby the increasing vulnerability of, system trust.

In such an order, uncertainties in the economic system can affect decisions about investment in a twofold, contradictory way, according to what level of generalization they reach, on the whole. Uncertainties can, if they make anticipation of economic events more difficult (or if they increase the costs of information and planning), strengthen the preference for liquidity as an equivalent of certainty and can cause investment to be cut back. They can also, on the contrary, shatter trust in money as a whole and can initiate a 'flight into material assets'. This double effect makes precise control of individual decisions through monetary policies difficult. As a result, individual decisions about both keeping and using money are, through the question of trust, made dependent on the whole system, and indeed, characteristically the more so, the more rationally they are calculated.

As a certainty-equivalent which can guarantee in the present the fulfilment of as yet uncertain future expectations, money is at the same time a functional equivalent for other forms of trust. Within the context of those needs which can be satisfied with money, it fulfils the same time-spanning and risk-absorbing function in a more precise and more effective form because it is specifically designed for such functions, and it thus renders trust redundant. Anyone who has money has no need, in that respect, to trust others. Generalized trust in the institution of money, then, replaces, through one all-inclusive act, the countless individual, difficult demonstrations of trust which would be necessary to provide a sure foundation for life in a co-operative society.

While in the case of money it is left to the individual to make the reduction of complexity conform with his situation and his needs, in the case of truth we are concerned with a complementary counter-principle which precedes the individualization of human beings into discrete points of view. The medium of truth is related to the experience of meaning, and encompasses all meaning which can be regarded as able to be transmitted intersubjectively. When confronted with true meaning, everyone must acknowledge it and accept the reduction which is accomplished thereby – or lose his role as a human subject involved with others in constitutive activities, as a fellow participant in the world, and with it his social identity. Truth is the medium which acts as carrier for the reduction of intersubjective complexity. Trust is only possible where truth is possible,[8] where people can reach agreement about any given entity which is binding upon a third party. Truth facilitates this understanding, and thus the reduction of complexity, by the assumption that the third party would also consider their view as correct.

In this, each individual must be able to presume that the orientation of the other is somehow related to truth. The amount of societal complexity which exists is overwhelmingly large. The individual can therefore make use of it only if it is presented to him in an already reduced, simplified, prearranged form. In other words, he has to be able to depend and to rely on the external processing of information. He knows who knows how the engine of his car works, how his gastritis can best be treated. He might distrust the newspapers but still assumes that their news is at least news. He relies on the fact that the representatives of his insurance firm give him factually correct information on insurance matters. In a highly complex environment this type of trust can no longer take the form of personal trust, although this form does still exist, for example when one's doctor is also a family friend.[9] Its typical form is trust in specialized and demonstrable abilities to process information, in functional authority,[10] and, ultimately, in the ability of science to function as an action system. For example, if a politician gauges his actions on the results of empirical electoral research, he must trust that the interviewers really did conduct interviews and did not, for example, substitute their own analyses of trends in place of interviews.

Typologies of authority which take account of this circumstance are among the topics of current interest, particularly in the sociological analysis of organizations.[11] To expose the trust problem which is contained in such analysis clearly depends on illuminating the background which permits authority to be authority in the first place. Authority is always a representation of a complexity which is not explained in detail.[12] Its style depends on how the possibility of explanation is projected. As the old cosmos of truth has broken down, radical changes have occurred in the

manner in which the world is knowable and recognizable as familiar. The
theme of factual experience always relates to other possible, but unrealized, experiences. The world gains unity solely from the horizon of this
'and so forth'. This experiential potentiality surrounds and influences
factual experience today differently from what obtained in earlier times.[13]
One knows, or senses, that behind every experience of objects there are
possible statements and that behind every statement there lie human
processes through which information has been worked on and worked
out – not some immutable Truth of Being. In principle these processes
are intersubjectively controllable, having the task of providing everyone
with accessible knowledge, and are thus independent of particular societal structures and, above all, independent of higher status based on, for
example, religious, political or economic functions.[14] This principle of
intersubjectivity, and hence the separation from particular given societal
structures, now underwrites the certainty value of statements and, in
this modern sense, their truth. It follows that whatever prevents the individual from uncovering his own premises can be only the complexity of
concrete relationships and not something like the hidden nature of truth,
or social constraints on revealing them. Accordingly, authority is not a
matter of wisdom bestowed by grace on a few people, but a matter of
some specific competence learned, and practised, within the framework
of the division of labour.

In this form, authority also has need of trust that communicates the
truth.[15] This differentiates it from other forms of takeover by alien sets of
assumptions coming, for example, from power. The advance made by one
who trusts consists here in the uncritical use of information which others
have drawn up – accordingly he commits himself to the danger that the
information may prove false, or not what he anticipated. On the other
hand, the object of trust in the case of functional authority, as with money,
is basically abstract and thus intangible. It is often the case that one has an
authentic sender, but he is only the last link in a long chain of information-
processing. Does one trust the chemist, or his assistant, or the doctor, or
is it medicine, science or technology? It is true that mistakes can usually
be located later. We know today why it was that thalidomide (marketed
in Germany as Contergan) had such frightful consequences. What previously was the basis for the total assurance that the information processes
leading to the advice 'Take Contergan' were not mistaken?

Here too we have to reckon with a sort of diffuse, encompassing trust.
We do not know the individual factors on which this trust in experts
depends.[16] It is related to knowledge, to technology, but also to the fact
that a huge amount of factual knowledge can be accumulated and stored
in highly differentiated societies. This knowledge is not a system in the
sense of a logically closed combination of sentences, but in the sense of an
ordering of communication behaviour which ensures a certain care and
attention to particular rules when selecting and utilizing the premises

for an utterance. In relation to such knowledge, everyone relies on there being sufficient controls over reliability built into the system, and on the fact that these controls function independently of the structure of the personal motives of any of the participants at any given time, so that one does not need to know personally those who have drawn up that knowledge.[17]

Finally, let us discuss a third and last example. Trust in legitimate political power. While the cases of trust in money and in an authority which dispenses information are concerned with typical decentralized forms for the reduction of complexity, the organization of political and administrative force tends to centralize the process of reduction, which amounts to an ability to make binding decisions.[18] The formation of political opinions, reaching consensus, and the articulation of interests with which state bureaucracies are confronted, as well as bureaucratic decision-making, are all processes in which there is an organized, and thereby strengthened, selectivity at work. This selectivity paves the way for decisions which are not in themselves to be understood, but which nevertheless have on them the seal of binding legitimacy. If necessary, these decisions are carried out by force. In this case, therefore, the medium of communication is neither money nor truth, but power.

It is not easy to say how far trust is necessary for this process of power-supported simplification, and where such trust is to be placed.[19] So it is not surprising that the old theme of political trust, which used to play such a large role, particularly in the period after the end of the religious civil wars,[20] has virtually disappeared from contemporary political theory.[21] Its place as a conceptual category is taken, in recent theorizing about the political system, by 'support'.[22] However, the connection between the apparatus of popular representation in democratic politics through which conditions of trust have to be operationalized, and the social processes which really build up trust, is still unclear. It is not achieved by means of an appeal (whether impassioned or matter-of-fact) for 'trust in the political leadership', although it is not unimportant if one finds that personalizing this one link in the decision-making process, which occurs at the summit of the political system, makes it possible to put some sort of quasi-personal trust in political service.

The lack of clarity in the mechanisms for the formation of trust is based, first of all, on the fact that, in politics, the impetus towards commitment – both the advance made by the person trusting, and whatever he is putting his trust in – evaporate into a cloud of uncertainty. The metaphor of the 'social contract', according to which naturally free people undertake to trust each other or the established sovereign, has no counterpart in real life. Certainly, the citizen casts his vote. But to vote is not to mandate someone to represent one's interests. What is declared as the main aim of this institution is for the elected representatives of the people to reach decisions according to criteria of the public good. But they demand sovereign power to take decisions, and one cannot trust a sovereign. An ultimate power to decide generates its own norms. In this case a trust can at most refer to an awareness of the limits on sovereignty.

However, this dilemma of sovereignty and trust is merely a conceptual specification in exaggerated form of the problem of the reduction of complexity in politics which, in reality, is not solved in this black and white way but in the many small steps by which information is processed – steps which at first articulate interests, sound out possible points of consensus, push people into positions, test general programmatic proposals, and then bring about, for the time being, a consolidation of what is binding, by decisions about legislation, the budget, or general directions of policy. These are then worked through detailed processes of 'interpretation' and 'application' into countless ad hoc decisions. Each stage attains a new level of selectivity which absorbs new information and excludes alternatives. In all this, what is sovereign is just this drive towards reduction, towards narrowing the scope for decisions, and excluding other possibilities. This process is made trustworthy because it is reached by many small stages and is open to information at all of them, so that, although the process is carried out centrally in order to guarantee the unanimity of the decision, sovereignty cannot be exercised at one stroke, i.e. arbitrarily. It would seem that even the social system learns that it is best to offer trust in small doses which individually do not put too much at risk.

In view of this ordering of information-processing, the citizen's trust can no longer take the simple form of trust in the legality and appropriateness of the exercise of official powers by those holding them. Instead, there is differentiation of the situation of trust. Political trust is demanded and given on two different levels of generalization.[23] On the one hand the citizen cherishes certain expectations about what will be decided, possibly about what concerns himself, or about the style of politics he favours, and he can use his vote as an expression of overall disappointment or satisfaction. On the other hand, he shows his trust in the political system as such by remaining in the country and counting on being able to lead a reasonable life. Individual expectations about decisions do, it is true, contain fairly clear criteria for trust, but they do not commit the citizen deeply and they commit each one in a different way. The expression of disappointment can remain generalized, can be made lightly and can remain almost of no consequence. Against this, system trust is to a great extent indefinite, but, on the other hand, involves commitment and consequence which can be a matter of life and death. The interlocking of both levels of trust results in the stability of the overall order – and makes the question of trust more complicated in comparison with notions of personal trust in officials which obtained in former times.

To give now a résumé and take the argument further. Money, truth and power are generalized media of communication, which serve as transmitters of reduced complexity. They offer, each in its own way, a capacity for the reduction of complexity for the communications in their area – and this is expressed in the concept of 'medium'.[24] The reduction of complexity assumes trust on the part of those who are expecting such reduction and of those who are supposed to accept it once it is accomplished. In both respects, in the style of complexity reduction, and in the kind of trust assumed, the media are affected and changed by the process of the development of civilization leading in the direction of greater social differentiation and greater social complexity. This development illustrates and sharpens the extent to which all human interaction is contingent. Differentiated communications media cannot therefore just be left with the slender hope that 'everything will turn out fine', but presuppose a processing of the selectivity of the experience and actions of others in the form of a media-specific trust.[25] At the same time one becomes aware of the reduction and of the transfer of reduced complexity as an organizational need for systems of human communicative behaviour. So the trust which is focused specifically on the money one has in in one's hand, on the person who provides information or on the blood relationship with those in power, no longer suffices as a basis for trust. The systems of reduction themselves demand trust and sustain it.

However, one must bear in mind that – with trust in generalized media of communication as with trust in general – a minimum of real foundation is required.[26] The pillars of trust must be built on solid ground. In the cases we have discussed, the supports of trust are mainly found in opportunities for effective communication, that is, in the possibility of exchanging money for things of real and lasting value,[27] in the possibility of reaching a definite agreement in the kinds of statement in which truth is demanded, in the possibility of activating the means of coercion which belong to the state on the basis of set rules. Given these opportunities for communication, the person who gives his trust is in possession of enough reality to be able usually to opt out of using them. Thus he places twofold trust in two different levels of generalization. Firstly, he trusts in the effectiveness of certain opportunities for communication as a safety valve, should it become necessary; secondly, he trusts in the general functioning of the system, which enormously increases the effectiveness of these opportunities. In this he does not normally separate the two aspects in his consciousness and this makes it possible to generalize trust as regarding highly abstract system processes.

The dimension of time becomes especially relevant in all these generalized mechanisms, and this explains at the same time why trust is a prerequisite for them. If a system has liquid assets, if it has power, it can postpone its decisions and nevertheless secure them within a given context of possible choices. The system can form long chains connecting selective events without being able to know or specify in advance the situations which are thereby co-ordinated.[28] It thus gains time for complex information-processing decisions, which make it possible to adapt to the environment at a higher level of complexity. The same can be said for truth. It enables certain structures in the environment to be held constant so that the system can relate to them. In so far as proven truths are established, the system does not need to reckon on everything changing at the same time. The gain in reaction time here is a result of being able, without danger, to be indifferent to a multiplicity of possible events in the environment.

While trust may expand the time horizon of a system, loss of trust may make it contract, thus diminishing the system's complexity and its potential for giving satisfaction. If many demands which, in the long term, could have been satisfied, are registered simultaneously or within a short space of time owing to lack of trust, this will destroy the system's possibilities of fulfilling those demands. The system must then take decisions about priorities and sequences with increasing harshness, which then accelerates the demands, until it must in the last resort reject the demands, and adopt drastic methods to reduce complexity, such as coercion or specific bargains with certain powerful interests.[29] Some social order capable of being institutionalized can, of course, be found even for this situation,[30] but it is at a lower level of complexity and achieves correspondingly less.

Of course, only empirical research can establish in detail how far the formation and generalization of trust does go, and how these things alter the style and the certainty of trust. Theoretical consideration of this area of abstraction cannot anticipate the result of such research. The overall set of connected propositions which it builds up does make it possible, however, to indicate possible directions of change.

All the components for the process of trust formation seem to lean on one another. These are the necessity and the method of learning, the partial shift of the problem areas to the internal from the external, and reference back to the environment in order to gain symbolic control over the object of trust. The shift to system trust seems to facilitate the learning of trust, to make inner guarantees largely dispensable, or rather to replace them with functioning interaction. But, on the other hand, it seems to make the control of trust more difficult. It makes trust diffuse and thereby resistant. It becomes almost immune to individual disappointments, which can always be explained away and passed off as a special case, while personal trust can be sabotaged by trivial treacheries. System trust does not always have to be learned anew from scratch.

Further, reference to a system seems to single out the special situation of the person trusting. It seems, for example, to bring to mind the situation of the person who does not check what others have worked out, or the kind of person who measures the political system according to his own individual expectations about decisions, or the situation of the person who can satisfy an individual set of needs with the help of money. On the other hand, trust in the large reduction mechanisms is so inevitable that it does not need to be consciously perceived as a subjective activity which one can continue or drop, as in the case of personal trust. Thus system trust hardly becomes an open matter for public discussion, and, again, the fact that it is something latent helps maintain its integrity.

In addition, a peculiar independence from motivation is characteristic of system trust.[31] As we have just remarked, an individual hardly has the opportunity to question his own motives about whether or not he wishes to place trust in money, political power or what is established as professionally attested truth. Motivation enters just as little into the question in the case of the person who, in a concrete instance, is trusted because what he communicates is accepted (in so far as concrete individuals appear relevant at all in this). All the same, this puts a different complexion on the problem of deception and the general problem of self-presentation which is basic to it. While, in personal trust, one must penetrate such presentation, anticipate deception and arm oneself against it, the case of system trust relieves one of these requirements for trust. No one would want to term as deception the fact that the bank lends out more money than it possesses, that the state issues more commands than it can enforce by using the police, that more information is divulged in professional advice than could be backed up empirically or logically. Trust is in these cases, through generalization and indifference to questions of motive, placed above the level where deceptions are to be expected and are dangerous.

Finally, control over system trust demands increasing expert knowledge. That goes without saying in financial affairs and truth. Here only an expert can make even a cursory examination of what are indications of trustworthiness. But today even an appraisal of political forces and developments demands an exacting amount of detailed knowledge, mainly about people, roles and organizations, which can only be gained by taking an active part in the political process. In practical terms, control over trust can be exercised only as someone's main occupation. Everybody else must rely on the specialist involved in such control, and thus is forced to remain on the periphery of events. In other words, if they are not organized, controls must be built into systems which require trust, and those controls must be made quite explicit within them. Trust in the ability of systems to function includes trust in the ability of their internal controls to function. The propensity to risk things must be kept under control within the systems themselves.

Indifference about individual motives for trusting creates its own problems in a highly complex society which individualizes anxiety on the individual, and which has even institutionalized the expectation of individualism. What should the individual make of himself in a situation where he is forced to give trust without being able to provide or control that trust himself?

This question opens up a large area for empirical research. It cannot be adequately answered here. It may be supposed that this situation will give rise to topics, problems and values of its own – such as the problem of 'security'.[32] One can also safely assume that in this way society sets long-term educational conditions for successful socialization. For example, it gives particularly positive opportunities to a type of person who is urbane and versatile, who is adaptable and who can, by adopting rational tactics, separate emotion from reality, a person with a high potential for 'taking things as they come'. On the other hand, it would be very wrong to speculate on definite psychological solutions to this problem. Since solutions to such problems are assumed to be *general* by a highly complex society, there must be *different* possibilities for a more or less happy personal adjustment to it; otherwise society would have to make a fatal reduction in its need for various highly individual personalities. It is just this essential multiplicity which makes it impossible to engage in further discussion of this question in the present context.[33]

All these considerations point to the conclusion that system trust has absorbed certain functions and attributes of familiarity (and therefore really stands beyond personally generated trust and distrust).[34] However, we are not simply concerned with familiarity with systems, but with a very much more problematic issue. Although system trust is shown to be more or less absorbed, more or less latent, it is fundamentally different from the 'naive' experience of familiarity with the everyday world. In system trust one is continually conscious that everything that is accomplished is being *produced*, that each action has been *decided on* after comparison with other possibilities. System trust *counts* on explicit processes for the reduction of complexity, i.e. on people, not nature. The great civilizing processes of transition to system trust give people a stable attitude towards what is contingent in a complex world, make it possible to live with the realization that everything could be otherwise. These processes make people able to be aware of the social contingency of the world. This thought gives rise to the question of transcendental trust in the meaningful constitution of the world.

Notes

1 See the basic points on this made by Schroder and Harvey (1963), for both social and personal systems.

2 A brief outline of this set of problems can be found in Habermas and Luhmann (1971), pp. 344ff.

3 Cf. Parsons' theory of a 'generalized mechanism' such as money, power, influence or commitment: see Parsons and Smelser (1956), pp. 70ff.; Parsons (1959a), pp. 16ff., and (1963a), especially pp. 47ff., on trust. In a German translation, Parsons (1964a), these mechanisms are termed '*Steuerungssprachen*' (languages of steering).

4 Of course, this is the case only within certain limits. To indicate these limits we need only remind ourselves of the problems of trade cycles or of the possibility of steering consumer decisions through monetary policies without interfer-

ing with individual freedom. However, what is decisive for sociology does not lie in these important insights, but is something which lies behind them, i.e. that it has been possible largely to immunize the social order against individual reductions of very complex ways of behaving and thereby to achieve a decentralization of decision-making, which then makes it possible to build up complex economic systems. An obvious comparable institution would be love (in the sense of individual passion) as a basis for marriage. This too does not only permit but even normalizes the choice of a partner within largely unlimited alternatives on the basis of individual desire, undirected by society. This too assumes that the indifference of the social order to the consequences of such decisions is guaranteed.

5 See Krüsselberg (1965), pp. 127ff., who gives a survey of the development of this idea by Keynes, Shackle and Schmölders; see also Paulsen (1950) or Tobin (1958). Keynes himself had come upon the phenomenon of trust when developing his theory of money but he declined to go into a theoretical analysis of this phenomenon, feeling it to be an empirical problem. See Keynes (1936), especially pp. 148f.

6 See Albach (1962) for the possibilities of rationally programming investment decisions from the point of view of considerations of liquidity.

7 For this reason Schmölders (1960) rightly demands a shift from a qualitative theory to a liquidity theory of money.

8 See the fundamental ideas put forward by Barth (1943), pp. 165ff.

9 See Strohal (1955), pp. 17ff., and Schottländer (1957), pp. 35ff., for an attempt to deal with authority as a relationship of personal trust.

10 Hartmann (1964) has made an especially noteworthy contribution with his analytical development of this concept.

11 See for example French and Raven (1959); Presthus (1960).

12 In his concept of authority, C. J. Friedrich explicitly points to a 'potentiality of reasoned elaboration'. See Friedrich (1958), p. 35; see also (1963), pp. 216ff.

13 See Husserl's portrayal of the significance of modern, objective science for the transformation of the world from within.

14 See Pool (1963), p. 242, for an interesting suggestion that a society which does without status as a source of cognitive credibility will have an unusually great need for trust.

15 Thus authority is here regarded as being founded in trust in every form and not vice versa, e.g. the acceptance of authority on the basis of trust as being one special type among other sorts of trust (thus, for example, Simon (1957a), pp. 111ff.).

16 In an empirical examination of this question of the variable guarantee of the presentation of expert judgement, Vesta, Meyer and Mills (1964) single out the content of the utterance (pure information and interpretation) and the acceptability of the judgement.

17 Lane (1966) opens up a series of structural problems which a 'knowledgeable society' presents, among them the problem of trust.

18 See Heller's (1934), pp. 228ff., emphasis on the nature of the state as an 'organized decision-making and executive unit', which anticipates recent American views of 'binding decisions' as the 'output function' of political systems.

19 See, however, remarks in Chapter 4 on the connection between criteria for success and the need for trust.

20 This was due to the situation of the time, prior to all theories of democracy. See, for example, the passionate appeal for the abolition of distrust and the reinstatement of trust in the Empire in Lapide (1674), Part III, Chapter 4, pp. 549ff.; see also the concept of government as trust which can be traced back to Locke (1953), Book II, Chapter 11, pp. 183ff. This, consolidated into the right of delegation, still dominates American constitutional law today. See Fraenkel (1960), pp. 180ff.

21 This is regretted by Hennis (1962), especially pp. 5ff. Krüger (1964), p. 209, mentions the idea that trust is the foundation for awareness of the state, but he does not develop it theoretically. It is revealed finally as a principle of uncritical obedience by the subject: it 'should push as far away as possible the point at which the subject, however ready to obey, must say to himself that the correctness of the order given to him must be tested'. Krüger (1964), p. 987.

22 See for example Parsons (1959b); Easton (1965b), pp. 153ff.

23 See also the remarks by Parsons (1959b) on 'political support'.

24 To this extent we are going beyond the views of Parsons, as we also did in dealing with truth as a medium for communication. For the detailed argument with Parsons, see Luhmann (1976).

25 See Baum (1976) in connection with the difference between hope and trust.

26 See the general discussion of this question in Chapter 5. An exposition of this idea, in particular for the case of generalized communications media, can be found in Parsons (1963a), especially pp. 46ff. (and 1964a). He assumes a 'basic unity of security' in each of the different media. See also the remarks by Bauer (1963), pp. 83f. and also Deutsch (1963), pp. 122ff. who uses this idea from the point of view of necessary 'damage control mechanisms'.

27 As opposed to daily consumer expenses, this must be concerned with *lasting* values, because this possibility alone can motivate the accumulation of money over and above what is needed for immediate and foreseeable use.

28 Blain (1971) sees this chain-building function as the chief significance of generalized communications media.

29 See Parsons (1964c), pp. 63f., also for the vicious circle set in motion by such loss of trust.

30 See Guzmán et al. (1962) for an extreme example.

31 This thesis could be repudiated if it were proved that readiness to establish personal trust and system trust depended on the same personality factors and that these vary in the same way. The results achieved by Rosenberg (1956, 1957) point in this direction but only deal with the disposition to make positive or negative utterances, and not the proportionate commitment. In any case we must cast some doubt on the notion that personality structures correlate so directly with the demands of social systems. It will probably be the case that system trust arises in no particular way but places a burden on the individual to a greater or lesser extent according to his personality, and he must then receive different kinds of psychological compensation. Accordingly, only the availability of the necessary compensating mechanisms makes this a social problem once more.

32 For this I must thank the stimulus given to this study by Kaufmann (1970).

33 Even Chapter 11, on readiness to trust, will not achieve this necessary division into differing, functionally equivalent, system mechanisms for building up trust, but will only be able to further the exposition of the problem.

34 The result of Kaufmann's empirical inquiry (1970) also points out that we must differentiate between two different levels, or scales, of the problem of trust.

8

The Tactical Conception: Trust as Opportunity and as Constraint

The two previous chapters have been concerned predominantly with systems which wish, or have to, bestow trust. We come now to those which want, or have to, earn trust. In both cases the location of the problem is the environment of the system. Once again we defer the question as to the system-internal conditions for the conferring or earning of trust. The analysis of trust has already afforded some occasion for tactical considerations. The learning of trust, its internalization, and the symbolic control of the object of trust have all raised the question of whether a system behaves more successfully in some particular way or in another. For us, however, as for the trusting system, analysis of the structures of the environment which make the placing of trust easier or more difficult takes precedence. The approach which we are now pursuing also gives predominance to tactical considerations. The problem is not who earns trust, but how one earns it.

It may be that in extreme cases there are people, or social systems, who earn trust simply by remaining fixedly and immovably what they are. Such an ontification of the substance of trust, together with an appropriate theoretical representation by means of the idea of trustworthy qualities or virtues, presupposes an environment which is immoveable and neither dangerous nor very complex (or else a compensating 'hereafter' which heals hurts and explains the inexplicable). In a changeable environment, the complexity of which becomes conscious, especially in its social aspects, this attitude implies dangers for the existence of the system and hence for the continuance of trust, too. Systems which are able to experience the trust they have in their environment as a problem, and are able to deal with it, are more elastic, more complex, and more durable. They lose in spontaneity and gain in reflexivity. Their self-presentation becomes more conscious, and adjustable to more complex conditions.

Trust placed in them has to rise up to the same level of reflexivity, otherwise it would experience continual disappointment. It is then no longer a matter of the other person remaining what he is, but rather of his continuing his self-presentation and of feeling himself bound by his past self-presentation. To the extent that this reflexivity becomes conscious, personal trust too becomes a variant of system trust. Only trust in the capacity for self-presentation to be reflected contains a guarantee for suitable continuity of behaviour under difficult, changing conditions. Only this form of trust regards the other person as truly free – and not merely as a being with certain constant characteristics. Only this form of trust can make itself conscious of the function of trust, the function of the reduction of complexity in the face of the freedom of the other person, and in this awareness find an orientation. Conversely, a functional theory of trust, such as is here being attempted, is only meaningful if, and in so far as, a social order is in a position to make trust in reflected presentations psychologically possible and, in social terms, to institutionalize it.

The basis of all trust is the presentation of the individual self as a social identity which builds itself up through interaction and which corresponds to its environment. Whoever presents himself from the outset as unapproachable – and this can be done in many different ways, such as by a snub, by walking past really quickly, by offending against customary demeanour or behaviour in a way which shows that one places no value on it – whoever distances himself in this way is in no position to acquire trust because he offers no opportunities for learning and testing. He may demonstrate that he is a relatively predictable factor in the situation, but one cannot trust him. Whoever wants to win trust must take part in social life and be in a position to build the expectations of others into his own self-presentation.

This is the basic rule. It must not, however, be confused with mere conformity – anything but! We have already seen that role-conformity offers little opportunity for the presentation of oneself.[1] Anyone who merely conforms will not be seen as a 'self' at all, and therefore can be trusted as little as the person who hurries past. The path to trust is through a transformative response to the expectations of others. One can fulfil them better than expected, or in a different way. Where indifference was expected, a certain outgoing quality can convince, provided it is not overdone. Where careful, reserved remarks are the norm, one can win out by being cautiously incautious. Even superiors, who are accustomed to be treated respectfully and by a restraint of criticism from their underlings, rarely appear put off by a carefree and brisk approach to business, as long as the approach is not overdone and does not degenerate either into pointlessness or into presumptuous familiarity. The tactical rule for such strategies of trust lies in recognizing functionally equivalent possibilities and in paying attention to their boundaries. To acquire personal trust means withdrawing standardized expectations, as it were, from one's partner, and replacing them with those that only he, as a distinctive personality, with a unique style, can guarantee to fulfil.

All self-presentation entails obligation – for the simple reason that it presents a self which claims to be one's identity. If one wants to remain the same, one must remain what one has shown oneself to be. In specific respects it may be possible to find good reasons for a discrepancy or so in reinterpreting one's past self-presentation, so that what is new appears as a consequence of what has gone before. Reformulations of this kind, however, are only feasible in a self which is otherwise constant and retains its integrity.[2] It is no accident that early sociologists could see that the unfamiliar stranger enjoys more freedom and is able to behave with greater freedom.[3] Anyone who has been around for some time, is already known, has trusted and enjoys trust, is thus entangled with his self-presentation in a web of norms which he himself has helped to create, and from which he cannot withdraw without leaving parts of himself behind – unless he disappears from the scene completely and simply leaves behind the illusion that he remains the same somewhere else.

In so far as the question of trust becomes a conscious, mutually culti-vated, focal point of a relationship, this self-commitment takes on a new, almost impersonal, character, and this presumes that the relevant aspects of trust have a certain degree of specification. The self is then presented from the outset as trustworthy. Self-commitment is anticipated by sub-mission to the conditions of trust. The actor in his self-presentation shows himself as interested in trust, as seeking to win trust. As this interest becomes obvious, and manipulation of the presentation transparent, the truster can rest his trust on it and control the behaviour of the actor by means of his interest, by signalling to him the conditions for the continu-ation or withdrawal of trust.

Thus in large organizations, in which the official extent of respon-sibility in the higher echelons far exceeds the individual's capacity for responsibility (i.e. the ability to process information), there arise very significant relationships of personal trust between superiors and underlings, between line executives and staff positions, between parlia-mentarians and the higher civil service. In these relationships one side, because of its overburdening responsibility, is obliged to confer personal trust, which cannot be admitted and articulated, and the other side seizes on this trust, is sensitive to its conditions and limits, cultivates it, uses it as a basis for personal influence over the truster – and justifies it by behaving in an appropriate manner. Otherwise the symbiosis, which is advantageous to both sides, cannot be maintained in the long run.[4] This arrangement hardly ever leads to serious deceptions since, in a continu-ing relationship, that would very quickly multiply demands on presenta-tion to an impossible extent. The truster exercises a short-term symbolic control of his trust, which makes any long-term discrepancy between illusion and reality exceptionally tiring for the person to whom trust is accorded to maintain and so, as a general rule, unrewarding.

Once again these analyses illuminate in the clearest possible way what constitutes the background to all trust – the problem of complexity. By means of trust, the truster unburdens himself of complexity which he cannot sustain. Anyone who wishes to abuse his trust must take this complexity upon himself. He will have to burden himself with complex demands on behaviour, to ensure the most wide-ranging command of the relevant information and complete control of the information available to the truster, with the result that he himself will be in danger of collapsing under the pressure of complexity.[5] Among the most important strategies for reducing fraud, therefore, is a time-limit on breach of trust, and also, if possible, on contact with the victim of the fraud. Adulterous relationships, in which this is not possible, require high expectations of behaviour, as is well known, and are seldom the result of balanced consideration. In all long-term relationships justifying trust is easier, even if this does not protect the truster from the exceptional circumstances of a well-secured individual, judiciously planted.

The communication of interest in the display of trust, the presentation of self as trustworthy, the engagement with and the reciprocation of trust are all efforts to intensify and generalize social relationships which prove, in long-term relationships at least, to be both opportune and constraining. Thus, an element of social control is built into relationships of trust. Trust accumulates as a kind of capital which opens up more opportunities for more extensive action but which must be continually used and tended and which commits the user to a trustworthy self-presentation, from which he can only escape with great difficulty. One can win trust by means of deceitful self-presentation, but one can only maintain it and use it as continually available capital if one continues the deception. Illusion then turns unnoticed into reality, the qualities which were at first deceitful grow into habits, the advantages of trust serve as an instrument of obligation. Trust educates. This is true on the emotional level as much as on the tactical level, and neutralizes the dangers which lie in a purely tactical control of trust relationships. The emotional bond given to trust is, as it were, a continuation of complexity reduction, internally simplifying reaction through an inertia in the expectations of the truster. This is not the only way of responding adequately to trust, and perhaps not the most mature. As against this, anyone who does not merely let himself be caught up and hemmed in by trust emotionally, but takes part in arranging the relationship of trust and what its subjects and its limitations are, is likely to recognize sooner the advantages of a joint reduction of complexity.

The consolidation of trust therefore constitutes an advantageous, but also a heavily presuppositional reformulation for the primordial problem of social order, the existence of a free *alter ego*. Instead of arming oneself against the unpredictability of the other person in the full complexity of all possibilities, one can seek to reduce complexity by concentrating on the creation and maintenance of mutual trust, and engage in more meaningful action in respect of a problem now more narrowly defined.

Presumably, with an increased awareness, those resulting possibilities arising from it can be put to better use.

Notes

1 Hence, it is not possible to make use of the concept of 'social identity' which has become widely accepted in the United States on the lines established by G. H. Mead, Kenneth Burke and Erving Goffman, and which amounts to the constitution of the self through the performance of role demands specific to individual situations. See Strauss (1959); Gross and Stone (1964). From the standpoint of its symbolic identity, the self is really more than a sequence of changing role identities, and its death cannot be resolved into a 'non-scheduled status passage', even when only the symbolic value of this event is under consideration. See Glaser and Strauss (1965). For a clear distinction between the two kinds of identity, see Goffman (1963b), pp. 51ff.
2 See Berger (1963), pp. 54ff.
3 See, for example, Simmel (1922), pp. 509ff.
4 On this see the informative account of trust relations among British civil servants in Dale (1941); of relations between the union base and intellectuals in Wilensky (1956) (in particular pp. 224ff., as concerns the anatomy of 'confidence'); between lobbyists and politicians in Washington in Milbrath (1963), pp. 286ff.; and on the relations between the representatives of administrative agencies and Members of Parliament on the occasion of discussions on the budget in parliamentary committees in Wildavsky (1964) (especially, on the problem of trust, pp. 74ff.); with reference to Germany, Mayer (1965), pp. 308ff.; further, on trust relations in general between the 'executive' and his 'principals', Braybrooke (1964), pp. 542ff. The frequently voiced view (amounting to a repetitive formula in organizational studies) that delegation requires trust (see, for instance, Alien (1958), pp. 135f.; Baum (1961), p. 86) gives no indication of the delicacy, the strategic demands and fraught moments which exist in such a relationship, but contents itself with a moralistic appeal directed to superiors, to provide themselves with the inward curb of trust. Again, the ordinary run of empirical studies of organizations, with their interview and questionnaire methods, can hardly come to terms with the subtle and complex reflexive strategies of presentation and of testing involved in these matters.
5 Goffman (1969) analyses this set of problems in detail.

9

Trust in Trust

The social mechanisms of cognition, norm-setting, learning, trust and the institutionalization of expectations of behaviour are, in their elementary, nonreflexive, forms simply not adequate for the constitution of highly differentiated social systems, the circumstances of which are so complex that it pays, indeed becomes essential, to make such social mechanisms reflexive. In this form they are applied to themselves and thus intensified in their effect.[1] Once their reflexive form has been institutionalized it offers so many advantages, and adapts the social system to itself to such an extent, that it becomes virtually impossible to return to a simpler state.[2] Reflexive mechanisms extend the potential for complexity of society and thus the prospect that the social system, in which they are institutionalized, will endure. They have, to be sure, serious dysfunctional consequences, particularly in periods of transition. Yet, on the new level of social organization, such problems are recognized as an inevitable accompaniment, and activate secondary efforts. In so far as these efforts succeed in reducing the problems to tolerable nuisances for behaviour, they contribute on their own account, as difficulties which have been overcome, to the stabilizing of the whole structure.

One of the important, far-reaching examples of a simple mechanism which is applied to itself is the learning of learning. In its elementary form learning occurs as it were incidentally, as a by-product of action and the perception of its consequences. Only when the learning process is differentiated and becomes functionally independent does it become possible to learn in a concentrated manner, systematically, and over a long period of time. It then becomes worthwhile to divert a part of the effort into the rationalization of the process of learning itself, and to learn to teach and to learn to learn. To a large extent the increase in the learning ability which can thus be achieved can only be realized if the differentiation of the learning process is transferred from the level of single actions to that of the social system. Learning can then be pursued co-operatively in social systems – in schools which are geared to it in functionally specific ways.

We find another example in the setting of norms for expectations of behaviour. There is a persistence of expectations even if they are disappointed, and this too originates purely as a by-product of living in a social community. Norms which are created in this way gain their stability by means of projection back into the past.[3] Old law is good law, and its normative status is completely divorced from human invention. Here too innovation is first set in motion by reflexivity,[4] and here reflexivity means that law becomes positive law. If, and in so far as, law can be set, norms must themselves be subject to norms. A system must create for itself a complex of formal controlling norms, for example, in the form of a 'constitution', which regulates procedure and provides an abstract pre-selection of permissible legal norms.

With the positivity of law and the parallel development of the positivity of purposes, the decision-making organization of the state can be made, in a true sense, sovereign. The state's powers too must then be organized in a reflexive way. Ways of overpowering power-holders and forms of legitimate change of power must be institutionalized. Only when the overpowering of power is assured can the potential of power be increased without hesitation.

It is to be supposed that with growing social differentiation other elementary mechanisms, as well as those which require more advanced conditions, will become reflexive – the fact that money can be bought is as well-known an example as the study of scientific study by means of reflexive disciplines such as epistemology, logic and methodology. The mechanisms of self-presentation and of trust formation are also subject to this tendency to reflexivity, even if reflexivity in this context takes on a less clearly differentiated form and so is not so easily recognizable. Here it takes the form of increasing functional awareness, of seeing through the foundations and functions of the creation of trust in society.

This seeing-through is of a different sort to the attempt to affirm trustworthiness directly. It does not seek to find out more and more precisely, by means of direct reference to the object, whether trust is justified, and so replace trust in the true sense with knowledge, making it superfluous. Rather, it distances itself and considers the function of trust and the conditions under which that function is performed, i.e. it takes as its starting point the necessity of going beyond the information available, and then places trust reflexively in the mechanisms for the formation of trust. It reveals the world of social contact, established by operating on symbols, as a manufactured illusion – but an illusion which provides a durable basis for the continuation of contacts so long as everyone observes the rules of the game and works together, in trust, to maintain the performance.

Essentially the ontological opposition of reality and illusion is inappropriate for the comprehension of this reflexive relationship.[5] For what we call illusion is reality, if it is used as a premise for further experience and action.[6] It is a second reality. The reality of symbolically represented identities, the reality of the social reduction of complexity, is certainly particularly susceptible to disturbance. In the end, however, every reality can be destroyed. That alone is no reason to call what can be destroyed 'illusion' and what destroys 'reality'.[7]

In the light of this reflexivity, personal trust becomes to a significant extent trust in tact and discipline in the way one expresses oneself.[8] In this form, it becomes transparent without its function being lost. Thus, one can see through one's partner's presentation, and, seeing it as a presentation, one is able to weigh and react in a balanced way and assess how far it is likely to go. One can estimate what strains personal trust can take without breaking down, in which role-context it belongs and in which it does not, and where its weak points lie, which should not be exposed – except if one does so intentionally and accepts responsibility for the consequences. Conversely, seeing through the tact of one's partner, particularly where it is socially institutionalized and expected, acts as a guarantee for the security of one's own self-presentation and thus makes it easier to learn a self-trust which is independent of emotion. Thus the uncovering of tact as a foundation of trust makes possible a reasonably frictionless control of social contact, a way around embarrassment and personal sensitivities, an avoidance of breakdowns or emotional reactions which get out of control, and, moreover, a greater reliability and durability of interaction as a building block for larger, complex, social systems.[9]

True seen-through trust has one serious disadvantage in comparison with spontaneous trust. It demands more caution, more consideration from the truster. He does not trust the other person directly, but rather trusts the grounds on which trust 'still works'. He is thereby continually conscious of other possibilities. What this means can be made clear with regard to the function of trust in reducing complexity. Seen-through trust fulfils this function less well than spontaneous trust. It places a greater burden of complexity on the actor and is thus psychologically more difficult. One would therefore be able to expect it only as a peak performance under particularly secure and continually sustained circumstances – for example, as the kind of behaviour associated with a higher educated class of society, or the upper levels of a bureaucracy, or with particular milieu, like political or economic spheres, where the effects on other areas of life can be relatively well controlled. An extension of seen-through trust as a general social attitude would be feasible only if and in so far as it became possible increasingly to stabilize personal and social systems of action and to make them transparent as regards the conditions under which they function.

These considerations confirm our conjecture that, under the conditions set by civilized society, personal trust becomes a type of system trust in the ability of systems to maintain conditions or performances which are, within certain limits, identical. Other examples of system trust also show this characteristically reflex engagement with fictions that is functioning.

For example, whether one is a member or outsider, one trusts large organized systems which process goods or data, although one knows that the objectives of these systems are not the goals of the people who work in them. Rather one knows that everyone concerned in them must be motivated by complex, prone-to-failure and not readily visible detours to produce four-fruit jam, insurance notices, or whatever. The purchasing power of money is trusted, although currency is known to rest on an overdraft, so to speak, and is not covered by a corresponding value in the institutions which issue the currency. It rests instead on the expectation, supported by experience, that not everyone wants to turn his money credits into real cash simultaneously.[10] One relies on the fact that the state has the power to guarantee peace and make decisions about problems, although one knows that its power of coercion is not adequate to do these things, if a considerable percentage of the population were to rebel at the same time or refuse to recognize decisions.

In all these cases it is a characteristic mark of civilizing trust that it incorporates an element of reflexivity. Trust is not concerned with knowing the essential truth about a matter but with the success of the reduction of complexity, with the fact that the taking of the risk involved has proved itself in social life and thus becomes a motivating force, which yields further attestation. Trust is concerned with itself in so far as it is necessary to ensure its ability to extend the fulfilment of its function. And in this form it can achieve more; it can absorb more uncertainty with less risk.

If one looks more closely, several different types of trust in trust can be distinguished according to which type one places trust in. The individual can trust his own trust, just as he can feel his feelings or think about his thinking. Furthermore, he can trust that others trust him, and finally that others trust third parties in the same way as he does. The possibilities for application, the risks and the consequent problems all vary according to which type is chosen.

The first two cases belong typically to the domain of personal trust. I can trust my own trust in another person if I attribute to my own trust the ability to motivate others, and if, furthermore, I find out the ways in which my partner is affected by being trusted. With this in mind, I can create for myself an additional motive for trust. This engenders more opportunities for trust in the face of increasing risk. Or I can trust the trust of others in me. This makes it possible for me to base my plans of action on the trust of others, whether it be to disappoint it or to discharge the resulting obligations. I can, for example, dismantle my own cautious strategies of self-presentation, if I am sure that the other person 'will know what I mean' if I criticize, tease or annoy him. This increasing of the potential of trust involves, like every reflexive process, a double risk – firstly in that I, myself, can suddenly doubt whether the trust of the other person really goes as far as I had supposed, and secondly in that the other person, without my noticing it, loses trust in my good intentions and my 'not so intended' action begins to undermine the relationship. On the other hand, the advantages of such double trust are obvious. It makes possible actions which could not come about by means of simple trust alone.

Whereas in personal trust reflexivity is an exception, system trust builds upon the fact that others also trust and that this common quality of trust becomes conscious. Certainly it is not necessary in each individual case to remember that the ability to function *rests* on trust in trust. It seems rather that familiarity with money, power and truth is learned as *behaviour* and that typically the reflexivity of this mechanism remains latent, as does its highly risky character. Such latency can make the creation of trust more simple and act as a safeguard against uncontrollable fears – what would happen if everyone suddenly wanted to cash in all their money, or if everyone appeared armed on the streets. Nevertheless, the rational basis of system trust lies in the trust placed in the trust of other people. The uncovering of this basis through sociological analysis can make the conditions under which this type of trust functions transparent and thus alleviates the type of latent insecurity which typically accompanies a reliance on mechanisms which are not understood.

Notes

1 See, for more extensive treatment of this point, Luhmann (1971), pp. 92ff.

2 See Parsons (1964b).

3 It is thus possible to make use of the temporal dimension in order to 'relieve' the social dimension. We rely in stating this on the previous discussion of the interaction of the temporal and social dimensions in the constitution of meaning and the world (see Chapter 2).

4 The medieval notion of a hierarchy of laws, with positive law on the lowest rung, played a significant transitional role in the passage from traditional to positive law. The notion of hierarchy entails the notion of reflexivity, of the application of something to itself, and at the same time legitimizes a certain amount of flexibility, by allowing at each level a certain mutability of the lower layer within boundaries set by the higher. On this see also Luhmann (1972), Vol. 1, pp. 190ff.; Vol. 2, pp. 213ff.

5 In ontological metaphysics the dichotomy of reality and illusion had a specific function. It explained that the being that appears in the world was also capable of not being, of changing, of passing away, of being merely possible, whereas it was not possible for the authentic being not to be. The appearing world thus became more and more an illusion, as the knowledge of other possibilities advanced. That dichotomy loses its function, and thus its meaning, as soon as one sets aside the ontological premise that being excludes not-being, and envisages the possibility that everything be otherwise.

6 The famous saying of W. I. Thomas and D. S. Thomas (1928), that a situation defined as real is real in its consequences, grasps this point, but only partially.

Not only the (erroneous) view of a situation as real, but also sociological-reflexive orientation to the Thomas theorem makes the definition of a situation become real, in so far as all participants allow that such defining operates in the way that the remark specifies.

7 In this sense also Goffman (1959), p. 65. See also Roethlisberger and Dickson (1939), pp. 276ff., who suggest that interviewers, when dealing with self-presentations and other social identifications, should not concern themselves with their truth in the sense of their relations to an underlying reality. The same exclusion of any naively credited actual reality constitutes part of the methodical procedure called 'reduction' in transcendental phenomenology. For a comprehensive presentation, see Husserl (1954). In these terms, also, the exclusive premise about being which is characteristic of ontological metaphysics is replaced by the principle of reflexivity.

8 Also Garfinkel (1963), p. 238, remarks that a trusting or trustworthy person can be characterized as one who can master the discrepancy of prescribed attitudes with respect to reality 'in such a fashion as to maintain a public show of respect for them'. See also the observations on the shifts in the threshold of shame and in the boundaries of carefulness in Elias (1978), especially Vol. II, pp. 397ff.

9 Cf. Luhmann (1964), pp. 358ff., p. 371.

10 Parsons (1964c), p. 45, strikingly expresses this reflexivity when he states: 'The rational ground for confidence in money is that others have confidence in money.'

10

Trust and Distrust

Someone who is thinking of buying a television set and weighs the advantages against the disadvantages normally sees no need also to compare expressly the advantages and disadvantages of not buying one. It would simply be the same list with the signs reversed. Thus it would hardly be worthwhile paying particular attention to distrust if it were simply a matter of lack of trust. Distrust, however, is not just the *opposite* of trust; as such, it is also a *functional equivalent* for trust.[1] For this reason one can (and must) make a *choice* between trust and distrust.

The qualitative difference and functional equivalence of trust and distrust become clear as soon as one pays attention to the function of trust. Trust reduces social complexity, that is, simplifies life by the taking of a risk. If the readiness to trust is lacking or if trust is expressly denied in order to avoid the risks involved of a premature absorption of ambiguity, this by itself leaves the problem unsolved. The function of trust would thus remain unfulfilled. Anyone who merely refuses to confer trust restores the original complexity of the potentialities of the situation and burdens himself with it. Such a surplus of complexity, however, places too many demands on the individual and makes him incapable of action. Anyone who does not trust must, therefore, turn to functionally equivalent strategies for the reduction of complexity in order to be able to define a practically meaningful situation at all. He must hone his expectations into negative ones, and so must, in certain respects, become distrustful.

These negative strategies give rise to distrust of an emotionally tense and often frantic character which distinguishes it from trust. Its repertoire extends from the definition of the role-partner as an enemy who must be fought, through a boundless accumulation of personal reserves for cases of emergency, up to the renunciation of all needs which can be written off. Strategies of combat, of the mobilizing of reserves, or of renunciation, make possible a conduct of existence based on distrust and define its situation in a way which makes it possible to act rationally within the circumscribed area. The consciousness of distrust is thus often lost and the strategies of reduction demarcated by it become autonomous, become a habitual outlook on life, a routine.

Consequently, distrust also achieves simplification, often drastic simplification. A person who distrusts both needs more information and at the same time narrows down the information which he feels confident he can rely on. He becomes *more* dependent on *less* information. The possibility of his being deceived thereby becomes something more open to account.[2] This is particularly true if distrust is honed towards a positive expectation of injurious action. However, distrust, virtually of necessity, is positively determined. Negative expectations are too complex for distrust, because they exclude less. In this way, strategies of distrust become correspondingly more difficult and more burdensome. They often drain the strength of the person who distrusts to an extent which leaves him little energy to explore and adapt to his environment in an objective and unprejudiced manner, and hence allow him fewer opportunities for learning. Relatively, trust is the easier option, and for this reason there is a strong incentive to begin a relationship with trust.[3]

These considerations also indicate the limits on the extent to which trust and distrust can be generalized into general attitudes towards the environment. Certainly, in personal systems, just as in social systems, there are learned general dispositions for preferring to resolve problematic situations in cases of doubt through trust, or through distrust. They simplify decisions between contrary mechanisms. On the other hand, a generalized invocation of trust or of distrust with reference to all possible meaning is unfeasible. No one can expect only good or only bad from everyone, and in every respect. The general, everyday attitude is rather expressed in the knowledge of one's immediate surroundings as familiar, as that attitude which has no particular frame of reference, of unquestioning security in relation to what is not expressly thought and intended, which we discussed in Chapter 3. In relation to this anonymously established, presupposed world of common experience, there is neither trust nor distrust in the true sense. Neither trust nor distrust are feasible as a universal attitude. That would be either too risky or too great a burden. Both positions (of trust and distrust) presuppose that one is conscious of the possible behaviour of others as a *specific problem*. One trusts if one assumes that this behaviour will fit in meaningfully with one's own pattern of life; one distrusts if one reckons that this will not be the case.[4]

Apart, therefore, from trust and distrust, one must take familiarity into account – a familiarity with the world which makes typical expectations possible at all, and which cannot be denied or rejected *in toto*. Even someone who suffers from fear or loathing of the world must take his medicine, pay his taxes, brush his teeth, take his car for testing and, in doing so, accept the world. The dependence on familiar world structures and types of meaning cannot be thrown off. It is, however, mitigated by a certain mobility of subject areas and attitudes in the world. One has the possibility of moving in certain respects, from pre-existent familiarity to trust or distrust, from distrust to trust, from trust to an unproblematic familiarity. Shifts of this kind in the world around us make it possible to use various strategies for the reduction of complexity, one after another, or in different ways, alongside one another.

Distrust can consequently develop out of unquestioning familiarity on the one hand, through the sudden appearance of inconsistencies – one hears an inexplicable noise in the middle of the night – and, on the other, through a reversal of trust, if symptoms are perceived which are symbolically discrediting. Past history will remain important to the way in which distrust is articulated, the emotional tone of its expression and its durability. Even if distrust arises directly from familiar situations, it does not completely negate the familiar but must first establish for itself particular aspects onto which it can fasten distrustful expectations.

For the distribution over time of the various attitudes (familiarity, trust and distrust) the existence of *thresholds* is important. The concept of thresholds, which was first developed in the psychology of perception[5] but which in its general function can be applied to all experience,[6] denotes an artificial discontinuity which levels out the area of experience before and after the threshold, and thus makes for simplification. A whole range of possible differences is thus drawn together under a single crude distinction and the rest are repressed into a sub-threshold latency. In an area of experience which is ordered by thresholds one can assume that the foundations of behaviour remain constant, or at least that one can remain indifferent about any distinctions until one crosses the threshold; then a small step brings about great changes.[7] Hence thresholds in experience are likewise mechanisms for the reduction of complexity to relatively simple problems. Instead of being faced with an immense mass of slightly differently shaded experiences, one is concerned with the substitute problem of recognizing the threshold, from whence one's orientation becomes essentially different. And this problem is easier to master.

Delimitation by means of thresholds is characteristic of the phenomenon of familiarity as well as that of trust, for in both cases it is a question of generalized attitudes, with considerable indifference towards numerous details and slight shadings of experience.[8] Not every discrepancy arouses doubts about the familiar features of the world, not every disappointment destroys trust. But precisely because of this there must be some limit to this power of absorption, where familiarity or trust abruptly turns into distrust. Not every discrepancy can be registered and its information value worked out, and, because of this, when suspicion is aroused, the effect is usually out of all proportion to what would have been the case if it had been seen in isolation and is the straw that broke the camel's back. Generalizing familiarity and trust, exceeding the information available, rests on the setting of boundaries which operate thresholds, the crossing of which sets off a new orientation of a much more pronounced kind, where the built-up tensions are discharged at a stroke.

If there is a swing from trust to distrust – and the same is true in the rarer reverse case – then the distruster adapts his behaviour to this new pattern of expectation and thus makes his change of attitude socially apparent. Distrust is made manifest by distrustful behaviour. Interpersonal behaviour is not a matter merely of ad hoc experience but something interpreted in terms of underlying 'attitudes', and used for the formation of expectations. Thus the distruster, willingly or unwillingly, can hardly avoid his distrust being perceived in him and attributed to him. Hostile feelings are difficult to keep hidden, and the cautious defences which now seem necessary betray the intention.

Someone who sees himself as the object of such expressions of distrust will hardly be disposed to look at himself from the perspective of distrust and seek the cause of it in himself. The distrust remains for him objectively inexplicable, and he therefore attributes it to the person who distrusts him. In so far as he continues the relationship at all, he will respond at first perhaps with explanations, with forbearance, then with caution and finally with distrust himself.[9] He finds himself relieved of moral obligation by the distrust which is brought against him and given the freedom to act in his own interests, or indeed he actually feels the need to revenge himself for this undeserved treatment. And thus he gives distrust additional justification and further nourishment.

Consequently, distrust has an inherent tendency to endorse and reinforce itself in social interaction – a good example, perhaps indeed the very kernel, of those processes to which Merton devoted a classic essay under the title of 'self-fulfilling prophecy'.[10] Underlying these processes is, as it were, an inverted feedback principle, that is, a wrongly or insecurely adapted system brings itself into equilibrium with its environment not by correcting itself on the basis of its effects but by finding its effects endorsed and hence offering occasions for new causes.[11] This reinforcing effect is verified by numerous observations, particularly in organizational milieus.[12] In particular, research into industrial subcultures has revealed, as one of its few 'tangible' results, that trust and distrust strengthen realities in a way which is difficult to trace back to specific causes.[13] We know even less about its limits, and its possible critical moments. Without such knowledge, the thesis of a 'tendency' for distrust to seek confirmation and reinforcement remains an inadequately specified assertion which does not lend itself to falsification.

The reason for this difficulty is that trust and distrust, as we saw, are symbolically transmitted, generalized, attitudes which do not vary with explicitly specifiable, objective causes, but are controlled by subjective processes whereby experience is processed and simplified. And in the simplifying, in the reduction of complexity, there always lies an unstable, incalculable moment. If the question of trust or distrust becomes acute then the situation becomes on the one hand more problematic, more complex, more rich in possibilities. On the other hand, simplifying processes of reduction, of orientation towards a few prominent key experiences, come into play. Objects and events, which appear to have value as indicators, gain special relevance, and control the interpretation of other situations. They capture attention. They become 'reasons', 'proofs', that trust or distrust is justified. Since in most cases the objective situation contains features to which both attitudes could be fixed, what is more decisive than anything is an indeterminate preconception about the selective tendency and the direction of symbolic fixing – often the result of a chance first impression.[14] It picks out the critical variables, the evidence which counts, and, with these, also defines the criteria whose variation in the objective situation takes on the character of a threshold experience and suggests the change from trust to distrust or vice versa.[15]

It is accordingly less a result of natural circumstances than of history where the thresholds and turning points lie at any given time, which events have symbolic value and accelerate or brake the process of the formation of trust or distrust. If one is to appraise how strong trust and distrust are, how strongly they are internally determined or bound to particular objects, and through which critical experiences they could be changed, one must be acquainted with the history of the system, the history of the self-presentation, the confirmation of the premises and symbols involved in the processing of experience, with defences against anxiety and means of simplification, and, moreover, with the biography of the given situation. Probably one would have to work out some kind of phenomenological psychology of everyday behaviour[16] in order to devise a usable body of research tools for this question and in order to make specific assertions.

Despite this openness and the uncertainty of detailed knowledge, at least one far-reaching systems theory hypothesis can be formulated – a social system, which requires or cannot avoid distrusting behaviour among its members for certain functions, needs at the same time mechanisms which prevent distrust from gaining the upper hand, and, from being reciprocated by a process of reciprocal escalation, turned into a destructive force. Above all there must be strategies and types of individual behaviour which are socially recognized and easily understood and which intercept and neutralize acts of distrust, thus rendering them, from the point of view of the system, 'accidental', insignificant, and therefore functionless aberrations. This function is performed above all by certain forms of presentation, or by the subsequent explanation of acts of distrust as involuntary actions, as determined purely by experience, as mistakes, as upsets caused by external factors, or as duties required by roles – that is, interpretations which make possible the carrying out of distrusting *actions* but which explain away distrust as an *attitude*. Furthermore, we have to reckon, at this point, with the institutions of punishment, penance and pardon. They have many functions, important among which is the fixing of deadlines by which an affair is closed and thus offers no further legitimate occasion for distrust.[17] Moreover, centralizing the right of punishment within the system has the function in 'difficult' cases of interrupting the circle of increasing distrust.

All such arrangements shift forward the threshold of effective distrust. They cannot, of course, be relied on to prevent distrust from emerging or swelling up, but at least they filter out numerous minor occasions for such a development. They thus reduce the probability of a social system being immediately destroyed by increasing distrust among its members, which can mean a gain in time, critical for the survival of the system in so far as it can employ this gain to learn trust and to accumulate trust capital, so helping it to become less sensitive and able to survive more serious situations.

Notes

1 See also the distinction between two kinds of polarity in Thompson (1963) – 'convertible polarity' is when to define one pole it is sufficient to negate the other; 'inconvertible polarity' is when this does not apply. The distinction performs a useful warning function, but gives little indication of the construction of inconvertible polarity which is dealt with only negatively. As far as the case at hand is concerned, we would say it is defined by means of the principle of functional equivalence.
2 Goffman (1969), pp. 3–81, is particularly suggestive on this point.
3 The same holds for a feature which bears distinctly upon the question of trust – the honesty of the presentation of self. Even when the presentation of a person's own essential being is highly artificial and occasionally devious, the person giving it will have an easier time of it if he believes in his own honesty. Also, Berger (1963), p. 109, observes that dishonesty requires an extent of self-mastery which is found excessively demanding by most people in most situations. On this account also, the very low capacity of man for grasping complex situations encourages human relations to oscillate on the axis trust-honesty-trust, even though this requires the bridging of certain discrepancies between being and appearance.
4 Both positions relate to the future with the help of the past. The thesis in Binswanger (1953), pp. 353f., seems to be untenable to the effect that trust is based on the future, distrust on the past. Past orientation leads if anything to familiarity and, when the future becomes problematical, can lead to trust as well as distrust.
5 See (on the basis of Fechner's views), Stern (1923/4), Vol. 1, pp. 353ff.; Vol. 2, pp. 190ff.; Vol. 3 (1924), p. 301; also the plentiful research evidence produced on this point by Gestalt psychology, for example, Koffka (1935), *passim*; Metzger (1963), pp. 114ff. See also the significance acquired in Ashby's cyber-

netic systems theory by the concept of threshold, used to define the concept of partial function: Ashby (1954), especially p. 163.

6 In making these generalizations, it must of course be borne in mind that thresholds are typically much less determinate in social systems than in organisms. See in this sense Vickers (1959), p. 56.

7 See Moore (1964), p. 334.

8 Reynaud (1957) argues for the application of the concept of threshold to studies of economic trends; see also Reynaud (1962), pp. 50ff.

9 The experiments on pretended distrust reported in Garfinkel (1964), pp. 233ff., support this point.

10 Merton (1957), pp. 421ff.

11 A parallel to this view can be seen in the outline of a creatively differentiating cybernetics put forward in Maruyama (1963). Here one starts with a simple, undifferentiated condition, wherein chance engenders a first, inconsiderable difference. This activates other causes (for example, erosion; initial concentration on an untextured plane), and thus becomes reinforced; out of this emerges a differentiated structure, which is now sustained through the well-known cybernetic processes by which complete systems are stabilized.

12 See, for instance, Gouldner (1954b), pp. 140f.; Worthy (1959), pp. 114f.; Guest (1962), especially pp. 17ff.; Braibanti (1963), pp. 388ff. In the industrial sociology of the Weimar era comparable remarks were made concerning the general distrust engendered by 'the class struggle', and which would attach a negative connotation even to well-meaning arrangements made by management. See, e.g., Geiger (1929); Jost (1932), pp. 63f.

13 Thus, e.g., Worthy (1959), pp. 119ff., locates the core of the problem of industrial subculture in the question of trust/distrust. See also Shepard and Blake (1962), pp. 90f. This may explain how and why organizational climate appears largely independent of the formal organizational structure, and how, while the structure remains the same, the climate may change from trust to distrust or vice versa, for instance through a change in leadership. See Gouldner (1954b); also (1954a) for the first and Guest (1962) for the second phenomenon.

14 See Daily (1952) concerning the significance of first impressions for the building up of further expectations. However, there is experimental evidence also for the effectiveness of contrasting views, the significance of last and of most frequent impressions. See in particular Postman and Bruner (1952). Such contrasts point to the fact that there are available several possibilities for the generalization and stabilization of expectations, and that perhaps what makes the difference are the concrete structures of the processing of experience in the systems involved.

15 In this connection, consider the striking example of the significance of a change of manager for the transformation of organizational climate; see the observations of Gouldner (1954b) and Guest (1962); also Pilisuk and Skolnick (1968).

16 See Heider (1958); Garfinkel (1964); a large number of studies in the area of 'symbolic interactionism', as well as the writings of Schütz already frequently cited.

17 Deutsch (1958), pp. 273f., speaks in this connection of the necessity for 'a method of absolution'.

11

Readiness to Trust

So far, what has been under consideration has been concerned predominantly with aspects of the formation and use of trust *external* to the system and has been oriented towards the environmental conditions and possible strategies of trust. This picture would remain incomplete, however, if the conditions for the formation of trust *internal* to the system were not also brought into consideration. We turn now to this question. How must a system be organized internally, in order to be in a position, and ready, to confer trust?

An adequate treatment of this subject would call for an outline of complete system theories for the personal and the social system. The material required for such an undertaking could not be extracted from the literature without difficulties, to say nothing of its being fitted thereafter into the framework of this study. We must therefore confine ourselves to a few very cursory reflections which should indicate the connection of the preceding exposition with detailed research on individual systems. The following statements have therefore an essentially functional orientation and do not allow one to judge directly the specific structures and processes by means of which particular systems can create trust.

Experience of everyday life tells us that people, just like social systems, are more willing to trust if they possess inner security, if they have some sort of inner self-assurance which enables them to anticipate possible disappointments of trust with composure, without turning what is merely conceivable possibility immediately into grounds for action.[1] This equation self-assurance = readiness to trust is, however, at first no more than a conjecture which needs to be substantiated and is, moreover, little more than a reformulation of the problem. For what is self-assurance?

It is precisely in regard to this problem that the ethical view of trust proves inadequate. It looks for an answer to the question under what circumstances one *ought* to trust, and arrives at the conclusion that, while in human society trust is an ethical command, one should not place trust blindly but only where it is earned.[2] Thus the problem of trust is transformed into a cognitive problem, despite the fact that it has its roots precisely in inadequate cognitive capacity. This 'solution', therefore, could be formulated thus: confer trust when there is no need for it. The real problem, however, is trust which is unjustified and which yet justifies itself and so becomes creative. Therefore, the inner foundations of trust which we are seeking cannot lie in cognitive capacity. We tied our investigation into the external conditions of trust to the fact that in an over-complex world one must act without adequate knowledge and involve oneself actively. We shall therefore take this point of departure also for the analysis, in consistent fashion, of the internal conditions of trust. What this means, then, is that complexity is reduced not only by external but also by internal structures and processes.

Treating the process of trust as an analogy of cognition – trust is only right where it is objectively justified – corresponds to a very widespread prejudice which is that stable structures within people could not be founded on unstable structures in their environment.[3] This prejudice, and the corresponding views in the theory of the social system, are unavoidable if one tries to derive a causal explanation of a system from its environment, for something unstable cannot cause something stable. In doing this, however, one ignores the system as a system, as a higher order performance in comparison with its environment. It is precisely in the realm of the stabilization of expectations, which is where the problem of trust belongs, that we know, as a result of experiments which have been widely debated, that insecure expectations are learned much more firmly than secure expectations.[4] Secure expectations in most cases collapse at the first disappointment. Insecure expectations, however paradoxical it may at first appear, are psychologically more stable. There exists within them the opposite expectation as well, without the positive expectation for that reason being abandoned. It is normalized, stereotyped and thus in various ways immunized against the refutation. Explanations of disappointment are built into it in such a way that a particular case of disappointment presents no problem but rather confirms the structure of the expectation as a whole.[5] Expectation is secured from *external* refutation, in that it incorporates a contradiction within itself, but it must then, however, be able to maintain and deal with the contradiction *internally*. The problem of the stabilization of the expectation is thus shifted from the environment to the system, because other, more effective, forms of problem-solving are available there.

Trust is then nothing other than a type of system-internal 'suspension' of this kind of contradiction in expectation. The possibility of a disappointment is not simply ignored, but anticipated and dealt with internally. In contrast to insecure expectations in general, the continuance of the expectation in the case of disappointment is not anticipated and prepared for as a routine form of behaviour. Rather the security of trust consists, in converse fashion, in the fact that a breach of trust must result in its withdrawal and hence in a radical change in the relationship. Disappointment is not played down but, on the contrary, is exaggerated in moral terms as an event which its extreme nature and exceptional shamefulness make improbable.

The problem of readiness to trust, accordingly, does not consist in an increase of security with a corresponding decrease in insecurity; it lies conversely in an increase of bearable insecurity at the expense of security.[6] Admittedly, this analysis remains superficial, for in no way is it being said that every person or every social system makes, or can make, use of these various possibilities for transforming unstable into stable, but nonetheless insecure, expectations. In order to be able to understand differences in this kind of system-performance we must return to the subject of 'self-assurance'. There is a connection here with recent ideas in group psychology concerning the creation of trust which attempt to achieve trust by dismantling defensive mechanisms and substituting more open foundations of security in conversations within the group.[7] As yet, however, this has produced no clear understanding of the inner psychological processes. In group psychology and in the practice of group therapy, these ideas are rather discounted and often replaced by strongly moralized postulates about 'healthy' personalities.[8]

From the functional point of view, self-assurance as a foundation for trust is to be traced back to the availability of internal mechanisms for the reduction of complexity. Trust can come about if these internal reduction mechanisms are stabilized in such a way that they complement the environmental reduction and thus are in a position to reinforce it at critical points. In other words, bestowing trust is made possible and easy by the fact that the trusting system has inner resources available which are not structurally tied up, and which, in the case of a disappointment of trust, can be put into action and take over the burden of the reduction of complexity and the solving of problems. What particular task must these internal mechanisms perform? And how must they be constituted?

The complexity of the world cannot be mapped within the system, for the system itself is not sufficiently complex to do so.[9] The response must take the form of a *generalizing* problem-solving capacity which is able to operate in terms of time and actual circumstance, so that, within certain limits, the system can remain indifferent to differences in time and circumstance. It must therefore be a question of a capacity applicable to circumstantially heterogeneous and individually unforeseeable problems. It then makes such foresight dispensable. Because of this generalizing of circumstance, moreover, the capacity must be generalized in terms of time, in the sense that it appears already assured, although it will only be put into action when it is needed in the future, at some as yet undetermined time. The inner knowledge that such resources are available then serves as an equivalent for certainty based on information about the environment. It makes foresight within the bounds to which it extends unnecessary, since it affords certainty that, whenever and however they appear, problems can be solved. Possibly the two most important examples of system-internal generalizing by psychological systems, emotional attachment and assurance in self-presentation, should help to clarify these notions.

One of the most elementary mechanisms of complexity reduction is the stabilization of feelings towards particular objects or people. The principle of the *generalization* of expectations in such relationships lies precisely in the *individuality* of their object. Familiarity with the object regulates and secures the formation of expectations. Feelings embrace in principle all aspects of their object – however different they may be and whenever they may reveal themselves and change. They motivate an input of energy for situations which are as yet undetermined, and presuppose a corresponding reserve of energy which is not determined elsewhere. Feelings are, to use the vocabulary of Parsonian pattern variables, attitudes orientated 'particularistically', 'qualitatively', 'diffusely'.[10] They exclude all other objects or relegate them to a position of comparative unimportance, even if in particular respects they produce equal, or better, results. Thus they attach a very far-reaching temporal indifference to circumstance and time, an insensitivity to other things, which remains astonishing for all witnesses, if they do not share that feeling.

Feelings accomplish external and internal reduction in a single operation – that is their strength and their weakness. They reduce the possibilities of the environment by settling preference on one object, and accordingly at the same time establish internal possibilities of processing experience. The affective system, as one says, 'identifies' with its object. In allowing no alternatives either outside or inside, feelings are inelastic, fixed, non-transferable. They can only be reorganized by being destroyed and remade. Every breakdown of the emotional relationship would restore the crushing complexity of the world. Anxiety therefore lurks in the background of feeling and motivates the continuance of the relationship, if it receives any kind of confirmation. Feelings try to make themselves immune from refutation, if at all possible. Love and hate make one blind.

This general structure of emotional relationships shows already that here we have a generalized medium of problem-solving, an equivalent for certainty, of the type which we are seeking as a foundation for readiness to trust. Positive emotional relationships between people can scarcely be maintained in the long run without trust. They lead, as the jealousy complex can illustrate, to an unstable state which reduces the emotion to ruins, but often cannot replace it, and hence cannot get away from it. Moreover, emotions form a foundation for entering into relationships of trust with other people to whom the emotion itself does not extend. Anyone who is emotionally rooted in a circle of people, a home, a role constellation with tasks and duties, is thereby supported in opening up relationships of trust outside this narrow circle. The emotional attachment of the child to his family is, for example, the foundation for the learning of all trust. In this way readiness to trust can survive as a habitual and proven attitude long after the emotions to which it owes its existence have faded.

A mobile, highly differentiated social system nevertheless cannot content itself with this foundation of trust alone. On the one hand it (the social system) individualizes feelings concerning subject and object and in doing so raises awareness of its own uniqueness and is hence a matter for self-indulgent reflection – which cannot be taken for granted. On the other hand, it prepares individuals for action and, therefore, favours more universally applicable, basic orientations, whose adaptation is not associated with such high costs.

Finally, it draws the object of trust further and further away from an intimate nearness. It increasingly demands trust for systems for which one can have no feeling. Under these circumstances one may antici- pate a need for functionally equivalent problem-solving mechanisms which partly replace feeling as a basis for trust and partly restrict it to increasingly private functionings. Such an alternative, *assurance in social self-presentation*, seems to gain in importance in the process of the develop- ment of civilization.

People and social systems strive, in their self-presentation, as we have already shown,[11] to draw a consistent picture of themselves and make it socially accepted. Since other people and social systems also have an interest in building up reliable expectations with regard to the people around them, in seeing them as enduring identities, there develops in social intercourse a type of expressive language which enables actions to be attributed to people or social systems, and not only causally but, indeed, also symbolically, as expressing their essence, their self.[12] The systems concerned move about in this medium of symbolic represen- tations with more or less great assurance, an assurance which is often misleadingly called 'self-confidence'. For self-presentation is difficult, threatened by inner contradictions, mistakes, facts and information which cannot be presented. So, on the one hand, it requires considerable expressive prudence and, on the other hand, the tactful co-operation of spectators. There often arise delicate or indeed embarrassing situations where the fact that the presented self is not the true self threatens to become obvious. Someone who then loses his self-control is lost. His self-presentation collapses – at least in relation to the spectators then present. A person who, on the contrary, retains his composure can save himself in various ways, for example, by giving the situation a humor- ous twist, by open admission, reinterpreting retrospectively his past self-presentation, playing the matter down, ignoring it with the help of co-operating spectators who see through his self-presentation but refrain from acting on it, by explaining the incident as an event of no importance, for example as a 'disturbance' brought about by something external.

The inner assurance which comes from being equal to the demands of self-presentation in all situations, and of always knowing a practicable way out even from bungled situations, is one of those inner resources which serve as a foundation for readiness to trust. For even bestowing trust is an act of self-presentation. The person who trusts presents himself as someone who is by his nature inclined to bestow trust. If the trust then turns out to be misplaced, the person who trusted is not only disappointed, but in some circumstances also exposed to ridicule. It then becomes obvious that he was too stupid to see through the situation, that he let himself be taken advantage of – a victim of the equivocal ethic which says that one should trust, but not too blindly. At this point, it comes to be something which depends on practice and expertise in self-presentation.[13] A person will certainly be more easily disposed to place trust to begin with if he is sure from the outset that, in the event of disappointment, his self-presentation will not be affected, or at least can be refloated without any great damage.

If one compares assurance in self-presentation with emotional attachment, the greater flexibility of the former becomes at once apparent. Its generalizing principle does not lie in the identity of an object, but in the identity of the presented self. In relation to its environment this self has selective interests. It can change its presentation's situations and its attributes, and make itself independent of the fate of specific objects in the environment. The mode of reduction in self-presentation is not the fusing of outer and inner, as in emotional identification, but separating and maintaining boundaries. Boundary maintenance is practised by control of all information about the self which leaves the system. Thus the presented self can harmonize with a more complex environment, and hence show more diverse trust than the emotionally bound self, not in the sense of an uninhibited readiness for assimilation, but, on the contrary, in the sense of distancing, of far-reaching indifference and readiness to substitute, and hence, further, of strategically rational attitudes which thrive in a highly mobile, strongly differentiated social system.

The sources of such assurance in presentation can be very varied. They include natural abilities of imagination and quick reaction, fortune or misfortune in inherited status, education, practical experience and career success, environmental conditions of having understanding, sensitive, like-minded partners or inferior opponents.[14] For the presentation of social systems what must be added above all is the institutionalization of what Goffman calls 'teams'.[15] Certainly there are several 'equifinal'[16] ways of reaching that state, just as very varied personality constellations can underlie an emotional attachment which is similar in its effect. Linear causal explanations in terms of single factors come to grief on this 'open' relationship of function and structure.

On the other hand, in these various equifinal causal constellations there probably exist various opportunities for social control of the process which offer different social groups ways of influencing it. Assurance in presentation, which is based on an elite education, is of a different sort, and has a mode of preparedness to take risks different from the inherent quick-wittedness of a campaign-hardened local politician or the irrepressibility of a commercial traveller, which is merely specific to that role. The certainty of never making a *faux pas* and therefore of always being able to attribute every upset to someone else is something quite different from the certainty of never being at a loss for an explanation or an evasive tactic. One may suppose that the style of social interaction in a society, and hence also the specific directions in which it is prepared to proffer trust, are very significantly determined by those social forces which influence the inner sources of trust, in that they open up possible channels of expression for emotions and opportunities for successful self-presentation.

Whether readiness to trust is achieved more through emotion or more through flexibility of self-presentation, in every case it rests on the *structure* of the system which confers trust. Only because the security of the system is structurally guaranteed is it possible to do away with the safety precautions for particular actions in specific situations. Readiness to trust is an important instance of the general rule that the absorption of complexity through structures can relieve the burden of action.

Until now we have been discussing the question of readiness to trust on supposition that the materialization of trust depends on whether a system is ready and in a position to create trust. That was the perspective of this chapter which we must at its close modify, and reveal as a variable.

We have already, in the chapter on system trust, encountered forms of relatively inevitable trust formation, which must function to a large extent regardless of individual motivational structures, and which furthermore are not controlled from outside but internally, within the systems which demand trust. Their security of function, and also the possibility of creating trust in trust, depend on this indifference. Thus the question as to the structures and processes of the systems which bestow trust recedes and becomes less meaningful; it does not depend so much on the readiness to trust. The trusting systems are, as it were, relieved of responsibility for their trust.

If one also takes this possibility into consideration then it becomes clear how complex and richly varied the social conditions for the formation of trust are. In part they operate through the structures of the system which invests trust; in part they affect it from outside. In the first case it is principally a question of social conditions for the expression of emotion or successful self-presentation – a social climate which honours personal bonds such as love or faithfulness, and does not expose them to ridicule, as in the figure of the cuckolded husband; which institutionalizes tact, and knows enough escape routes for self-preservation in difficult situations. In this way system structures for trust are reinforced. In the second case, due to the provisions made in their environment, system structures themselves are relieved of the burden of absorbing the uncertainty resulting from this engagement. This occurs in the case of system trust in so far as their possibilities of choice are narrowed down or interpreted away, and trust is confirmed in the short term during the course of interaction. Or it may be that the breach of trust is controlled by sufficiently tight sanctions to reduce the truster's risk.

The very multitude of the ways of creating trust makes it fruitless to search for general formulae. Rather one is forced to recognize that it is just this multitude of possibilities which provides some safeguard against the breakdown of trust in society. Trust is created – one way or the other. And highly differentiated societies, which need more trust for the reduction of their complexity than simple societies, must perhaps also hold in readiness correspondingly more varied mechanisms for the creation and stabilization of trust. They must therefore make more demands on the readiness to trust inherent in their systems and at the same time ease the burdens placed on that readiness to trust to a greater extent than is the case in simple societies.

Notes

1 In this sense it is often argued that 'self-confidence' is the basis of all 'genuine' trust; thus for instance Hauke (1956), pp. 34ff. On the other hand, it can just as easily be said that self-confidence can only be learned when one is the object of trust from others; thus, e.g., Kwant (1965), p. 96.

2 See the reference in Chapter 1, Note 2.

3 On this question see Horwitz (1956), p. 163.

4 See Humphreys (1939); lrwin (1944); Stogdill (1959), pp. 68ff.

5 On this also Luhmann (1972), Vol. I, pp. 40ff.

6 Thus, for psychological structures in general, Garner (1962), especially pp. 338ff.

7 See for instance Gibb (1964); Pilisuk and Skolnick (1968).

8 See Gibb (1964), p. 292. The employment of the word 'healthy' as cipher for a morality one can no longer profess would itself be worth some investigation.

9 A critique of this early modern theory of the world picture can be found in the essay 'Die Zeit des Weltbildes' [The Age of the World Picture] in Heidegger (1950), pp. 69ff.

10 See Parsons and Shils (1951), pp. 76ff.

11 See above, pp. 81ff. and pp. 138ff.

12 These two aspects of causal and symbolic imputation naturally cannot be wholly separated, for the imputation of cause is guided by the prior assumption of the identity of nature, which is symbolically constituted. See also Heider (1944).

13 Assistance by others, even by the deceiver himself, also comes into this. Goffman (1952) throws light from this standpoint on situations of disappointment.

14 Apropos of these considerations, it seems doubtful whether higher status can be reckoned to constitute in itself a basis for trust. So far as the political system is concerned, it would appear from investigations in the US that those in possession of higher social status have a more favourable picture of the leading personalities of their political systems, and this applies to politicians as well as to civil servants. See Agger, Goldstein and Pearl (1961). But it will not do to extend such views to all kinds of trust.

15 Goffman (1959), pp. 77ff. See also Luhmann (1964), pp. 314ff., on collegial arrangements.

16 A concept drawn from the general systems theory of Bertalanffy (1949), pp. 127ff.

12

The Rationality of Trust and Distrust

Ethics posed the question of whether trust was rational, right and morally necessary but it was incapable of resolution. Some preference for trust can be perceived in the statements cited in Chapter 1,[1] but such a preference cannot be expressed without reservations. There are obviously some cases which call for trust and other cases which call for distrust. This is rationally indisputable. It therefore follows that trust cannot be a maxim for conduct which is valid without exception. Ethics must, therefore, presuppose that whether in particular instances one should trust or not follows from the objective features of the situation, from common human understanding. Therefore, even if a general rule is formulated about trust as a principle, the decision as to whether it should be followed or not must be delegated and left to the situation. Furthermore, it must be presumed that the situation, and in particular the object of trust, displays sufficient objective features to ground a judgement that can serve the development of trust, and that these features can have the same meaning for all people and the same relevance for trust. Only thanks to these basic suppositions, which conceive the world as consisting of multiple forms and pervaded by malice and deceit but nevertheless socially objectified and stable, could the ethical mode of treating the problem be meaningful.

One could keep to the old view that this way of treating the problem is determined by its subject of reference and, to that extent, is correct. To demand more precision than the subject offers would be irrational and could lead to erroneous, excessive abstractions. This long-established argument is not to be refuted by direct rebuttal. But that does not settle the questions of its cognitive value, of whether it is even answering the right question of what its basic premises are, and, above all, of how it stands in relation to the structure of the social order which it presupposes in its premises.

A moral principle which also acknowledges its opposite must be reliant on practical situations that can be unanimously and unequivocally interpreted, and where it can be firmly settled whether the principle or its opposite is to be applied. In so far as situations for such interpretation are lacking, the principle loses both its value as a means of orientation and its normative function. For it could provide justification for each and every decision. Consequently, the normative character of such maxims becomes important only if, and so far as, one can expect social situations where the factual and social complexity has already been reduced to a considerable extent. This can be the case in a relatively simple social world, or, again, in fairly strongly regulated parts of a more complex reality – for example in the field of law, or in organizations.[2] Trust is, however, typically demanded precisely where other means for simplifying the orientation of action and guaranteeing it fail to work. If one adds that the social world in general nowadays is, with some reservations, much too complex to permit an ethics of principles to function as a theory of action, then it becomes questionable whether we should continue to apply the ethical mode of thinking to the problem of trust. In particular, lowering the scope of the social dimension through social psychology and phenomenology to provide insight into the impact of social relationships upon all experience, makes it doubtful whether an ethic which seeks to offer instruction in correct personal decision-making is adequate for our problem of the rationality of trust.[3]

If it is not, then the rationality of trust and distrust must be seen anew and in a different way as a problem. To that end one must first discover where the cardinal point of the problematic, the heart of the difficulty, lies. Obviously social reality is much too highly differentiated for it to be abstracted into a simple but instructive ethical maxim for decisions regarding trust. The problem of the orientation and directing of action must be solved by very many differentiated means. The sciences of human action can no longer allow themselves the illusion of laying down to the actor, if only in terms of vague principles, how to act correctly, in some direct, immediate, fashion, of telling him what he ought to do. Scientific-analytic and practically oriented perspectives must be more rigorously separated and consciously worked out separately from each other. Such a difference in style between theoretical analyses and practical information-processing is no drawback to the collaboration of theory and practice, but rather precisely the basis for it, and a meaningful division of labour in the joint mastering of an exceedingly complex environment.

If one focuses the relationship of theory and practice, so understood, upon the problem of complexity, then it seems obvious to locate the problem in the difference between modes of selection, and thus to summarize it in a nutshell.[4] A usable division is then offered by the distinction between system-perspective and action-orientation which seems to be gaining ground in recent developments in the social sciences. Psychology and sociology have strong theoretical tendencies to becoming sciences of personal and social action systems respectively – to becoming sciences which in their systems theory include unconscious, latent and incongruous action-oriented perspectives, which make comparative research possible, recognize structural contradictions in systems, and in all this achieve a potential for complexity which overtaxes the actor-in-a-situation. Under the pressure of this expansion of the field of vision, other sciences which pursue prescriptive aims must transform themselves, by means of stricter specialization and a greater awareness of their problems, into theories of the rational reduction of complexity – into decision theories. In their final form they endeavour to work out and establish a calculus which the actor can apply in predetermined, constructed 'model-like' situations, without having to think through and decide anew on the functional context of his behaviour in each case. He must be able to presuppose that system structures and decision programmes have already taken over this part of the work from him, that, in other words, the social world is organized.

What, then, does the pronouncement 'rational' refer to in such a social order when the problems are set out in this way, and to what does trust refer? If one were to take as a yardstick the concept of rationality in decision-making theories – be it that of rational choice in the employment of means, or that of optimality – one would from the outset fall into a too narrow conceptual frame of reference which cannot do justice to the facts of trust. Trust is not a means that can be chosen for particular ends, much less an ends/means structure capable of being optimized. Nor is trust a prognosis; its correctness cannot be measured by the occurrence of the predicted event and after some experiences have been reduced to probability values. These types of techniques, which are significant within the framework of decision-making models, have, as does trust, the function of reducing complexity. They are functional equivalents for trust, but not acts of trust in the true sense. As far as they extend, trust is unnecessary. They can replace trust, just as, conversely, the need for trust as a complementary way of absorbing uncertainty is a result of the limited effectiveness of those decision-making techniques. Trust is, however, something other than a reasonable assumption on which to decide correctly, and for this reason models for calculating correct decisions miss the point of the question of trust.

In a more widely conceived sociological theory of rationalization, the preparatory work for which is missing in the prevailing empirical-descriptive orientation of sociological research, the evaluation 'rational' could follow from functional analysis. All activity which helps to orient human action more meaningfully in an exceptionally complex world, thus increasing the human capacity for comprehending and reducing complexity, would then have to be judged rational. This can only be done by means of system formation. So, from this point of view, the label 'rational' would not refer to decisions about particular actions but rather to systems, and functions for maintaining systems.[5] We will take this idea as a basis, especially as it was already implicit in our functional analysis of trust, and see what it leads to.

Trust is rational in regard to the function of increasing the potential of a system for complexity. Without trust only very simple forms of human co-operation that can be transacted on the spot are possible, and even individual action is much too sensitive to disruption to be capable of being planned, without trust, beyond the immediately assured moment. Trust is indispensable in order to increase a social system's potential for action beyond these elementary forms. Completely new types of actions, above all such as are not immediately satisfying and hence have to be artificially motivated, become possible in a system which can activate trust. Through trust a system gains time, and time is the critical variable in the construction of complex system structures. The satisfying of needs can be delayed, and nevertheless guaranteed. Instrumental action, oriented towards distant effects, can become institutionalized if the temporal horizon of a system is suitably extended by means of trust. The availability of liquid financial resources, power and truth, all mechanisms dependent on trust, makes possible an indifference on the part of the system towards numerous events in the environment and thus a gain in reaction time.

This judgement of trust as system-rational can nevertheless not remain unqualified and be interpreted simply as an assertion about trust. Of course, trust is never the only mechanism for the reduction of complexity; the need for trust depends on the availability, or non-availability, of functional equivalents. Trust requires numerous auxiliary mechanisms of learning, symbolizing, controlling, sanctioning; it structures the processing of experience in a way which demands energy and attention. Above all, however, not just in individual cases, but much more at the system level, trust depends on the inclination towards risk being kept under control and on the quota of disappointments not becoming too large. If this is correct, then one could suppose that a system of higher complexity, which needs more trust, also needs at the same time more distrust, and therefore must institutionalize distrust, for example in the form of control.

Accordingly, system rationality cannot be attributed to trust alone. It lies rather on a level that encompasses both trust and distrust, namely in the *binary schematization* of a more elemental relation to the world into the structured *alternatives* of trust and distrust.[6] The advantages of such a schematization should be compared with more strongly formalized and specialized binary codes – for example that of right/wrong or that of true/untrue. In all these cases the definitions of the situation which are set against each other are at first logically inconvertible entities.[7] By means of binary schematization they are treated, however, as if one could be turned into the other by mere negation. Thus the transition from the one form to the other is made easier, both come closer together precisely in that they are thought of as opposites, and in this lies the gain in rationality. For the simplicity and directness of the transition to the opposite makes tolerable a greater risk in determining the system. The relative inferiority, the relatively low 'level of technicality', of the trust mechanism in comparison with the truth-code or the legal-code can be seen, among other things, in the greater difficulty of reversing negation – trust is easier to transform into distrust than is distrust into trust.

Such thoughts are distantly analogous to the position which used to be adopted in ethics, namely, that trust should be the rule and distrust the exception, that trust is therefore to be preferred in cases of doubt but must leave room for distrust. However, there is a difference in that these considerations cannot be converted into the currency of directives which action may follow. In deciding about the particular case, trust and distrust exclude one another. Their relationship must therefore be constructed by a science of action such as ethics in the sense of an either/or, according to the rule/exception schema. When related to systems and seen as general mechanisms, trust and distrust can be increased side by side, in so far as aspects and situations can be sufficiently differentiated. Admittedly, no further indications can be gained on this abstract level of consideration as to whether one should trust or distrust in any particular case.[8] Only very much more exact analyses of particular systems could help to form a basis for a decision on that issue. Systems theory can, however, found a judgement on the rationality of the trust mechanism and on the particular system conditions under which it can perform its function.

A system-rational increase in the effectiveness of trust will depend on all the aspects of trust formation which we have treated in the course of our inquiry and cannot catalogue once again here. Nevertheless, perhaps the decisive question remains open as to whether and how it is possible for trust and distrust to be co-ordinated through the creation of systems, and so increased in tandem. For reasons of general systems theory which cannot be adequately developed here, two closely connected processes ought to be decisive. These are the differentiation of the system from its environment, i.e. the drawing of boundaries, and the inner differentiation of the system, i.e. the functional specification of its subsystems and mechanisms.

It is a basic thesis of systems theory that systems constitute themselves by means of the distinction between inner and outer and maintain themselves by stabilizing this boundary.[9] If we conceive rationality in the sociological sense as system rationality, it is plausible to seek in *this inner/outer distinction a rational criterion for the distinctive location and the joint increase of trust or distrust.* In working out this idea, care must be taken to distinguish different system references. The reference system whose inner/outer distinction we are now considering is not the system which trusts or distrusts. It is not therefore a matter of distinguishing external and internal conditions for trust, which was dealt with earlier. We are referring now rather to the case where a system, be it a person or a social system, takes part in another social system, so that it becomes enmeshed into a social system through membership and is called upon to decide, in questions of trust, whether from the point of view of this membership system trust is required for system-internal or for system-external processes. Although system nestings of many sorts are involved, we can, to simplify matters, consider the case of the membership of people in organizations.

As a first, rough, approximation, one can suppose that internal processes earn and maintain more trust than external ones, that one trusts one's colleague in his role more than an outsider, a fellow club or party member more than a stranger. That such a differentiation is widespread and can be rational, that the dividing line between the familiar and the non-familiar person supports it, is not something to be dismissed out of hand. One finds system boundaries characterized as trust boundaries particularly in all social systems engaged in operations which are not supposed to be revealed to the outside or are even illegal and therefore have to be kept secret.[10] A functional analysis of the problems of complex social systems certainly does not give this simple picture. For many systems it can be vitally necessary that they are in a position to invest trust in their environment so that they can take part in relationships which are only to be achieved through mutual trust. The system members must then be able to display trust externally also. In the lower positions in modern large organizations, for example, internal relationships can be programmed in such detail that trust between members becomes virtually unnecessary because uncertainty in behaviour is overcome by other mechanisms. For some systems also, it is precisely in their internal relationships that substantial injections of distrust are needed for them to remain alert and capable of innovation, so as not to fall back into their customary pedestrian ways of relying on one another.

The inner/outer differentiation should therefore not be equated unproblematically with the boundary between required trust and justified distrust. With greater social differentiation and system specialization especially, there exists a tendency for internal distinctions to increase and for those connected with the environment to decrease.[11] Even then, however, system boundaries make possible a different strategy for the apportioning of trust and distrust in the case of internal processes than in the case of external ones, in the sense that members trust or are distrustful in a different way and for different reasons. The internal world of a system is quite different from the external world and, therefore, no one is obliged to be 'consistent' in trusting beyond the system boundaries. One can, for example, accept without question the opinion of one's colleague about a technical matter but nevertheless not risk lending him money 'personally'. System boundaries act as critical thresholds, in the sense discussed above,[12] at which familiarity and trust can switch to distrust, system trust to personal trust or distrust, or distrust to indifference.

A greater measure of trust can be established internally by means of selective processes for the choice of members within the framework of the selection criteria. On the other hand, on this basis a sharp distrust of a quite specific kind can be elevated to the level of formal duty, for the purposes of supervision, for example. In the case of external relationships such system-structural reasons for trust and distrust are irrelevant and things come to depend more on the specific learning and confirming of trust relationships in the contact between system and environment, on the freedom of traffic allowed by the system boundaries, or on the strength of the system and the cover it guarantees its members in the case of distrustful behaviour leading to disruptions and conflicts in relationships with the environment.

It is precisely this differentiation of the approaches to trust and distrust which is, from the point of view of the system, rational. For it assists it in preserving the higher level of inner order in comparison to its environment, or, in other words, in stabilizing, in an extremely complex environment, a simpler, less complex system-order which is suited to human capacities for action, and in reducing the complexity gap between system and environment. In the repertoire of system strategies and latent functions which serve such system maintenance, trust naturally plays only a limited role, both internally and externally. The more effectively the environment of a system is protected by more encompassing systems from too intense, unpredictable fluctuations, the more effectively the system can move over to directing its actions by internally rationalized decision-making techniques, and replace trust with calculations of probability. Whether, and under what conditions, such a process of substitution is itself rational can likewise only be judged within the framework of our comprehensive idea of rationality, whereby trust, which has apparently come about 'irrationally', may appear rational if and in so far as it performs the functions which serve the maintenance of the system.

A further aspect which can contribute to the rationalization of trust and distrust in social systems has already been mentioned on numerous occasions in the preceding pages and must now be worked out in its particular problematic. *This is the specifiability of the respects in which one trusts or distrusts.* As soon as, and in so far as, the boundaries of a system are defined, it can allocate specific functions internally to subsystems and mechanisms and thus define more precisely actions, situations and roles with regard to which trust or distrust is expected. What would be absurd as a general rule of conduct, or could not be motivated, can be achieved within the boundaries of specific systems which themselves enjoy the trust of their members.

Admittedly, trust and distrust are, in the way in which complexity is reduced, confused in principle and oriented towards concrete persons or groups or the objects and events symbolizing their trustworthiness. That does not mean, however, that trust relationships cannot be restricted to specific aspects. One can trust someone in matters of love but not in money matters; one can trust his knowledge but not his skill, his moral intention but not his ability to report objectively, his taste but not his discretion. The reason for this specificity can be simply that trust was learned in this restricted sphere and has foundered in other respects. It may, however, also go back to a selective interest of the system to which the parties concerned belong and which even structures the learning process itself.

The possibilities of system rationalization seem to lie in such a pre-structuring and legitimation of specific opportunities for trust and distrust. In this way systems are able to provide for trust and distrust alongside one another, indeed, interlocking them in a variety of ways so that they intensify one another. Where the mobility of a two-year-old son is concerned, different members of a family have a legitimate distrust and, at the same time, mutually trust their distrust. In organizations, checks can be set up which operate under a specified order to distrust, and here too place others, often even the people who are themselves controlled, in a position of trusting the functioning of this distrust.[13] There are even roles, for example, those of researchers or judges, where, within the specific horizon of their task, trust is allowed to be treated as distrust, and where reports about trust are regarded with distrust.[14] Trust in systems as a whole can, as we saw, depend decisively on trust being interrupted at critical points and distrust being switched on. Conversely, only in systems which are trusted can distrust be so institutionalized and restricted that it is not regarded as personal and reciprocated, so remains protected from escalating into conflicts.

If the effect of these various mechanisms is to be increased, their combination must be secured independently of personal motivational structures and proclivity for risk. This can only be done through organization, which brings into play new, impersonal, motives for action. To this extent, moreover, a differentiation of the system to be trusted is a prerequisite for extensive inner specification. Organization in no way makes trust and distrust superfluous but it depersonalizes these mechanisms. The person who trusts no longer does so at his own risk but at the risk of the system. All he has to do is to take care still that no detectable mistakes creep into his bestowing of trust. The person who distrusts no longer does so by going back to personal modes of reduction, such as personal animosity, hostility or safety precautions, but does so on the basis of the system, which has already programmed in advance the mode of behaviour for cases of disappointment, and guards the distruster against any excess.

Characteristically, the organization in which trust and distrust are the object of expectations with regard to aspects of a work task does not completely remove the choice between these two possibilities from the actor. Even the truster must retain a modicum of distrust – he must, for instance, intervene if his colleague gives an opinion which is obviously false. And neither can the distruster, as in the case of supervision, take his justified distrust to extremes without becoming a liability to the organization. What in ethics is expected from the nature of things is performed by means of the organization and specification of the system, that is, clear directions in a particular case as to whether trust or distrust is appropriate and rational.

All in all, system theory accomplishes more than ethics in that it makes comprehensible the system's specification mechanisms. It too, in the final analysis, cannot tell the actor how he should act and whether he should trust or not. It does, however, possess the possibility of showing clearly how systems can be set up in which, despite high complexity, it can be left to the actor to decide whether to trust or not. Systems are rational to the extent that they can encompass and reduce complexity, and this they can only do if they possess understanding of how to make use of trust and distrust without placing too heavy demands on the person who finally shows trust or distrust, that is, on the individual.

These considerations lead us back to our starting point, to the problem of social complexity. Historically as well as factually, trust takes on many various shapes. It has a different character in archaic social systems from what it has in civilized social orders; it can be trust which arises spontaneously, or which is personal and built up in a tactical-insightful manner, or it can be trust in general system mechanisms. It avoids a clear-cut ethical instruction. Only from the point of view of its function can it be understood as a whole and compared with other functionally equivalent mechanisms. Trust reduces social complexity by exceeding available information and generalizing expectations of behaviour in that it replaces missing information with an internally guaranteed security. It thus remains dependent on other reduction mechanisms developed in parallel with it, for example those of law, of organization and, of course, those of language, but it cannot, however, be reduced to them. Trust is not the sole foundation of the world. But a highly complex yet nevertheless structured representation of the world could not be established without a fairly complex society, which in turn could not be established without trust.

Notes

1 Chapter 1, Note 2.
2 Useful evidence for consideration of this problem is constituted by the discussion concerning the 'logic' and rationality of juristic modes of reasoning; see, in general, Viehweg (1965), or, directly pertaining to the topic, Miller (1956); see also the similar controversy concerning the significance of 'organizational principles' initiated by Simon (1946), as well as, for instance, Urwick (1948). In both cases the defenders of principles which allow for their opposite are in a relatively good position, because they refer to social situations which are thoroughly regulated and on that account not excessively complex; here even principles which give no unequivocal directives for behaviour may afford sufficient security from case to case.
3 It has become clear today in many ways that ethics can no longer constitute

the sole discipline in which the problems of human collective existence receive their fundamental treatment. See, for instance, Löwith (1962), p. 2; Kwant (1965), pp. 48ff.

4 See also Luhmann (1971), pp. 253ff.

5 For greater detail, see Luhmann (1968). In the first edition the formulation did not take into account that if one considers the complexity of the decision situation a corresponding concept of rationality can be developed for decision theory also.

6 See Weinrich (1967) on improbability in the lifeworld and on the linguistic particularities of 'double paradigms'. Definitions of the situation which confer upon the partner a decisive either/or in social intercourse are seen as constituting an imposition. This raises the interesting question of under which assumptions they can be treated as if they were normal.

7 In the same sense as Thompson (1963). See also above, Chapter 10, Note 1.

8 It is for functional analysis to compare functional equivalents, not to give grounds for a decision favouring one or the other operation. Such a decision presupposes evaluations which may, under certain circumstances, be suggested by the analysis of concrete systems with reference to the consequences and side-effects of all thinkable alternatives, but never conclusively laid down by it. Such inquiries into concrete systems may indicate the existence of bottlenecks with reference to given functions, because the relative operations result in serious problems, but cannot easily be replaced by equivalent ones. It may then be the case, in view of the problem framework peculiar to the system, that it appears sensible to demand more or less trust or distrust. More trust, for instance, to lay the basis for new combinations of actions; more distrust, for instance, in order to keep down the incidence of error and disappointment. But even in such cases the decisions for or against such changes presuppose an evaluation of their consequences.

9 See the concept of 'boundary maintaining system' in Parsons; see for instance Parsons and Shils (1951), pp. 108f.; Parsons (1953), p. 623; and similar views in Optner (1960), pp. 20ff.; Herbst (1961), especially pp. 78ff.; Easton (1965a), especially pp. 24f., pp. 60ff.

10 See, for a striking example, Bensman and Gerver (1963), and the detailed discussion in Goffman (1959), pp. 77ff.

11 See Simmel (1890).

12 See p. 81.

13 For instance when a punch-operator can work faster and less carefully, because she knows the tester is nearby.

14 Organizational sociology has clearly established that in spite of their specialization and depersonalization, such distrust roles still carry the seeds of many intra-organizational conflicts. Hence their critical evaluation in connection with control and supervision, and their positive evaluation in the context of innovation. See, for a typical example, Gouldner (1954b); also Thompson (1961, 1965); Kahn et al. (1964), pp. 125ff.

References

Adler, M. (1936) *Das Rätsel der Gesellschaft Zur erkenntnis-kritischen Grundlegung der Sozialwissenschaft*. Vienna.

Agger, R. E., Goldstein, M. N. and Pearl, S. A. (1961) Political cynicism: measurement and meaning. *Journal of Politics* 23, 477–506.

Albach, H. (1962) *Investition und Liquidität*. Wiesbaden.

Alien, L. A. (1958) *Management and Organization*. New York, London and Toronto.

Allport, F. H. (1955) *Theories of Perception and the Conception of Structure*. New York and London.

Ashby, W. R. (1954) *Design for a Brain*. 2nd edition. London.

Atkinson, J. W. (1957) Motivational determinants of risk-taking behaviour. *Psychological Review* 64, 359–72.

Bales, R. F. (1951) *Interaction Process Analysis: A Method for the Study of Small Groups*. Cambridge, MA.

Barth, H. (1943) *Fluten und Dämme. Der philosophische Gedanke in der Politik*. Zurich.

Bauch, B. (1938) Das Vertrauen als ethisches Problem. *Die Tatwelt* 14, 67–74.

Bauer, R. A. (1963) Communication as a transaction: a comment on 'On the Concept of Influence'. *Public Opinion Quarterly* 27:1, 83–6.

Baum, B. H. (1961) *Decentralization of Authority in a Bureaucracy*. Englewood Cliffs, NJ.

Baum, R. C. (1976) On societal media dynamics: an exploration. In: J. J. Loubser, R. C. Baum, A. Effrat and V. Lidz (eds), *Explorations in General Theory in the Social Sciences*. New York.

Bednarski, J. (1957) La reduction husserlienne. *Revue de Metaphysique et de Morale*, 418–35.

Bensman, J. and Gerver, I. (1963) Crime and punishment in the factory: the function of deviancy in maintaining the social system. *American Sociological Review* 28, 588–98.

Berger, P. L. (1963) *Invitation to Sociology: A Humanistic Perspective*. Garden City, NY.

Berger, P. L. and Kellner, H. (1965) Die Ehe und die Konstruktion der Wirklichkeit: Eine Abhandlung zur Mikrosoziologie des Wissens. *Soziale Welt* 16, 220–35.

Berger, P. L. and Luckmann Th. (1966) *The Social Construction of Reality: A Treatise in the Sociology of Knowledge.* Garden City, NY.

Berger, P. L. and Pullberg, S. (1965) Verdinglichung und die soziologische Kritik des Bewusstseins. *Soziale Welt* 16, 97–112.

Bergson, H. (1889) *Essai sur les données immédiates de la conscience.* Paris.

Bertalanffy, L. von (1949) Zu einer allgemeinen Systemlehre. *Biologia Generalis* 19, 114–29.

Binswanger, L. (1953) *Grundformen und Erkenntnis menschlichen Daseins.* 2nd edition. Zürich.

Blain, R. R. (1971) An alternative to Parsons's four-function paradigm as a basis for developing general sociological theory. *American Sociological Review* 36, 678–92.

Blau, P. M. (1960) Patterns of deviation in work groups. *Sociometry* 23, 245–61.

Blau, P. M. (1964) *Exchange and Power in Social Life.* New York, London and Sydney.

Braibanti, R. (1963) Public bureaucracy and judiciary in Pakistan. In: J. La Palombara (ed.), *Bureaucracy and Political Development.* Princeton, 360–440.

Brand, G. (1955) *Welt, Ich und Zeit. Nach unveröffentlichten Manuskripten Edmund Husserls.* The Hague.

Braybrooke, D. (1964) The mystery of executive success re-examined. *Administrative Science Quarterly* 8, 533–60.

Bruner, J. S., Goodnow, J. J. and Austin, G. A. (1956) *A Study of Thinking.* New York and London.

Burns, T. (1953) Friends, enemies, and the polite fiction. *American Sociological Review* 18, 654–62.

Canaris, C.-W. (1971) *Die Vertrauenshaftung im deutschen Privatrecht.* Munich.

Cazeneuve, J. (1958) La connaissance d'autrui dans les societés archaiques. *Cahiers Internationaux de Sociologie* 25, 75–99.

Claessens, D. (1962) *Familie und Wertsystem. Eine Studie zur 'zweiten, sozio-kulturellen Geburt' des Menschen.* Berlin.

Claessens, D. (1970) *Instinkt, Psyche, Geltung: Zur Legitimation menschlichen Verhaltens. Eine soziologische Anthropologie.* 2nd edition. Opladen.

Craushaar, G. von (1969) *Der Einfluss des Vertrauens auf die Privatrechtsbildung.* Munich.

Daily, C. A. (1952) The effects of premature conclusion upon the acquisition of understanding of a person. *Journal of Psychology* 33, 133–52.

Dale, H. E. (1941) *The Higher Civil Service of Great Britain.* London.

Darmstaedter, F. (1948) Recht und Jurist. *Süddeutsche Juristen Zeitung* 3, 430–6.

Davis, K. (1959) The myth of functional analysis as a special method in sociology and anthropology. *American Sociological Review* 24, 757–72.

Deutsch, K. W. (1963) *The Nerves of Government: Models of Political Communication and Control.* New York and London.

Deutsch, M. (1958) Trust and suspicion. *Journal of Conflict Resolution* 2, 265–79.

Deutsch, M. (1960a) The effect of motivational orientation upon trust and suspicion. *Human Relations* 13, 123–39.

Deutsch, M. (1960b) Trust, trustworthiness and the F-scale. *Journal of Abnormal and Social Psychology* 6:1, 138–40.

Deutsch, M. (1962) Cooperation and trust: some theoretical notes. *Nebraska Symposium on Motivation*, 275–319.

Dewey, J. (1926) *Experience and Nature.* Chicago and London.

Diesel, E. (1947) *Die Macht des Vertrauens.* Munich.

Easton, D. (1965a) *A Framework for Political Analysis.* Englewood Cliffs, NJ.

Easton, D. (1965b) *A Systems Analysis of Political Life.* New York, London and Sydney.

Edelman, M. (1964) *The Symbolic Uses of Politics.* Urbana, IL.

Eichler, H. (1950) *Die Rechtslehre vom Vertrauen. Privatrechtliche Untersuchungen: Über den Schutz des Vertrauens.* Tübingen.

Elias, N. (1978) *The Civilizing Process.* Oxford.

Etzioni, A. (1961) *A Comparative Analysis of Complex Organizations: On Power, Involvement, and Their Correlates.* New York.

Etzioni, A. (1965) Dual leadership in complex organizations. *American Sociological Review* 30, 688–98.

Evan, W. M. (1963) Peer group interaction and organizational socialization: a study of employee turnover. *American Sociological Review* 28, 436–40.

Evans, G. (1964) Effect of unilateral promise and value of rewards upon cooperation and trust. *Journal of Abnormal and Social Psychology* 69, 587–90.

Eyferth, K. (1964a) Lernen als Anpassung des Organismus durch bedingte Reaktion. *Handbuch der Psychologie*, Vol. 1. Göttingen, 76–117.

Eyferth, K. (1964b) Das Lernen von Haltungen, Bedürfnissen und sozialen Verhaltensweisen. *Handbuch der Psychologie*, Vol. 1. Göttingen, 347–70.

Feinberg, J. (1961) Supererogation and rules. *Ethics* 71, 276–88, reprinted in *Doing and Deserving: Essays in the Theory of Responsibility.* Princeton, 1970, 3–24.

Fink, E. (1958) *Sein, Wahrheit, Welt: Vor-Fragen zum Problem des Phänomen Begriffs.* The Hague.

Fraenkel, E. (1960) *Das amerikanische Regierungssystem: Eine politische Analyse.* Opladen.

French, J. R. P. and Raven, B. (1959) The bases of social power. In: D. Cartwright (ed.), *Studies in Social Power.* Ann Arbor, 150–67.

Frenkel-Brunswik, E. (1949) Intolerance of ambiguity as an emotional and perceptual personality variable. *Journal of Personality* 18, 108–43.

Friedeburg, L. von (1963) *Soziologie des Betriebsklimas: Studien zur Deutung empirischer Untersuchungen in industriellen Grossbetrieben.* Stuttgart.

Friedrich, C. J. (1958) Authority, reason, and discretion. In: *Authority (Nomos I).* Cambridge, MA, 28–48.

Friedrich, C. J. (1963) *Man and His Government: An Empirical Theory of Politics.* New York.

Gäfgen, G. (1961) Zur Theorie kollektiver Entscheidungen in der Wirtschaft. *Jahrbücher für Nationalökonomie und Statistik* 173, 1–49.

Gäfgen, G. (1963) *Theorie der wirtschaftlichen Entscheidung: Untersuchungen zur Logik und Ökonomischen Bedeutung des rationalen Handelns.* Tübingen.

Gale, R. M. (1968) *The Language of Time.* London.

Garfinkel, H. (1963) A conception of, and experiments with, 'Trust' as a condition of stable concerted actions. In: O. J. Harvey (ed.), *Motivation and Social Interaction: Cognitive Determinants.* New York, 187–238.

Garfinkel, H. (1964) Studies of the routine grounds of everyday activities. *Social Problems* 11, 225–50.

Garner, W. R. (1962) *Uncertainty and Structure as Psychological Concepts*. New York and London.

Geiger, Th. (1929) Zur Soziologie der Industriearbeit und des Betriebs. *Die Arbeit* 6, 673–89; 766–81.

Gibb, J. R. (1964) Climate for trust formation. In: L. P. Bradford, J. R. Gibb and K. D. Benne (eds), *T-Group Theory and Laboratory Method*. New York, 279–309.

Glaser, B. G. and Strauss, A. L. (1965) Temporal aspects of dying as a non-scheduled status passage. *American Journal of Sociology* 71, 48–59.

Goffman, E. (1952) On cooling the mark out. *Psychiatry* 15, 451–63.

Goffman, E. (1955) On face work. *Psychiatry* 18, 213–31.

Goffman, E. (1957) Alienation from interaction. *Human Relations* 10, 47–59.

Goffman, E. (1959) *The Presentation of Self in Everyday Life*. 2nd edition. New York.

Goffman, E. (1963a) *Behavior in Public Places: Notes on the Social Organization of Gatherings*. New York.

Goffman, E. (1963b) *Stigma: Notes on the Management of Spoiled Identity*. Englewood Cliffs, NJ.

Goffman, E. (1969) *Strategic Interaction*. Philadelphia.

Golembiewski, R. T. (1964) Authority as a problem in overlays: a concept for action and analysis. *Administrative Science Quarterly* 9, 23–49.

Gouldner, A. W. (1954a) *Wildcat Strike*. Yellow Springs, OH.

Gouldner, A. W. (1954b) *Patterns of Industrial Bureaucracy*. Glencoe, IL.

Gouldner, A. W. (1959) Reciprocity and autonomy in functional theory. In: L. Gross (ed.), *Symposium on Sociological Theory*. Evanston IL, 241–70.

Gouldner, A. W. (1960) The norm of reciprocity: a preliminary statement. *American Sociological Review* 25, 161–78.

Gross, E. and Stone, G. P. (1964) Embarrassment and the analysis of role requirements. *American Journal of Sociology* 70, 1–15.

Guest, R. H. (1962) *Organizational Change: The Effects of Successful Leadership*. Homewood, IL.

Gurwitsch, A. (1962) The common-sense world as social reality: a discourse on Alfred Schutz. *Social Research* 29, 50–72.

Guzmán, G., Borda, O. F. and Luna, E. U. (1962) *La Violencia en Colombia: Estudio de un proceso social*. Bogota.

Habermas, J. and Luhmann, N. (1971) *Theorie der Gesellschaft oder Sozialtechnologie. Was leistet die Systemforschung?* Frankfurt.

Hartmann, H. (1964) *Funktionale Autorität: Systematische Abhandlung zu einem soziologischen Begriff*. Stuttgart.

Hartmann, N. (1962) *Ethik*. 4th edition. Berlin.

Harvey, O. J. and Schroder, H. M. (1963) Cognitive aspects of self and motivation. In: O. J. Harvey (ed.), *Motivation and Social Interaction: Cognitive Determinants*. New York, 95–133.

Hauke, H. (1956) *Die anthropologische Funktion des Vertrauens. Seine Bedeutung für die Erziehung*. (Dissertation) Tübingen.

Heidegger, M. (1949) *Sein und Zeit*, Vol. I. 6th edition. Tübingen.

Heidegger, M. (1950) Die Zeit des Weltbildes. In: *Holzwege*. Frankfurt.

Heider, F. (1944) Social perception and phenomenal causality. *Psychological Review* 51, 358–74.

Heider, F. (1958) *The Psychology of Interpersonal Relations*. New York and London.

Heller, H. (1934) *Staatslehre*. Leiden.

Hennis, W. (1962) *Amtsgedanke und Demokratiebegriff. Festgabe für Rudolf Smend*. Tübingen.

Henslin, J. M. (1968) Trust and the cab driver. In: M. Truzzi (ed.), *Sociology and Everyday Life*. Englewood Cliffs, NJ, 138–58.

Herbst, P. A. (1961) A theory of simple behaviour systems. *Human Relations* 14, 71–94, 193–239.

Hocking, W. E. (1953/4) Marcel and the ground issues of metaphysics. *Philosophy and Phenomenological Research* 14, 439–69.

Hofstätter, P. (1959) *Einführung in die Sozialpsychologie*. 2nd edition. Stuttgart.

Hohl, H. (1962) *Lebenswelt Und Geschichte Grundzüge der Spätphilosophie E. Husserl*. Freiburg and Munich.

Horwitz, M. (1956) Psychological needs as a function of social environment. In: L. D. White (ed.), *The State of the Social Sciences*. Chicago.

Hülsmann, H. (1967) Hermeneutik und Gesellschaft. *Soziale Welt* 18, 1–28.

Humphreys, L. G. (1939) Acquisition and extinction of verbal expectations in a situation analogous to conditioning. *Journal of Experimental Psychology* 25, 294–301.

Husserl, E. (1928) Vorlesungen zur Phänomenologie des inneren Zeitbewusstseins. Ed. M. Heidegger. *Jahrbuch für Philosophie und phänomenologische Forschung* 9, 367–496.

Husserl, E. (1948) *Erfahrung und Urteil*. Hamburg.

Husserl, E. (1950) *Cartesianische Meditationen und Pariser Verträge*. Husserliana, Vol. 1. The Hague.

Husserl, E. (1952) *Ideen zu einer reinen Phänomenologie und Phänomenologischen Philosophie*, Vol. II. Husserliana, Vol. IV. The Hague.

Husserl, E. (1954) *Die Krisis der europäischen Wissenschaften und die transzendentale Phänomenologie*. Husserliana, Vol. VI. The Hague.

Irwin, F. W. (1944) The realism of expectations. *Psychological Review* 51, 120–6.

Janowitz, M. (1960) *The Professional Soldier*. Glencoe, IL.

Jennings, H. H. (1950) *Leadership and Isolation: A Study of Personality in Interpersonal Relations*. 2nd edition. New York.

Jennings, M. K., Cummings, M. C. and Kilpatrick, F. P. (1966) Trusted leaders: perception of appointed federal officials. *Public Opinion Quarterly* 30, 368–84.

Jones, E. E., Davis, K. E. and Gergen, K. J. (1961) Role playing variations and their informational value for perception. *Journal of Abnormal and Social Psychology* 63, 302–10.

Jones, E. E., Gergen, K. J. and Jones, R. C. (1963) Tactics of ingratiation among leaders and subordinates in a status hierarchy. *Psychological Monographs* 77.

Jones, E. E. and Thibaut, J. W. (1958) Interaction goals as bases of inference in interpersonal perception. In: R. Tagiuri and L. Petrullo (eds), *Person Perception and Interpersonal Behavior*. Stanford, CA, 151–78.

Jost, W. (1932) *Das Sozialleben des Industriellen Betriebs*. Berlin.

Kahn, R. L., Wolfe, D. P., Quinn, R. P. and Snoek, D. J. (1964) *Organizational Stress: Studies in Role Conflict and Ambiguity.* New York, London and Sydney.

Kaufmann, F.-X. (1970) *Sicherheit als soziologisches und sozialpolitisches Problem: Untersuchungen zu einer Wertidee hochdifferenzierter Gesellschaften.* Stuttgart.

Keynes, J. M. (1936) *The General Theory of Employment, Interest and Money.* London.

Kidd, J. L. (1962) A new look at system research and analysis. *Human Factors* 4, 209–16.

Koch, H. (1960) Zur Diskussion in der Ungewissheitstheorie. *Zeitschrift für handelswissenschaftliche Forschung* 12, 49–75.

Koffka, K. (1935) *Principles of Gestalt Psychology.* London.

Krüger, H. (1964) *Allgemeine Staatslehre.* Stuttgart.

Krüsselberg, H.-G. (1965) *Organisationstheorie, Theorie der Unternehmung und Oligopol. Materialien zu einer sozioökonomischen Theorie der Unternehmung.* Berlin.

Kwant, R. C. (1965) *Phenomenology as Social Existence.* Pittsburgh.

Landgrebe, L. (1940) The world as a phenomenological problem. *Philosophy and Phenomenological Research* 1, 38–58.

Landgrebe, L. (1963) Phänomenologische Bewusstseinsanalyse und Metaphysik. In: *Der Weg der Phänomenologie.* Gütersloh, 75–109.

Lane, R. E. (1966) The decline of politics and ideology in a knowledgeable society. *American Sociological Review* 31, 649–62.

Lapide, H. A. (1647) *Dissertatio de ratione status in Imperio nostro Romano-Germanico.* Freistadt.

Lenz, K.-H. (1968) *Das Vertrauensschutzprinzip.* Berlin.

Locke, J. (1953) *Two Treatises of Civil Government.* Ed. W. S. Carpenter. London.

Löwith, K. (1962) *Das Individuum in der Rolle des Mitmenschen.* Darmstadt.

Long, N. E. (1962) Administrative communication. In: S. Mailick and E. H. van Ness (eds), *Concepts and Issues in Administrative Behavior.* Englewood Cliffs, NJ, 137–49.

Loomis, J. L. (1959) Communication, the development of trust and cooperative behaviour. *Human Relations* 12, 305–15.

Luce, D. R. and Raiffa, H. (1957) *Games and Decisions: Introduction and Critical Survey.* New York.

Luhmann, N. (1962) Der neue Chef. *Verwaltungsarchiv* 53, 11–24.

Luhmann, N. (1964) *Funktionen und Folgen formaler Organisation.* Berlin.

Luhmann, N. (1965a) Die Gewissensfreiheit und das Gewissen. *Archiv des Öffentlichen Rechts* 90, 257–86.

Luhmann, N. (1965b) *Grundrechte als Institution. Bin Beitrag zur politischen Soziologie.* Berlin.

Luhmann, N. (1965c) Spontane Ordnungsbildung. In: F. M. Marx (ed.), *Verwaltung: Eine einführende Darstellung.* Berlin, 163–83.

Luhmann, N. (1968) *Zweckbegriff und Systemrationalität: Ober die Funktion von Zwecken in sozialen Systemen.* Tübingen.

Luhmann, N. (1971) *Soziologische Aufklärung. Aufsätze zur Theorie sozialer Systeme.* 2nd edition. Opladen.

Luhmann, N. (1972) *Rechtssoziologie.* 2 Vols. Reinbek.

Luhmann, N. (1976) Generalized media and the problem of contingency. In: J. J.

Loubser, R. C. Baum, A. Effrat and V. Lidz (eds), *Explorations in General Theory in the Social Sciences*. New York.

Mainka, J. (1963) *Vertrauensschutz im Öffentlichen Recht*. Bonn.

Marcel, G. (1935) *Etre et Avoir*. Paris.

Marcus, P. M. (1960) Expressive and instrumental groups. *American Journal of Sociology* 66, 54–9.

Marschak, J. (1954) Towards an economic theory of organization and information. In: R. M. Thrall, C. H. Coombs and R. L. Davis (eds), *Decision Processes*. New York, 187–220.

Marschak, J. (1955) Elements for a theory of teams. *Management Science* 1, 127–37.

Maruyama, M. (1963) The second cybernetics: deviation-amplifying mutual causal processes. *General Systems* 8, 233–41.

Mayer, F. (1965) Geschäftsgang. In: F. M. Marx (ed.), *Verwaltung: Eine einführende Darstellung*. Berlin, 298–314.

McTaggart, J. E. (1908) The unreality of time. *Mind* 11, 457–74, reprinted in *Philosophical Studies*. London (1934).

Mead, G. H. (1934) *Mind, Self and Society*. Chicago.

Mead, G. H. (1938) *The Philosophy of the Act*. Chicago.

Merleau-Ponty, M. (1945) *Phenomenologie de la perception*. Paris.

Merton, R. K. (1957) The self-fulfilling prophecy. In: *Social Theory and Social Structure*. 2nd edition. Glencoe, IL, 421–36.

Metzger, W. (1963) *Psychologie. Entwicklung ihrer Grundannahmen seit der Einführung des Experiments*. 3rd edition. Darmstadt.

Milbrath, L. W. (1963) *The Washington Lobbyists*. Chicago.

Miller, L. S. (1956) Rules and exceptions. *Ethics* 66, 262–70.

Moore, W. E. (1964) Predicting discontinuities in social change. *American Sociological Review* 29, 331–38.

Nadel, S. F. (1957) *The Theory of Social Structure*. Glencoe, IL.

Neumann, J. van, and Morgenstern, O. (1944) *Theory of Games and Economic Behavior*. Princeton.

Nitschke, A. (1952) Angst und Vertrauen. *Die Sammlung* 7, 175–80.

Optner, S. L. (1960) *Systems Analysis for Business Management*. Englewood Cliffs, NJ.

Ossenbühl, F. (1972) Vertrauensschutz im sozialen Rechtsstaat. *Die Öffentliche Verwaltung* 25, 25–36.

Parsons, T. (1951) *The Social System*. Glencoe, IL.

Parsons, T. (1953) Some comments on the state of the general theory of action. *American Sociological Review* 18, 618–31.

Parsons, T. (1959a) General theory in sociology. In: R. K. Merton, L. Broom and L. S. Cottrell, Jr. (eds), *Sociology Today*. New York, 3–38.

Parsons, T. (1959b) 'Voting' and the equilibrium of the American political system. In: Eugene Burdick and Arthur J. Brodeck (eds), *American Voting Behavior*. Glencoe, IL, 80–120.

Parsons, T. (1960) Pattern variables revisited. *American Sociological Review* 25, 467–83.

Parsons, T. (1961a) The point of view of the author. In: M. Black (ed.), *The Social Theories of Talcott Parsons*. Englewood Cliffs, NJ, 311–63.

Parsons, T. (1961b) An outline of the social system. In: T. Parsons, E. Shils, K. D. Naegele and J. R. Pitts (eds), *Theories of Society*, Vol. I. New York, 30–79.

Parsons, T. (1963a) On the concept of influence. *Public Opinion Quarterly* 21, 37–62.

Parsons, T. (1963b) On the concept of political power. *Proceedings of the American Philosophical Society* 107, 232–62.

Parsons, T. (1964a) Die jüngsten Entwicklungen in der strukturell-funktionalen Theorie. *Kölner Zeitschrift für Soziologie und Sozialpsychologie* 16, 30–49.

Parsons, T. (1964b) Evolutionary universals in society. *American Sociological Review* 29, 339–57.

Parsons, T. (1964c) Some reflections on the place of force in social process. In: H. Eckstein (ed.), *Internal War: Problems and Approaches*. New York, 33–70.

Parsons, T. (1968) On the concept of value-commitments. *Sociological Inquiry* 38, 135–60.

Parsons, T. (1970) Some problems of general theory in sociology. In: J. C. McKinney and E. A. Tiryakian (eds), *Theoretical Sociology: Perspectives and Developments*. New York, 27–68.

Parsons, T. and Bales, R. F. (1955) *Family, Socialization and Interaction Process*. Glencoe, IL.

Parsons, T. and Shils, E. A. (eds) (1951) *Toward a General Theory of Action*. Cambridge, MA.

Parsons, T. and Smelser, N. J. (1956) *Economy and Society*. Glencoe, IL.

Parsons, T., Bales, R. F. and Shils, E. A. (1953) *Working Papers in the Theory of Action*. Glencoe, IL.

Paulsen, A. (1950) *Liquidität und Risiko in der wirtschaftlichen Entwicklung. Ein Beitrag zur dynamischen Wirtschaftstheorie*. Frankfurt and Berlin.

Peabody, R. L. (1964) *Organizational Authority: Superior–Subordinate Relationships in Three Public Service Organizations*. New York.

Piaget, J. (1955) *Die Bildung des Zeitbegriffs beim Kinde*. Zurich.

Pilisuk, M. and Skolnick, P. (1968) Inducing trust. A test of the Osgood proposal. *Journal of Personality and Social Psychology* 8, 121–33.

Plessner, H. (1964) *Conditio Humana*. Pfullingen.

Pool, I. de S. (1963) The mass media and politics in the modernization process. In: L. W. Pye (ed.), *Communications and Political Development*. Princeton, 234–53.

Postman, L. and Bruner, J. S. (1952) Hypothesis and the principle of closure: the effect of frequency and recency. *Journal of Psychology* 31, 113–25.

Presthus, R. V. (1960) Authority in organizations. *Public Administration Review* 20, 86–91.

Prior, A. N. (1957) *Time and Modality*. Oxford.

Prior, A. N. (1968) *Papers on Time and Tense*. Oxford.

Rapoport, A. (1960) *Fights, Games and Debates*. Ann Arbor.

Rapoport, A. and Chammah, A. M. (1965) *Prisoner's Dilemma. A Study in Conflict and Cooperation*. Ann Arbor.

Rescher, N. (1968) Truth and necessity in temporal perspective. In: R. M. Gale (ed.), *The Philosophy of Time*. London, 183–220.

Reynaud, P.-L. (1957) Recessions et seuils economiques. *Revue Economique* 8, 1032–52.

Reynaud, P.-L. (1962) *Economie généralisée et seuils de croissance. Etude de la psychologie économique du développement: U.R.S.S., Tunisie, Portugal.* Paris.

Roethlisberger, F. J. and Dickson, W. J. (1939) *Management and the Worker.* Cambridge, MA.

Roos, L. L., Jr. (1966) Toward a theory of cooperation-experiments, using nonzero-sum games. *Journal of Social Psychology* 69, 277–89.

Rosenberg, M. (1956) Misanthropy and political ideology. *American Sociological Review* 21, 690–5.

Rosenberg, M. (1957) Misanthropy and attitudes toward international affairs. *Journal of Conflict Resolution* 1, 340–5.

Sartre, J.-P. (1950) *L'être et le néant.* 30th edition. Paris.

Sartre, J.-P. (1960) *Critique de la raison dialectique,* Vol. I. Paris.

Schmölders, G. (1960) The Liquidity Theory of Money. *Kyklos* 13, 346–60.

Schottländer, R. (1957) *Theorie des Vertrauens.* Berlin.

Schroder, H. M. and Harvey, O. J. (1963) Conceptual organization and group structure. In: O. J. Harvey (ed.), *Motivation and Social Interaction: Cognitive Determinants.* New York, 134–66.

Schütz, A. (1932) *Der sinnhafte Aufbau der sozialen Welt. Eine Einleitung in die verstehende Soziologie.* Vienna.

Schütz, A. (1957) Das Problem der transzendentalen Intersubjektivität bei Husserl. *Philosophische Rundschau* 5, 81–107.

Schütz, A. (1962–6) *Collected Papers.* 3 Vols. The Hague.

Shepard, H. R. and Blake, R. R. (1962) Changing behavior through cognitive change. *Human Organization* 21, 88–92.

Simmel, G. (1890) *Über sociale Differenzierung.* Leipzig.

Simmel, G. (1922) *Soziologie: Untersuchungen Über die Formen der Vergesellschaftung.* 2nd edition. Munich and Leipzig.

Simon, H. A. (1946) The proverbs of administration. *Public Administration Review* 6, 53–67.

Simon, H. A. (1947) *Administrative Behavior.* New York.

Simon, H. A. (1957a) Authority. In: C. M. Arensberg (ed.), *Research in Industrial Human Relations.* New York, 103–15.

Simon, H. A. (1957b) *Models of Man, Social and Rational: Mathematical Essays on Rational Human Behavior in a Social Setting.* New York and London.

Slater, P. E. (1959) Role differentiation in small groups. *American Sociological Review* 20, 300–10.

Solomon, L. (1960) The influence of some types of power relationship and game strategies on the development of interpersonal trust. *Journal of Abnormal and Social Psychology* 61, 223–30.

Stendenbach, F. J. (1963) *Soziale Interaktion und Lernprozesse.* Berlin.

Stern, W. (1923/4) *Person und Sache: System des kritischen Personalismus.* 3 Vols. Leipzig.

Stocker, M. (1968) Supererogation and duties. In: *Studies in Moral Philosophy,* American Philosophical Quarterly Monograph Series, No. 1. Oxford, 53–63.

Stogdill, R. M. (1959) *Individual Behavior and Group Achievement.* New York.

Stratenwerth, G. (1958) *Verantwortung und Gehorsam. Zur strafrechtlichen Wertung hoheitlich gebotenen Handelns.* Tübingen.

Strauss, A. L. (1959) *Mirrors and Masks: The Search for Identity*. Glencoe, IL.

Strickland, L. H. (1958) Surveillance and Trust. *Journal of Personality* 26, 200–15.

Strohal, R. (1955) *Autorität. Ihr Wesen und ihre Funktion im Leben der Gemeinschaft*. Freiburg and Vienna.

Swinth, R. L. (1967) The establishment of the trust relationship. *Journal of Conflict Resolution* 11, 335–44.

Tenbruck, F. H. (1972) *Zur Kritik der planenden Vernunft*. Freiburg and Munich.

Theunissen, M. (1965) *Der Andere: Studien zur Sozialontologie der Gegenwart*. Berlin.

Thibaut, J. W. and Kelley, H. H. (1959) *The Social Psychology of Groups*. New York.

Thibaut, J. W. and Riecken, H. W. (1955) Some determinants and consequences of the perception of social causality. *Journal of Personality* 24, 113–33.

Thompson, J. W. (1963) The importance of opposites in human relations. *Human Relations* 16, 161–9.

Thompson, V. A. (1961) *Modern Organization*. New York.

Thompson, V. A. (1965) Bureaucracy and innovation. *Administrative Science Quarterly* 10, 1–20.

Tirpitz, A. von (1920) *Erinnerungen*. 2nd edition. Leipzig.

Tobin, J. (1958) Liquidity preference as behavior towards risk. *Review of Economic Studies* 25, 65–87.

Thomas, W. I. and Thomas, D. S. (1928) *The Child in America: Behavior Problems and Programs*. New York.

Turner, R. H. (1962) Role taking: process versus conformity. In: A. M. Rose (ed.), *Human Behavior and Social Processes: An Interactionist Approach*. Boston, 20–40.

Urwick, L. (1948) Principles of management. *British Management Review* 7, 15–48.

Vesta, F. J. di, Meyer, D. L. and Mills, J. (1964) Confidence in an expert as a function of his judgements. *Human Relations* 17, 235–42.

Vickers, G. (1959) *The Undirected Society: Essays on the Human Implications of Industrialization in Canada*. Toronto.

Vickers, G. (1965) *The Art of Judgement: A Study of Policy Making*. London.

Viehweg, Th. (1965) *Topik und Jurisprudenz*. 3rd edition. Munich.

Weigert, E. (1949) Existentialism and its relation to psychotherapy. *Psychiatry* 12, 399–412.

Wichman, H. (1970) Effects of isolation and communication on cooperation in a two-person game. *Journal of Personality and Social Psychology* 16, 114–20.

Wildavsky, A. (1964) *The Politics of the Budgetary Process*. Boston and Toronto.

Wilensky, H. L. (1956) *Intellectuals in Labor Unions: Organizational Pressures on Professional Roles*. Glencoe, IL.

Worthy, J. C. (1959) *Big Business and Free Men*. New York.

Wrightsman, L. S. (1966) Personality and attitudinal correlates of trusting and trustworthy behaviors in a two-person game. *Journal of Personality and Social Psychology* 4, 328–32.

Zand, D. E. (1972) Trust and managerial problem solving. *Administrative Science Quarterly* 17, 229–39.

Part II
POWER

Introduction

There have been numerous and conflicting attempts to conceptualize the phenomenon of power in a way which is both theoretically and empirically satisfactory. Faced with this situation, a theory of power cannot content itself with a descriptive statement, with an analysis of its essence, which virtually incorporates by way of assumptions the results it elicits. Even attempts to analyse the concept on its own, and to divide the term into its different meanings, take us no further – unless towards wariness and, in the end, resignation. In such circumstances it is not possible to proceed step by step and thereby presuppose what power is. Instead, we must try to use more general concepts, which are in use elsewhere and which might serve the transfer of already established questions, and conceptual frameworks, which facilitate comparison and offer the possibility of relevant examination of other areas of interest.

If we look for issues of this kind, we find first of all the idea that power involves causing outcomes despite possible resistance, or, in other words, is causality in unfavourable circumstances. We also find recent concepts in exchange and game theory which emphasize the calculative side of a process which remains conceived in causal terms, but which is rich in alternatives.[1] Analysis of these matters can pursue different paths.

There is first the possibility of examining such conceptual frameworks directly in terms of their logical consistency, of the possibilities of verification they offer, of difficulties in measurement and, finally, of their conceptual predilections.[2] Up to the present at least, this approach has led to fragmentation of the theory of power rather than to its consolidation. This appears to be the consequence of over-hasty theorizing about one phenomenon in isolation. Alternatively, one could make use of a sociological technique (of proven value ever since Durkheim) of framing questions so as to reveal the basic premises of the institutions of the lifeworld, their existing interpretations and understandings. The questions might be the following: If power has to be a causal process, what non-causal foundations of causality are there? If power is to be reckoned with as exchange, what non-exchangeable foundations are there for exchange? If power is a game played between opponents, what are the non-game-playing foundations of the game? This question-framing technique refers back to society as a condition of the possibility of power, and seeks a theory of power indirectly, by way of a theory of society.

This detour we shall take in what follows. We shall be examining a particular macro-sociological system of reference, namely that of the encompassing societal system, and shall ask, primarily, about the functions of power formation at this level.[3] This does not exclude the possibility of having recourse to experimental, socio-psychological research. But, in addition, we can take for granted instances of symbolic generalization which cannot be produced by individual cases of interaction, but only by society as a whole – for example the development of law. Above all, in this type of analysis at the societal level, we can go beyond the mere designation of power as expression or dependent variable of the social fact, 'society', and make use of the fact that recent social theory works with three different but compatible concepts, namely: (1) a theory of system formation and system differentiation; (2) a theory of evolution; and (3) an as yet emerging theory of symbolically generalized communication media. The objects of these theories must be seen as interdependent at the societal level of system formation, in the sense that social evolution leads to larger, more complex and more strongly differentiated social systems. In order to bridge a greater degree of differentiation, these systems develop more highly generalized and, at the same time, more highly specialized communication media, which are assigned to societally more significant subsystems. This connection cannot be further elaborated here. Our current, partial, task consists in clarifying what is involved when power is treated as a symbolically generalized communication medium, and when analyses of power are placed in the context of a theory of society.

Notes

1 Cf. for example Harsanyi (1962a, 1962b); also Tedeschi et al. (1971); Baldwin (1971c); and Bonoma et al. (1972).
2 See for example Riker (1964); Danzger (1964); March (1966); Wrong (1968); or Luhmann (1969b).
3 Lehman (1969) in particular has highlighted the significance of this way of putting the question.

1

Power as a Communication Medium

Using the theory of communication media as a basis for a theory of power has the advantage of making it possible to draw a comparison between power and other communication media, applying identically composed questions, comparing it, for example, with truth, or with money. Thus, these questions not only serve to clarify the phenomenon of power, but at the same time help produce a more broadly orientated comparative interest and facilitate the exchange of theoretical insights between different media areas. In addition to such new insights, the theory of power gains a general perspective over forms of influence which will be discussed separately from a more designated concept of power. This makes it possible to avoid what has so often been remarked on, i.e. overloading the concept of power with attributes of a very broadly and loosely defined process of influence.[1]

By way of introduction, therefore, a few cursory remarks about the theory of communication media are necessary.[2]

1. Societal theory is, according to the main elements it has inherited from the nineteenth century, on the one hand a theory of social differentiation into strata and into functional subsystems and, on the other hand, a theory of socio-cultural evolution. Both aspects are intertwined through the assumption that socio-cultural evolution leads to increasing differentiation. Within this frame of reference, issues of communication and questions of motivation for accepting and complying with communications remain incompletely illuminated. Partly they were seen as merely psychological actions and attributed to the individual, so that they could be passed over in a macro-sociological approach. Partly they were subsumed under such special concepts as consensus, legitimacy, informal organization, mass communication, and the like. Both ways of dealing with the problem led to concepts of a lesser order and of more limited range in comparison with the concepts of differentiation and evolution. Questions of communication and motivation were thus not entirely excluded from societal theory but they did not rank with the main

concepts. Against this one could speak out in the name of a supposed humanism and deplore the loss of humanity without achieving any more than articulating protest at a quite inappropriate level.[3]

The attempt to formulate a general theory of symbolically generalized communication, and to tie it in with the concept of societal differentiation as well as with statements about mechanisms and phases of socio-cultural evolution, is aimed at filling this gap. In this we are aiming to avoid recourse to the 'subject', in the way that transcendental philosophy has used the term, as well as any claim to deal with the physiologically and psychologically concrete individual. The one alternative would be too abstract, the other too concrete for sociological theory.[4] Instead, we shall proceed from the basic assumption that social systems are only ever formed through communication, i.e. they always assume that multiple selection processes determine one another by anticipation or reaction. Social systems first arise from the need for agreed selections, just as, on the other hand, such needs are first experienced in social systems. The conditions which make this correlation possible are the result of evolution, and change alongside it. Just as evolution articulates the temporal, and differentiation articulates the material, so communication articulates the social dimension of the societal system.

Communication comes about only if one understands the selectivity of an utterance, and that means the ability of the system to use as a selection one of the conditions which allow for its own existence.[5] This implies contingency on both sides, and thus also the possibility of rejecting the selections on offer transmitted by the communication. These possibilities of rebuttal, as possibilities, cannot be eliminated. A rejection communicated in return and the application to subject areas of that rejection within social systems constitutes conflict. All social systems are potential conflicts; it is only that the degree to which this conflict potential is realized varies according to the degree of system differentiation, and according to societal evolution.

Under such constitutive terms, the choice between 'Yes' and 'No' cannot be guided by language alone, for it is precisely language which guarantees both possibilities; neither can it be left to chance. Therefore, in every society there are devices additional to language which guarantee the transmission of selections to the appropriate degree. The need for these devices increases and their form changes with the evolution of the societal system. In simple societies these functions are mainly fulfilled by 'reality constructions' founded on shared, lifeworld experiences, which underlie the communication processes and are taken for granted.[6] To a great extent language serves to confirm such assumptions, and its potential for negation and information does not become exhausted.[7] Only more advanced societies develop the need for a functional differentiation between the language-code in general and special, symbolically generalized communication media, such as power or truth, which condition and regulate in particular the motivation for accepting offered selections. By means of this differentiation, potentials for conflict and consensus in society can be mutually extended. The evolutionary mechanisms for the variation and selection of usable, socially effective, transferable selections part company and this speeds up socio-cultural evolution, since new choices can be made under more possibilities from more specific points of view.

The invention and spread of writing seem historically to have been the especial cause of the development of symbolic communication media. Writing greatly widened the potential for communication in society beyond the interaction of people immediately present and thus removed it from control by concrete interaction systems.[8] Without writing it is impossible to create complex power chains in political and administrative bureaucracies, let alone democratic control over political power. Ostracism requires writing. The same applies to the discursive development and perpetuation of more complex elaborations of truth statements.[9] The classifying function of a logically schematized truth-code is needed only when a body of thought formulated in writing is available. But even the moral generalization of a special code for friendship/love (*philía, amicitia*) in the Greek *polis* is a reaction to the written culture of the city, a compensation for a density of interaction among neighbours (*philói*) which can no longer be assumed. Above all, this dependence on writing is evident in the money-code. It is only through the second coding of language through writing that the societal communication process is released from the bonds of social situations and unproblematical assumptions to the extent that, in order to motivate the acceptance of communications, special codes have to be created which, at the same time, also condition what can successfully be maintained and assumed.

2. Accordingly, communication media shall be defined as a device additional to language, namely, as a code of generalized symbols which guides the transmission of selections. Language normally guarantees intersubjective comprehension, i.e. the recognition of the selection of the other party as a selection. Communication media add to this by providing a motivating function in that they urge the acceptance of other people's selections and as a rule make that acceptance the object of expectations. Accordingly, communication media can always be formulated when *the manner of selection of one* partner serves simultaneously as a *motivating structure for the other*. The symbols of this connection between selection and motivation then take on the function of a transmission and make clear the connection between the two aspects, so that this anticipatory connection can strengthen and, in addition, motivate the selectivity.

This concept contains a number of assumptions and implications which also apply to the theory of power and steer it in a particular direction. The first and most important assumption is that media-guided communication processes bind partners who *both* complete their *own* selections and know about this from each other.[10] Let us use the terms *'alter'* and *'ego'*. All communication media assume social situations with the possibility of choice on both sides, in other words, situations of double contingent selectivity. That is precisely what gives these media their function of transmitting selections from *alter* to *ego* while preserving their selectivity. To this extent, the initial problem in all symbolically generalized communication media is the same; what applies to love or truth applies to power. In each case the influential communication relates to a partner who is to be directed in the making of their selections.[11]

According to this, transmission of selection outputs means precisely the *reproduction* of those outputs in simplified form abstracted from the requirements of their initial configuration. It is precisely in view of this simplification and abstraction that symbols are needed to replace the concrete beginning, the initial link in the selection chain. For this purpose communication media develop symbolically generalized codes which then act as shared orientations for their operations. Yet each subsequent phase of the process continues itself to be self-selection. Communication media consequently provide the ability to orient around widely different situations while, at the same time, enabling particular (non-identical) selections to be made. It is only under this basic condition that power, too, functions as a communication medium.[12] It organizes social situations through double selectivity. Therefore, the selectivity of *alter* must be distinguished from that of *ego*, for very different problems are raised in relation to their respective positions, particularly in the case of power.

Accordingly, a fundamental assumption of all power is that *uncertainty* exists in relation to the selection of the power-holding *alter*.[13] For whatever reasons, *alter* has at his disposal more than one alternative. He can *produce and remove* uncertainty in his partner when he exercises his choice. This deviation via the production and reduction of uncertainty is an absolute precondition of power. It determines the latitude which exists for the generalization and specification of a particular communication medium – and is not, for instance, one particular source of power among others.

Power also assumes openness to other possible actions on the part of the *ego* affected by power. Power invokes its performance of transmitting by being able to influence the selection of actions (or inactions) in the face of other possibilities. Power is greater if it is able to assert itself even in the face of attractive alternatives for action or inaction. And it can be increased only in combination with an increase in freedom on the part of whoever is subjected to power.

Power must therefore be distinguished from coercion (*Zwang*) to do something concrete and specified. The possible choices of the person being coerced are reduced to zero. In borderline cases coercion resorts to the use of physical violence and thereby to the substitution of one's own action for unattainable action from others.[14] Power loses its function of bridging double contingency the closer it comes to coercion. Coercion means the surrender of the advantages of symbolic generalization and of steering the partner's selectivity. The person exercising coercion must himself take over the burden of selection and decision to the same degree as coercion is being exercised – for many cases we can even say that coercion has to be exercised, where there is a lack of power. The reduction of complexity is not distributed but is transferred to the person using coercion. Whether this is the sensible thing to do depends on how complex and variable are the situations where decisions about action have to be made.

The use of coercion itself can only be centralized in very simple societal systems. More complex systems can only centralize decisions (or even decisions about deciding the premises for making decisions) about the use of force. That means that they must develop power to make coercion possible. The concept of a 'coercive apparatus' introduced by Max Weber covers this situation.

Even these simple initial reflections show that a closer definition, operationalization and measurement of concrete power relationships is an extraordinarily complex enterprise. A *multidimensional* measure would have to be used to assess the complexity of the possibilities from which *both* sides (or, in chain foundations, *all* participants) can choose an action.[15] The power of the power-holder is greater if he can choose from more and more diverse types of decisions for power-like assertions and it is greater if he can do this in opposition to a partner who himself has more and more diverse alternatives. Power increases with freedom on *both* sides, and, for example, in any given society, in proportion to the alternatives that society creates.

According to this, not only scientific and methodological problems are indicated.[16] Further, the result of this complication for society itself is that it must develop *substitutes for an exact comparison of power constellations* and that these substitutes themselves become a factor in power. Firstly, hierarchies which postulate an asymmetrical distribution of power serve as substitutes. It is assumed that a superior has more power than an inferior (although in bureaucratic organizations the opposite may be normal).[17] Another substitute is the history of the system; cases of past successes in obtaining desired outcomes in conflict situations are recalled, normalized, and generalized as expectations. This function, as a basis for comparison, goes together with the symbolic explosiveness of concerns about status and single events, which are used in a way that brings present power constellations too much to the foreground. Thirdly, there are important possibilities for substitution in semi-contractual arrangements, whereby a too-powerful partner comes to terms with those who might withdraw or be disloyal.[18] In all these cases the direct communicative recourse to power is replaced by reference to symbols which commit both sides normatively, and at the same time take into account the presumed power differential.

These are all functional equivalents for measuring power and for tests of power as decision premises in societal reality. The institutional anchoring and practicability of such substitutes renders exact calculations unnecessary, and even makes any attempt to do so problematic. The result of this is that if science were to produce a way of measuring power, it would alter social reality; that is to say, it would destroy the substitutes and reveal them as false assumptions. More within the bounds of probability, however, is that science will develop its own substitutes for measuring power, which would be dealt with in other areas of society, as purely and simply the province of science.

3. The function of a communication medium lies in transmitting reduced complexity. The selection made by *alter* limits *ego*'s possible selections by its being communicated under particular and specified conditions. Dependencies that pass through communication media are distinguished from general interference and mutual hindrance (such as *alter* listening to the radio and *ego* being unable to go to sleep) in that they presume some process of communication which can be pre-conditioned by symbols. Thus they are subject to cultural formation, can be changed by evolution, and are compatible with a large number of system conditions.

Also, in the case of power, it is this transmission of the results of selection which is the main point of interest, not, for example, the concrete causes of certain effects. Power does not arise only in the borderline case where *alter* concretely lays down *ego*'s action, for instance to insert a given screw as tightly as possible. It is more typical, and satisfactory, to view power, in the same way as every other communication medium, as putting limits on the partner's range of selections.[19] The causal notion hitherto guiding theories of power[20] is not to be dismissed but is abstracted. It does not designate an invariable link between concrete conditions in the world – expressions of power, and behaviour – nor does it restrict the effectiveness of power to the case where the behaviour of *ego* would have taken a different course without the power-transmitting communication from *alter*.[21] If such were the case, it would be assumed, wrongly, that there always exists a ready resolve (that can be empirically determined), by now in existence, which is then broken. In fact, however, the existence of a power differential and the anticipation of a power-based decision make it quite senseless for the subordinate even to make up his mind. And it is in precisely this that the function of power lies. It secures possible chains of effect independent of the will of the participant who is subjected to power – whether he wishes it or not. The causality of power lies in neutralizing the will, but not necessarily in breaking the will of the inferior. It also affects him, and that most precisely, when he intended to do that same thing and then learns that he has to do it anyway. The function of power lies in the regulation of contingency. As with every other media-code, the power-code relates to a possible (!) and not necessarily an actual, discrepancy between the selections of *alter* and *ego* by creating the impression of equality between the two and so removing this assumed discrepancy.

Accordingly, the power of the power-holder is not satisfactorily described as a cause, or even a potential cause. It can be compared rather with the complex function of a catalyst. Catalysts accelerate (or decelerate) the triggering of events; without themselves changing in the process, they cause changes in the ratio of effective connections (or probability) expected from chance connections between system and environment. Thus, in the end they produce a gain in time – always a critical factor for the construction of complex systems. In this respect – and this we will term, following Kant, the concept of schematism – they are more general than their respective products. In the process of catalysis, they do not change, or do not change to the same extent as the accelerated (or decelerated) process produces or inhibits effects.

Bearing in mind that we are here talking about a real structure (and not only an analytical summary),[22] one can then say that power is an opportunity to increase the probability of realizing improbable selection combinations.[23] Real probabilities contain a tendency to be self-reinforcing. If one knows that something is probable, one prefers to reckon that the event will happen, rather than that it will not, and the more relevant it is, the lower the threshold which starts such a process moving. The same applies to improbabilities – as every driver knows. Therefore, a prior decision is necessary each time to decide whether to view an uncertain event as (very/quite/not very) probable or as (not very/quite/very) improbable. Here purely psychological laws can play a part.[24] In addition, social definitions of the situation will come into play and influence the perception of the probable or improbable. And for their part these situational definitions can be presented by means of symbolically generalized communication media and be conveyed as general formulas. The catalyst function of power is, therefore, based on very intricate causal complexes. This is precisely why power is to be understood only as a symbolically *generalized* communication medium. The development of abstract formulations by way of symbolically controlled selection complexes ensures at the same time that power is not seen as something dependent on direct action and interference by the power-holder on the power-subject.[25] It is only by assuming a process of communication, that is, that the power-subject always learns by some indirect route of the selectivity (not only of the existence!)[26] of past or future power-acts by the power-holder. It is especially a function of generalizing the communication medium of power to make possible such deviations without thereby cancelling out the identification of the power-code and the topics of communication.

4. It is typical of all communication media that at the base of their differentiation lies a *special interaction constellation* and, within this framework, a specific fundamental problem. Communication media are raised above the taken-for-granted reality of normal life only where influence is contingent and thereby, for once, rather improbable. Only when, and in so far as, goods are scarce does the active claim to some of them on

the part of one person become a problem for others, and this situation is then regulated by a communication medium, which transfers the action selected by the one person into the experience of the others and so makes it acceptable.[27] In the context of scarcity, influence becomes precarious in a special way, so that, in view of this unusual situation, a specifically generalized communication medium can take shape, which makes possible the transmission of reduced complexity in this case, but not in others. This is also how truth arises. Here too, with the framework of unproblematical assumptions and beliefs, a certain improbability of information must first arise before test criteria start to function, and before a special code can be formed to regulate the identification of truth and untruth. Truth is doubt overcome. It can be triggered by the simple disappointment of cognitive expectations, but also by a set of cognitive instruments with sharply increased capacity for resolving the issue.

Such a focus, a passage through increased contingency, is also necessary for the formation of the communication medium of power. Not every execution of a proposed action becomes problematical. One does not let go of something one has been given, but accepts it and holds it tight, etc. But in special cases, if the proposer, shall we say, restricts himself to proposing, and his own action restricts itself to prescribing the action of others, the actual context of circumstances can no longer perform all the transmission of selections which are required. The temptation to negation also increases with the contingency of the selection. Then transmission of selection can occur only under special presuppositions and the power-code reconstructs and institutionalizes these presuppositions. Only with the help of a symbolically generalized communication medium do they become the basis of reliable expectations.

It is difficult to encapsulate this problem in a definition which states categorically what power is and is not. The terms of the problem, however, evoke distinctive and describable sets of circumstances. One can state that the greater the extent to which influence becomes contingent, on account of it being recognized as an action whose selectivity refers only to the activation and guidance of someone else's action, the less the extent to which a natural-situational congruence of interest can be subsumed; that the more problematical the motivation becomes and the more necessary a code which regulates the conditions of transmission of selection and the attribution of personal motives. This approach, which proceeds from interaction configurations, can then be taken over into the theory of societal evolution in the thesis that, as societal differentiation increases, so does the frequency of situations in which, no matter how high the degree of contingency and specialization, transmission of selection must take place if an achieved level of development is to be maintained. In important functional areas, situational congruence of interests no longer occurs frequently enough or with enough specialization for this to suffice. Then the development of a special code for power, tailored to such problems, becomes an unavoidable priority for further evolution.

This line of argument, moreover, has its parallels in other media areas and is supported by them. Only from a certain stage of development onwards does daily communication become so loaded with information that truth itself becomes a problem. Only from a certain stage of development does the stock of goods become so large that it becomes meaningful to keep it open to contingent intervention in situations of scarcity. It could further be said that love becomes necessary as a special communication code only when others' emotions and images of the world are so strongly individualized – and that means, have become so contingent – that one can no longer be sure of them, and therefore, according to cultural standards, one has to love for its own sake. And even art, as a communication medium, depends on increased contingency, i.e. the contingency of works manifestly produced, but no longer sustained by the context of specific, lifeworld purposes. Designated in all of these are problematic areas of interaction, namely variants of the problem of selection transmission and, at the same time, stages in the evolution of the societal system.

5. Perhaps the most important difference as against older theories of power is that the theory of communication media conceptualizes the phenomenon of power on the basis of a difference between the code and the communication process and is therefore not in a position to attribute power to one of the partners as a property or as a faculty.[28] Power 'is' code-guided communication. Attribution of power to the power-holder is regulated in this code with wide-ranging results concerning the reinforcement of motivations to comply, responsibility, institutionalization, giving specific direction to wishes for change, etc. Although *both* sides are acting, whatever happens is attributed *solely* to the power-holder.[29] Scientific analysis, however, should not let itself be side-tracked by rules of attribution which are contained in their object. Such rules do not cause the power-holder to be more important or, in any sense, 'more causal' in the formation of power than the power-subject.[30] The rules of attribution contained in the media-code are themselves another possible object of scientific analysis.[31] One can, yet again, also raise questions about their functions. To this end, the analytical apparatus must first abstract pre-decisions from attributions. At the same time this demands a greater differentiation of society's scientific subsystem, in our case a more far-reaching differentiation between science and politics.

The difference between the generalized code and the selective communication process will constantly be with us in what follows. The symbolic generalization of a code, according to which expectations can be formed, is a prerequisite for the differentiation of power as a specialized medium capable of being related to particular combinations of problems; it produces certain actions and is subject to certain conditions. Further, the generalized media-code contains the starting points for cumulative development in the course of societal evolution. From these points of view, power is of interest for the theory of society. This should not exclude the possibility that theories of organization and interaction could work with simplified concepts of power, such as those which already presume in their conception of power differences of status or sufficient possibilities for information and calculation. However, it would be impossible within the frame of such circumscribed premises to reach any conclusion about the implications of power for wider society.

6. In a much acclaimed, extensive critique of the work of Parsons, and of his power theory in particular, Alvin Gouldner expresses his surprise that Parsons, in his treatment of power as a symbolically generalized medium, identifies it so closely with legitimate power, with 'establishment power', and that he takes this as normal for society.[32] Pointing to the brutality and selfishness of power-holders, he dismisses this view, across the board as well as in its individual formulations, as unrealistic, as intellectually absurd, as utopian, as misleading. This astonishment on the part of a sociologist is itself astonishing to sociologists, even more so because it is formulated in the framework of a sociology of sociology. Of course, it is indisputable that sociology can and should concern itself with the phenomena of the brutal and selfish exercises of power. Such an interest, however, should not grow into a prejudiced view concerning social reality, built into concepts and theories.

The real achievement of Parsons' theory was to replace the prejudices of sociology as a science of crisis and opposition with a relatively non-issue-driven theoretical design (one thus open in its turn to criticism). However one judges the adequacy of this analytical apparatus, it is indisputable that the institutionalization of enforceable legitimate power is a phenomenon of greater social significance in comparison with brutality and selfishness. Everyday social life is determined to a much greater extent by recourse to normalized power, i.e. legal power, than by the brutal and selfish exercise of power. Exceptions limited to certain areas actually serve to illuminate this state of affairs.[33] Intervention by legitimate force is more considerable; one simply cannot think it away without disrupting and transforming almost all normal social life. Brutality and selfishness are phenomena which are compatible with many social conditions so long as they do not undermine the dominance of institutionalized power. Such an argument, of course, does not justify any single brutal act, and, moreover, does not justify tolerating or accepting it, as one knows from the history of theodicies[34] and welfare. But this kind of accounting problem is really secondary – both historically and theoretically. It presumes the introduction of a binary schematism to differentiate debit from credit, or right from wrong, or conformity from non-conformity.

By working out a theory of symbolically generalized communication media, we are trying to avoid such controversy. The conditions for forming a dichotomy between 'ruling order' and 'critique' are part of the theory itself. The theory treats such disjunctions as elements of a communication code and asks about their genetic preconditions, their functions, their results, their complementary mechanisms, their chances of development. Such a theory can also be characterized, as Gouldner would have it, as moralistic and conservative, if one assumes that the theory confirms the social characteristics that it has exposed. It is conservative in the sense that it wishes to retain and keep open the option of expressing an opinion either for or against a manifestation of power according to prevailing circumstances.

Notes

1 Social psychologists in particular run this risk. Typical examples would be: Raven (1965), and Clark (1965).
2 The treatment of power specifically as a communication medium begins with Parsons (1963a). For other suggestions, applications and criticisms, see Chazel (1964); Mitchell (1967); Lessnoff (1968); Giddens (1968); Turner (1968); also Baldwin (1971a) and Blain (1971). In what follows the concept of the communication medium is used in a way which is independent of Parsons' interchange paradigm; it is therefore not built up on an idea of exchange, and also differs in other respects from Parsons' concept. The differences depend on the interpretation of the contingency problem (see Luhmann (1976)).
3 Cf. for example Homans (1964) and Maciejewski (1972).
4 This statement is meant at the same time to show how problematic it is to designate the individual as subject. With such equivocations it becomes all too easy to step from the abstract into the concrete.
5 For this concept of communication, cf. MacKay (1969).
6 Cf. Berger and Luckmann (1969); McLeod and Chaffee (1972); also Arbeitsgruppe Bielefelder Soziologen (1973).
7 See, for example, Marshall (1961).
8 On this cf. Goody and Watt (1963) and Goody (1973).
9 'Dialogue' is then cultivated as a *literary* form, as a self-contradictory protest against the demands of literacy; and only in this way does it achieve stylistic perfection.
10 Parsons accommodates this by using the idea of a double contingency as a prerequisite for the formation of complementary expectations. Cf. Parsons and Shils (1951), pp. 14ff.; see also the remarkable definition of authority as the laying down of decision-making *premises* (not decisions!) of others in March and Simon (1958), p. 90.
11 Accordingly, in the context of a general power theory, it is not really sensible to give a one-sided emphasis to the decision-making problems of any one side. In particular power areas this may well be different. Thus Fisher (1969) recommends that offices which deal with foreign affairs concern themselves less with making their own policies more precise than with paying attention to

other states and above all working out what decisions from other governments would be acceptable before any exercise of power.

12 Abramson et al. (1958) in particular emphasize that power theory must take into account the majority of possible actions by *both* sides.

13 Cf. Crozier's observation (1963), especially pp. 193ff., that in heavily structured organizations power shifts to where, in relation to choices of action on which others depend, there is still a remnant of uncertainty. For an elaboration on a general 'strategic contingency theory' of power see Pennings et al. (1969); Hinings et al. (1974).

14 This case of using physical force – moving different bodies in order, for example, to cause them to change their position in space – must be carefully differentiated from the symbolic use of physical force in order to form power. We will return to this in Chapter 4.

15 One problem, which can only be noted here, is that all these measures are relative to the conditions of possibility which one takes as a basis. Measurement thus always takes for granted that participants belong to one system and are restrained by common conditions of the possible.

16 See Danzger (1964), pp. 714ff.

17 See, for example, Walter (1966) and a criticism of this: Mayhew and Gray (1969). See also pp. 117ff.

18 Cf. on this a series of experiments which proceed specifically from alternatives open to both sides: Thibaut and Faucheux (1965); Thibaut (1968); and Thibaut and Gruder (1969).

19 This is sometimes taken into account explicitly in power theories, but is usually implicit. For a corresponding definition of the concept of power, see van Doorn (1962/3), p. 12.

20 A more recent survey of problems in a causal theory of power can be found in Dahl (1968), pp. 46ff. Cf. also Gamson (1968), pp. 59ff.; also Stinchcombe (1968), pp. 163ff., who suggests an information theory formulation of the causal concept of power.

21 This characteristic is frequently taken account of in the form suggested by Max Weber. One assumes power only where the power-holder can assert himself even against opposition (see Weber 1948, p. 28). Emerson (1962) and Holm (1969), for example, use this conceptualization. Initially only the selective definition, the 'processing of contingency', is important on the level of a general theory of communication media. We will return to the specific characteristics which this process takes on in the case of power.

22 This conception goes back to Max Weber's concept of 'chance'. Wrong (1968), pp. 677f. points out quite correctly that the assessment of the power-subject is being referred to and not the statistical analysis by sociologists of cases of the actual exercise of power.

23 In this sense Dahl (1957) formulates not only power itself as 'chances' but also the causality of power as a change of probabilities.

24 For example, a generally observable tendency to prefer positive situation definitions, which probably only seldom lets the case of double negation (less improbable) occur. Cf. for example Jordan (1965); Kanouse and Hanson (1971). Another question would be whether negative or positive verdicts possess

greater interference with alternatives, whether the improbable or the probable block or leave open more varied possibilities.

25 Both for and against this see Nagel (1968), pp. 132f.; Gamson (1968), pp. 69f.; and Wrong (1968), pp. 678f.; also Schennerhorn (1961), pp. 95f., using the example of the local political power of large corporations.

26 Thus Nagel (1968).

27 See Luhmann (1972a).

28 This redistribution has an even more decisive effect in the context of other communication media. Truth, seen as a communication medium, can no longer be characterized as a quality of ideas or sentences, love no longer as feeling, money no longer as possession, belief no longer as an inner binding of the person. For the sociology of communication media, such ideas and attributions do not characterize the theory but its object: simplifying aids to understanding social life orientated to generalized codes.

29 As we know from experimental research, even hierarchies in general guide the process of attribution in this sense. Cf. Thibaut and Riecken (1955).

30 The reverse of course applies equally little, that is, viewing the power-subject as the decisive cause of the formation of power. Thus numerous American definitions of authority with reference to Barnard (1938), pp. 161ff.; Simon (1957); Peabody (1964); also, concerning threats, Lazarus (1968), pp. 339ff.; Fisher (1969).

31 Lehman (1969), for example, points out the increased significance of a stable, predictable imputation of power on the macro-sociological level. I do not know of any more detailed examinations.

32 See Gouldner (1971), especially pp. 290ff.

33 Cf. Guzmán et al. (1962).

34 Editors' note: Theories of why God allows evil to exist in the world.

2

The Action Framework

Power differs from other communication media in that its code assumes that there are partners on *both* sides of the communication relationship who reduce complexity through *action* – and not only through experiencing. Since human life assumes the existence of both acting and experiencing as being inextricably linked, the contrast between the two seems somewhat artificial.[1] This is not in dispute here, but it cannot be used as an objection to the theory set out in this book. In other words, the artificiality of a mechanism which is quite specifically adapted to the formation of action chains is not an analytical fabrication driven by an obsession with scientific abstraction, but an abstraction made by society itself, a prerequisite for societal systems in advanced stages of evolution. A theory of power which is developed as the theory of a particular, symbolically generalized communication medium must, however, be able to work out how such a specialization in the transmission of action-reductions is at all possible in social life and what problems result from it. A mirror image of the same problem would be a theory of truth which aims to explain how specialization in the transmission of reduced possibilities available for experiencing can occur without the interference of the participants' actions, and preferences for acting in particular ways, distorting the facts.

1. We wish to refer to acting only when selective behaviour is attributed to a system (and not to its environment).[2] This attribution relates to the form of selection itself, offering, as it were, explanation in place of the conjuring trick of reduction. There can be, and is in many cases, some argument about attributing something to experiencing or action. But there is also a societal interest in clarifying this question, at least for problematic situations. Depending on whether selective behaviour is attributed to system or environment, *this might have consequences for other systems in society, faced with using the same selection, or if, as a consequence of this, alternative selections for making attributions become available.* One can have the same experience, while the action giving rise to that experience can differ. This difference precedes the question of whether the availabil-

ity of a different type of action is again limited – for instance by moral or legal demands, or by power. In relation to experiencing, these forms for limiting contingency would have been meaningless. Mistaken interpretations of experience are treated as errors and are sanctioned differently, if at all.[3] On the other hand, acts are subject to special social controls which are formulated at the same time as the action itself becomes possible. The high risk involved in making an action possible is apparent. It is revealed, inter alia, in the fact that where acting is concerned, it is easier to deny that it was intended than in the case of experiencing and hence the complications which arise over the problem of negation in a normative theory or even a logic of action.

The categorizing of selection as action must therefore be evaluated as a mechanism which releases systems from the imposition of equality and which makes differentiations possible. As this cannot happen on an unlimited scale, action has, as it were, again to be made captive and domesticated. The primary function of the social construction of the possibility of acting, and the specialization of control mechanisms related to this, lies in the emergence of an indirect avenue leading to the production of increased social complexity. This consists of the creation and limitation of the possibility of different selections in an intersubjectively constructed world of meaning.

Interest in attributions and labelling follows categorizations, which presuppose and explain the fact of acting, and thus order the *experiencing* of one's own or other's *actions*. This includes the concept of will (as opposed to reason), the notion of contingency in the selection process as freedom (as opposed to chance) and, in more recent times especially, the attribution of *motives*[4] and intentions.[5] Free will is an old European attribute of action, motivation a modern one – in each case, it is not a primary fact, such as a 'cause' of the act,[6] but an attribution, which makes possible the socially comprehensible experiencing of action. Motives are not necessary for acting, but are necessary if actions are to be experienced as having meaning. A social order will thus be much more closely integrated at the level of the attribution of motives than at the level of action itself. The understanding of motives, therefore, helps retrospectively in recognizing whether an action has occurred at all.[7]

One cannot adequately describe the function of the communication medium, power, solely in terms of simply having the power-subject accept directives. The power-holder himself must be made to exercise his power, and there, in many cases, lies the greatest problem. Is it not easier for the more independent party, when in doubt, just to hold back and let things take their course? Even the motivation of the one who transmits the selection is constructed and attributed only in the communication process. And because of his power, the power-holder himself will have successes and failures attributed to, and suitable motives imposed on, him, whether he wants this or not. Thus power does not become the instrument of an already present will, it first of all generates that will. Power can then make claims on the will, can bind it, can make it absorb risks and uncertainties, can even lead it into temptation and let it miscarry. The generalized symbols of the code, the duties and insignia of office, ideologies and conditions of legitimation serve to help the process of articulation, but the communication process itself only crystallizes motives when power is being exercised.

2. It is against this background that one must understand the specialization of a medium which performs the transmission from one selected action to another, and which thus assumes *both* partners to be systems and attributes their selection as an act. The power-subject is expected to be someone who chooses his own action and thus possesses the possibility of self-determination. It is for that reason alone that the instruments of power, such as threats, are brought to bear against him, in order to direct him towards carrying out the choice himself. And even the power-holder claims not just to represent what is true but also that he is acting according to his own will. For this reason it is possible to propose the possibility of attributable 'localized' differences in the relationship between the two of them. A transmission of reduced complexity takes place when, and in so far as, *alter*'s action is involved in determining how *ego* selects his actions. The success of any ordering of power consists in increased, but bridgeable, situational and selection differences.

For this we need an *indirect route via negations* which makes certain demands on the power-code. If power is to make available a combination of *chosen* alternatives, and if other alternatives are still in play, the probability of this combination can be sustained only by means of co-ordinating, in parallel, the *elimination* of alternatives. Power assumes that *both* partners see in alternatives the realization of what they wish to *avoid*. For both sides, over and above the simple plurality of possibilities, there must thus be an order of preferences which must be schematized in terms of, on the one hand, a positive, and on the other, a negative evaluation, and the other side must be aware of this.[8] Under this assumption, both sides are able to produce a *hypothetical combination* of avoidable alternatives – most simply by means of the threat of sanctions, which the power-holder himself would rather avoid. 'If you don't do it, I'll hit you!' But even that is not sufficient. Power is not exercised unless the relationship of the participants to their respective avoidable alternatives is *differently* structured, in such a way that the power-subject, *rather* than the power-holder, would have a preference for avoiding his alternative – in our example, violence – and that this relationship between the way the participants relate to their avoidable alternatives can be recognized by the participants. In short, the power-code must bring about a relationability of relations. On this assumption there arises the *possibility of conditionally linking the combination of avoidable alternatives to a less negatively evaluated combination of other alternatives*. This linking motivates the transmission of action-selections from the power-holder to the power-subject.

This gives power to the one who can decide whether such a conditional linking of combinations of possibilities is to be made or not.[9] Thus power rests on the fact that there are possibilities, whose realization is *avoided*. The avoidance of sanctions (which are and remain possible) is *indispensable* to the *function* of power.[10] Each actual recourse to avoidable alternatives, each exercise of violence, for example, changes the communication structure in an almost irreversible way. It is in the interests of power to avoid such an occurrence. Thus, already in terms of its structural quality (and not only by reference to laws), power rests upon controlling the exceptional case. It breaks down whenever the avoidable alternatives are realized.[11] As a result, among other things, highly complex societies, which need far more power than simpler societies, have to modify the ratio of the exercise of power to the application of sanctions, and must manage with an ever decreasing incidence of factual realization of avoidable alternatives.[12]

These propositions need to be clarified further as concerns the relationship between negative and positive sanctions. In spite of the feasibility of their being logically symmetrical, negative and positive sanctions differ so basically in the assumptions they work from and in their results[13] that the differentiation and specification of communication media cannot ignore their dissimilarity. Love, money and persuasion towards consensus about values cannot be defined as instances of power. We shall, therefore, limit the notion of power to the case which was referred to as the concept of the negative sanction (although this concept itself needs further clarification).[14] Power is used only when a more *unfavourable* combination of alternatives is constructed in the face of a given expectation. The differentiation between favourable and unfavourable is dependent on expectation and therefore also on a given point in time.[15] The initial premises of a power situation may well rest on positive performances on the part of the power-holder, for instance on promises of protection, demonstrations of love, or promises of payment. However, it is transformed into power when not just the initial premises themselves but also their suspension is made dependent on the conduct of the power-subject. If, for instance, central government makes the grant of funding dependent upon a local authority's commitment of its own resources to a given project, this does not in itself constitute an expression of power; just as a normal purchase does not do so. Power comes in at the point when the threat of withdrawing the matched funds is used in order to exact from the local authority a form of conduct (say, abstention from making any remarks critical of central government) not originally envisaged in the programme of central grants. Here lies the difference – in the case of previous conditioning through positive rewards, the subject involved is free to reckon that, should a later revision of the conditions for these rewards occur through threats to withdraw them, he has already taken into account their availability and has, therefore, gained stronger protection against these changes. For this reason positive and negative sanctions differ also in their needs for legitimation. On the other hand, it is precisely this possibility of transforming positive performances into negative sanctions which makes available to the power-holder motivational resources and opportunities to effect matters, which might not otherwise be open to him. Power formed through organization rests to a considerable extent on this indirect route.

Having given this explanation, we return to our main subject. Under the influence of such a complexly constructed media structure, operated through negations, which brings out in an emphatic, exaggerated way the selectivity of *both* partners' conduct, *acting becomes decision*, i.e. consciously selective choice. The evolutionary improbability of such a differentiated, symbolically generalized code is reflected in the operational process for imposed decisions which may become uncomfortable for the power-subject as well as for the power-holder himself. One therefore cannot be surprised if, in fields which offer increasingly complex selections, power problems in the final instance turn out to culminate in decision-making difficulties.

3. The basic structure of power as a communication medium, that is, as a combination, which is made conditional in reverse (unfortunately it cannot be formulated more simply), of pairs of alternatives which are comparatively speaking quite negative and again comparatively speaking quite positive, accounts for the fact that power appears as *possibility* (potential, opportunity, disposition) and also *acts effectively as such*.[16] On this basis communicative interactions are rendered into different *modalities* from the standpoint of power. When communicating on factual matters, what is taken into account is that one side has the possibility of enforcing its views. By generalizing as possibility, power is equalized vis-à-vis its contexts and to certain extent made independent of a reality which is only fragmentary and existing only in particular situations. The projection of the possibility allows – in Nelson Goodman's formula[17] – the gaps in reality to be filled in.

A typical problem resulting from such modalization is one which has already concerned science in both its theory and its method.[18] Modalization creates a surplus of possibilities. Power, which is a constantly appearing possibility and appears as if it is an attribute, an ability or quality of the power-holder, cannot, however, be used on all people and in all issues within the field of power all the time and, above all, not continuously. To expect all power to be exercised all the time would not only overstrain the power-holder – according to the prescriptions of the power-code it would also prevent the accumulation of worthwhile power. The power-holder must behave selectively in regard to his own power; he must consider whether he wants to bring it into play; he must be able to discipline himself. The power-holder needs additional directives and aids to rationalization for those types of decision which are unavoidable.[19] For this reason, a recent version of power theory in economic terms has attempted to offer cost-benefit calculations.[20] It is at present an open question how far that can be taken. In any case, the social fact of the modalization of the medium of power makes it necessary for power theory to take account of two levels simultaneously – the genetic and structural conditions for the constitution of power as potential, and the structural and situational conditions for the exercise of power.

This distinction between potentiality and actualization entails two things. At the level of the symbolic code, it is possible for indications to be given about where to employ power, but they cannot be entirely specified, because that would eliminate the disposable surplus of potentiality. If the code is to symbolize sustained potential, it must be underspecified in this respect. This puts particular limitations on the juridification of power which might force the power-holder constantly to intervene. Or, to put it another way, the juridification of power endangers it by making it challengeable. Secondly, a decision to use power can involve a loss of power at the level of the process of actual power behaviour, i.e. it may mean sacrificing uncertainty, openness, the 'liquidity' of the possible.[21]

At the same time, modal generalization makes power sensitive to certain information about opposing realities – in so far as the power-holder is dependent on projective information-processing, he cannot allow himself to be defeated in any individual case. In some circumstances he must even fight to maintain the facade of his power.[22] At the same time as communication about the projected action is taking place, a *meta-communication* about power takes place.[23] It can take the form of tacit, anticipatory agreement or of the foreseeable expecting of expectations. It can also be actualized and, in the last resort, can be explicitly *formulated*[24] by means of hints and unanswerable allusions. In the communication process, formulated power takes the character of a threat. It exposes itself to the possibility of an explicit negation. This forms a first step towards realizing the unavoidable alternatives, a first step towards destroying power, and thus is avoided wherever possible. One may, for example, instead of directly referring to force, make reference to a legal claim which, in turn, contains within it the ultimate back-up of force.

The formulation of power which can appear necessary in order to clarify and bring about an agreed modal definition of the situation is difficult and problematical, particularly in simple systems of primary interaction. In organized social systems and on the level of encompassing societal systems, there are institutionalized equivalents to cater for this – such as recognized competence or valid legal norms to which one can refer. These equivalents serve to facilitate and depersonalize the exercise of power in interaction systems, and so provide motives for the exercise of power, although, in respect of these, inhibitions in power formulation can also arise (as every supervisor knows, if he has to rely explicitly on the orders that he gave to a subordinate, who is 'deaf in one ear', to carry out his duties).[25]

We cannot here go into the details of the forms in which meta-communication relating to power can be pursued. For our purpose we are mainly interested in seeing that distinguishing between code and process takes the form of a modalizing of communicative acts. This modalizing – and not, for instance, an ability, strength or potential inherent in the power-holder, and also not merely the means at his disposal – forms the basis of the fact that power is effective as a bare possibility, even without engaging the so-called instruments of power. Conceptualizations in terms of 'chance' or power potential do not adequately convey this point.

4. Further, we need our analysis of the modalizing of power as combining relatively negatively evaluated and relatively positively evaluated combinations of alternatives in order to clarify certain problems in the temporal structure of power relationships.

On the level of interactional processes, *decisions can be made over an extended period*, if power as a possibility is secured on the basis of possible actions which one would like to avoid being realized. A social system which has this possibility available can, thereby, organize complexity so as to gain time. Something which cannot occur simultaneously becomes possible in an ordered sequence. This is a way of extending a system's repertoire of actions which can be integrated and yet related to one another.

To begin with, these temporal structures occur in the power-holder's own sphere of action. First, he can sketch out the desired course of action both experimentally and without committing himself, knowing full well that he has power at his disposal. He can attempt to ascertain if this alone will suffice because of the other person knowing where power lies. If there is a show of resistance, he can become more definite, and implicitly or explicitly begin communicating about power, in other words, he can threaten. There are, at this point, different degrees of intensity. Ultimately he can decide whether, if all else fails, he wishes to carry out the sanction, i.e. to realize the avoidable alternative, or not. The unity of such a chain is laid down on the one hand by the system in which it occurs, and on the other by the power-code itself, that is by assessing whether potential is being maintained or has increased. It is thus not purely a matter of chance if one step follows another and if expressions of power are stepped up in the way described. In such a course of action, system and code function as complementary identities which define the possibility/impossibility of taking the subsequent steps. At the same time, such chains consist of decisions made in new, changed situations. Whether the power-holder starts making reference to his power, should the situation not go smoothly, may depend upon the power-holder himself or on the situation; the same applies to whether he also carries out a threatened sanction. The system and the potentiality of his power leave the decision up to him, but it is not to be taken at will, rather in conjunction with more or less sharply defined conditions of consistency. Here too we can see the surplus of possibilities mentioned above.[26] An important question, therefore, is what latitude in conduct is left open to the power-holder himself with regard to his decision-making chain; how open his future still is, once he has started to communicate.[27] The scope and security of his power potential may be just as important in this instance as the degree of differentiation, thus as the possible thoughtlessness in connection with his other roles, and ulti- mately the form taken by the power symbolization – for example, whether a normative form of legitimation or even a legal formulation of power puts more pressure on the power-holder to be consistent. The openness of his future and the flexibility of his actions are dependent not least on whether the power-holder is free to act opportunistically.

These are decision-making chains relating to one power-holder which must be carefully distinguished from those chains which link several decision-makers. Both types of time-organized decision contexts are made possible by increasing the ways that the increased potential in the use of power is formulated, and both serve to order complexity in a temporal sequence. Only on the basis of relatively complex assumptions about a power-code does power begin to 'flow', i.e. to take the form of a process which transmits reduced complexity from one decision to another.[28] The liquidity of power is the effect of its being a suitable code – just as with money.[29] The impression of 'flow' arises because events (here, actions) take place *sequentially*, their selectivity being related to one another by means of a code in the sense that selections presuppose or complete one another reciprocally. In the case of power, the consistency of the context is guaranteed by means of *subject areas* and it appears that individual power processes can be identified only through the integration of these subject areas.[30] Here we also find important limitations on the formation of power chains, which we shall return to later.

Mobilization, chain formation, generalization, and the thematic specifi- cation of power processes increase socially available resources by making possible combinations of actions and increments in selectivity, which, so to say, would not arise of their own accord.[31] In this way it is possible to achieve a certain independence from motive bases made accessible from the natural lifeworld. The fact that one cannot take such distinctions and connections between power processes for granted makes the problematic nature of power understandable. One can see that what came most readily to hand in the process of development towards advanced societies was *not* the actual specialization of an appropriate decision-making power, but the claim that knowledge was identical to decision-making compe- tence, and that truth was identical to power. Under these circumstances, as can be readily ascertainable from accounts of Far Eastern civilizations,[32] it can be presumed that there are few alternative-rich situations available to the power-subject. Neither is there any need, in instances of such incomplete code differentiation, for the construction of a complex legal system sufficient for the codification of power.

Conflicts and conflict-laden binary schematizations are morally discredited. The postulated absolute power here remains as a minor form of power, because one does not have available any choice-situations in which it could intervene. In these circumstances, society does not indicate the clear primacy of any one of the differentiated fields of politics, power and law, the contingency of which, and their capacity for distinguishing on the basis of action, seem to be a necessary stage in social evolution.

Notes

1 See also the critique of Habermas in: Habermas and Luhmann (1971), pp. 202ff., from the viewpoint of the functional equivalence of experience and action, and of Loh (1972), pp. 48ff., from the viewpoint of a differing relationship to the identification of systems.

2 Social psychology also uses the differentiation between internal and external imputations, especially at the important meeting-point of cognitive psychology and motivational psychology. Cf. Lefcourt (1966); Kelley (1967); Jones et al. (1971); Meyer (1973).

3 Cf. Luhmann (1970), p. 233. Research in social psychology has established especially that emotive factors also appear if cognitive expectations are disappointed – probably because of this presumption of equality. Cf. for example Carlsmith and Aronson (1963); Keisner (1969).

4 On the concept of motive intended here, cf. Blum and McHugh (1971).

5 For a more recent survey of research see Maselli and Altrocchi (1969).

6 Not a cause, simply because will and motive cannot be determined at all independently of the action which they determine. Cf. Melden (1961), pp. 83ff.

7 The category of *interest* too belongs in this context, and was *even developed especially for it* when interest received a definite form in the early days of bourgeois society. Interest is that motive of *action* which can (only) be achieved in reflection, i.e. (only) *in experience*, which can be recognized at once in the perspective of experience as a problematic act of separation and which, for the bourgeois society, is linked with societal differentiation primarily in economic terms. Here the need for social unanimity is linked with the transfer of action differentiation into experience categories. In bourgeois society, however, this cannot be achieved either by religious fervour (Fénélon) or by the concrete morality of the state (Hegel), not to mention the non-concept of 'public interest', but it can only be achieved by money as the formula for harmonizing the interests which are still involved. On the history of the concept of 'interest', see Spaemann (1963), especially pp. 74ff.; Hirsch-Weber (1969), pp. 50ff.; Neuendorff (1973).

8 We do not take any transitive order of preferences for granted. To the extent

that such an order exists, it makes calculations about power and its use easier, except in borderline cases. Otherwise, for the binary schematism of preferences, see pp. 151ff.

9 Therefore the contingency of power already occurs in the context of mere possibility, not just in the decision about 'the engagement of power sources'. See the thoroughgoing differentiation between non-contingent and contingent threats and promises in Tedeschi (1970).

10 Different from this is a widespread theory of threat which in the mere threatening sees only a 'substitute' for the real exercise of power – a substitute with certain characteristics which can release generalizing forces. See, for example, Clausen (1972), p. 8. This concept very closely resembles the ideas about the generalization of power which will be discussed below. In my view, however, we should not speak of 'substitutes', because this concept takes the functional equivalence of sanction and threat for granted; and this is what is lacking.

11 This idea could link up with a theory and the art of *provocation*. Provocation challenges the power-holder to reveal his avoidance alternative or even to realize it, and thus to destroy his power himself (!) – a typically childish test but one which is also recommended as a socio-political strategy.

12 Thus, e.g. Riggs (1957), p. 70 and p. 86. Cf. also Parsons (1964a); Coser (1967), pp. 93ff.

13 Although the distinction is old and familiar, there is relatively little empirical research on a comparison between negative and positive sanctions. A survey appears in Raven and Kruglanski (1970), pp. 86ff. With reference to readiness to cooperate as a dependent variable, see especially Miller et al. (1969); Schmitt and Marwell (1970); Chenney et al. (1972).

14 On this explicitly Parsons (1963a); Blau (1964), p. 117; Bachrach and Baratz (1970), pp. 21ff. Cf. also Baldwin (1971b), who shows that political science predominantly tends in this direction, and works out the important differences between negative and positive sanctions, and then, surprisingly, still opts for a concept of power which overlaps both types of sanction. My main objection to such a broad concept of power is that it includes money and love as forms of influence.

15 Blau (1964), p. 116, speaks of an 'initial baseline', i.e. of a status quo with reference to which punishment and reward can first be differentiated.

16 We are not concerned here with a distinction between actual and potential power (as it is frequently formulated), but with the real and effective orientation to possibilities – with Friedrich's law of anticipated reactions. Cf. Friedrich (1941), pp. 589ff., and also (1963). See also the distinction between 'power as potential' and 'potential for power' in Rose (1967), p. 47, and Wrong (1968), pp. 678ff. Despite all the effort which has gone into this distinction, its logical and theoretical foundations in the final analysis remain unclear. The difference between a merely possible power and a potential for power, the exercising of which is probable and which, as such, works just by anticipation, can only be clarified by referring back to different conditions of possibility, and that means by differentiating between system references.

17 See Goodman (1965), p. 50.

18 Cf. March (1966), pp. 58ff.

19 The simplest principle of this type is that one only uses power to the same extent that opposition is manifested (thus, e.g. Clark (1965), pp. 12ff.). The broader question is, however, whether an 'economic' handling of power does not also involve the surrender of enforcement in the same way that economic rationality in general does not maximize particular outputs but relationships between expenditure and outputs.

20 Harsanyi (1962a, 1962b).

21 Thus for example Abramson et al. (1958), p. 17. Parsons brings this problem out in analogy with the medium of money, using the notion that each use of power is a 'spending of power', i.e. means a loss of power. Cf. Parsons (1963a), p. 246; (1964a) pp. 50f.; (1966), pp. 97ff.

22 Provocation can also help to reveal this situation, particularly trifling provocations, which serve to elicit and make obvious the exercise of power for power's sake.

23 Cf. on this concept Watzlawick et al. (1967).

24 'Formulated' in the sense used by Garfinkel and Sacks (1970). This 'formulation' of a code reference in everyday interaction must be strictly differentiated from the general formulated nature of the code, such as its availability in the form of a written text. Texts too still have to be quoted, and this is what is meant here by formulation.

25 Of interest in this context are the results of an empirical study of communication relationships between superiors and subordinates by Burns (1954). Cf. also in confirmation of this tendency Webber (1970), especially pp. 244ff.; Zaleznik et al. (1970), pp. 97ff.

26 See pp. 136ff.

27 Fisher (1969), especially pp. 27ff., sees in this question also a problem of strategy and advises the power-holder not to act according to routine or under the pressure of the engagement, but to make a new decision about each step with regard to the situation and to the decision-making possibilities of the addressee. Parallel with this, one would have to examine what structural preconditions the openness of the power-holder's future depends on.

28 On this comparison see also Talcott Parsons – in an admittedly somewhat different sense of the 'spending of power' by establishing 'binding decisions', which involves a transmission of the expended power. See Parsons (1963a), p. 246; (1964a), pp. 50f.; and (1966), pp. 97ff.

29 Research on community power in the United States speaks of 'issues'.

30 It is different in the economic system where the media-oriented processes have to abandon thematic integration and therefore function as substitutes for the subject-matter of 'transferable' money symbols, whose identity guarantees the consistency of the selective events. This makes it possible to make clear to oneself the 'flow' of the economic process, despite changes in thematic interest around the circulation of money symbols. The comparison between the circulation of power and of money finds its limits in this greater abstraction of money.

31 Eisenstadt (1963) examines this problem using the example of older formations of large empires.

32 Cf. for example Hahm (1967).

3

Code Functions

The starting point we have chosen for developing a theory of power has consequences for the way in which one perceives and follows up the question of how power is increased. If one treats power, along with Kurt Holm, for example,[1] as ability to do damage, increase in power corresponds to the extent of the damage which the power-holder can cause, and/or in the extent of the counter-power which could effectively prevent the damage. Such a starting point does have advantages for methodology and measurement. However, it does not grasp the function characteristic of power of creating order – or does so only indirectly, by way of a theory of the threat of power.[2] The close association of the powerful with the dangerous is really only adequate for archaic societies and archaic ways of thinking,[3] for societies without differentiated communication media. Concept formation must go hand in hand with societal development. With a theory of communication media, a concept of power is developed which makes it possible to see how the performance of particular functions may be increased under differing social conditions. The function to be performed is the transfer of reduced complexity, which becomes more critical the more complex the intersubjectively constituted world turns out to be. The conditions for increasing this transfer of reduced complexity are institutionalized in the code of the medium.

All possibilities for increase go back to what is basic in the distinction between code and process – the generalization of symbols.[4] What is meant by generalization is a generalizing of meaningful orientations, which makes it possible for an identical meaning to be adhered to when different partners face one another in different situations, so that the same, or similar, conclusions are drawn. Reducing the *relative significance of the immediate situation* diminishes the burden of obtaining and evaluating information in individual cases and removes the need for a complete reorientation in shifting from one case to another. At the same time, in this manner it absorbs uncertainty. It becomes possible to form complementary *expectations*, and conduct on the basis of expectations, but at the *risk* of an expectation-oriented, but not quite situation-adequate behaviour which does not exploit the possibilities that the concrete situation may offer (for instance not exploiting a momentary weakness in the power-holder) and misses opportunities for learning. Flexibility of conduct in different types of situation under a code is, at least for the moment, paid for by the inflexibility of the code. That applies particularly to normative, conscious, counter-factual generalizations.

By symbolization (symbols, symbolic codes) it must be understood that a very complexly structured interaction-situation is expressed in simplified form and, in this way, experienced as a unit. The conditions for the formation of power as a medium of communication, analysed in the previous section, cannot as such be a theme which both sides are permanently conscious of. These conditions are summarized and performed in word-symbols or signs, or again by symbolizing people's identity. The forms of expression vary – for example, in their relationship with power sources, in their degree of personalization, in the extent of their legal formulation, etc. Symbolization as such is a vital prerequisite for power formation. Language – and not by any means only the theoretical language of science – has 'dispositional concepts', such as strength, ability, potential, ready for this purpose. Such expressions hide the fact that power is a modalization of communicative processes because they combine the expression of possibility with an attribution of power to the power-holder. In this function they are parts of the power-code itself.

As symbolized potentials, conceptual arrangements have identifiable characteristics. They achieve simplification by dispensing with illustrating or anticipating what is possible. They are not models, maps or plans; they do not need to resemble what is possible. Instead they take for granted – almost as a functional equivalent for similarity – time, and opportunities which arise with time. Symbols express a stabilized possibility, a readiness of the system to act as its own catalyst which can become productive, if further conditions arise.[5]

On the basis of symbolic generalization and potentiality a different code can be developed for each different medium. Not every series of generalized symbols, not every text, nor every structure is necessarily a code in the more precise sense. By code we mean a structure which is in a position *to look for and assign to any item which lies within its range of relevance some other complementary item.* One can clarify the function of such codes in the special codes for the rewriting of texts into other media for transmission or computer-processing of data. But there are numerous other cases – for example, on the basis of enzymes, even in pre-organic evolution (genetic codes).[6] For socio-cultural evolution the most important code is formed with the help of language, because language is bound up with capacities for negation, so that, for important language functions, there is available a negation which corresponds exactly with the utterance.[7] It is precisely because of this ability of linguistic communication to negate a communicative offer that those devices, additional to language, which we have combined under the heading of communication media, become necessary. They have to guarantee their ability to operate as a code in another way. We shall return to this later, in the context of the discussion of binary schematization.[8]

Structures with the characteristics of a code seem to be extremely significant, perhaps even indispensable, for the construction of complex systems. The reasons for this capacity lie in the type of selection possible on the basis of a code and, more precisely, in its combination of universalism and particularity. The code is in a position to attach to each item an exactly corresponding complement, relatively independent of distributions already existing in the system's environment. Thus, for example, to each linguistic communication is attached the negation which corresponds exactly to it, to each true statement its exactly corresponding negation, to each outlay of income the corresponding cross-entry, to each sound its corresponding letters, etc. In this way the code produces, as opportunity requires (though independently of the distribution of opportunities, except as concerns the duration or probability of the process), system-specific couplings as a prerequisite for further operations.

In a very elementary or interactional sense power is always a code – that is in so far as it attaches at every stage avoidance alternatives to the action-selections whose transmission is being sought, thereby immediately doubling the possibilities under consideration. As has been shown, this duplication, typical for a code, makes it possible to attach an unwanted outcome of the power-subject to a wanted outcome of the power-holder. A person who wanted to study as a student becomes someone who did not want to be called up for military service, because of, and just because of, conscription,[9] and thus the issue is brought around to the complemental nature of wanted and unwanted outcomes, capable of being decided in the context of power. Through power, what started out as diffuse impulsiveness and the spontaneous striving for social goals become an 'unnatural' distribution of the wanted and unwanted as a precondition for specific actions. This is the starting point, a necessary prerequisite for every increase of power.

As a result of this duplication rule for forming complementary avoidance alternatives, power is always a code. In each case it opens up the situation to two tracks, according to, or against, the intent of the power-holder. That is power in its raw state, as it were. The relationship between these two tracks can be coded once more, i.e. it can be doubled again, for instance as permitted or forbidden combinations. Such *secondary codification* relates precisely to the *relationship* which is formed by the duplication rule of the primary code, and its problems of reference lie in a specific problem area of this relationship. In the case of power the excessive degrees of freedom offered by possible combinations with avoidable alternatives must be brought within the scope of expectations.

In our own theoretical tradition *secondary codification* of power thus results from the binary schematism of right and wrong.[10]

In the area of communication media even this is not an isolated case. Thus, in the economic code of property the simple rule that one party's assets mean, simultaneously and to an identical degree, the lack of assets of another is, at a certain stage in the development of the code, given a secondary codification through the mechanism of money. The money-code doubles the opportunities of becoming an owner of property by means of money symbols (in themselves worthless). This puts material property in motion; it can, as it were, change people and, because of this possibility, increase its value by being handed over in return for money. As non-owners of certain goods, those with money get an opportunity to acquire them, and vice versa. A comparable problem arose in the logical scheme of the medium of truth as soon as the process of negation was legitimized reflexively and was accepted in the medium-code as more reflexive. Then, to use a formulation of Bachelard's, truths became 'dialecticized' with respect to their potential for becoming untruth, and vice versa for untruths.[11] To contemporaries of this change it appeared that the mind itself had become placed within the framework of history. But history is not a code. The secondary codification of truth is designated by such titles as dialectic or polyvalent logic, but up to the present its structure has not been clarified.[12]

Secondary codifications are one, but only one, element that increases the communication media's capacity for performing the task of transmission required by the changing societal structure. They would have to be examined more closely in the context of a general theory of communication media. In addition, increasing power in proportion to the demands which develop in society depends on further symbols which can become associated with the power-code. This increase must not be understood solely as a heightened generalization of the code-symbols on a one-dimensional scale. Rather, changes in the level of power in societies which are becoming more complex come up against a multiplicity of different problems, the solutions to which have to be institutionalized into the power-code. Not every form of problem-solving is compatible with others, and all have their malfunctions. Their overall effect determines the respective level at which socially differentiated power functions.

In what follows we go through a list of such problem situations, although we shall not be able to do complete justice to existing interdependencies. In this we will keep throughout to issues which could also be worked out for other media-codes.

1. Symbolic generalizations make it possible to shift partially the process of the transmission of reduced complexity *from the level of explicit communication to the level of complementary expectation* and thereby to take some of the pressure off the communication process, which is time-consuming, clumsy and crudely served by language.[13] The anticipation

by the power-subject then runs on *two levels*. It relates not only to the reactions of the power-holder if his wishes are not fulfilled, thus to the avoidance of alternatives, but also to the wishes themselves. The power-holder does not even have to give orders, for even his unordered commands are already followed. Even the initiative to give the order can be shifted onto the subject, if, when the order is not clear to him, he asks what the order would be. Explicit communication is limited to an unavoidable residual function. To some extent, with this form of power augmentation, power is transferred to the power-subject. He decides when to tune into the power-holder and thereby gains not only influence but also power, namely alternatives which avoid stimulating the power-holder into giving no orders at all or giving orders all the time.[14] Along with dysfunctions, a non-communicated, exercised power acts as barrier to power's formalization and centralization.

2. Dual level anticipation of (a) power and (b) the subject area with which power is concerned demands a certain differentiation of these two levels and thus different guarantees of possible anticipation on both. This necessity points to a further characteristic of fully developed media-codes – *the two-stage nature of symbol formation*. The code of the medium itself must be differentiated from those symbols which signal selections, or readiness to make selections, communicate subject-matter and opinion, and determine the contents of expectation. Therefore, the code can even guarantee power which is relatively independent of any consideration of subject-matter by means of suitable symbols, e.g. position and qualifications.[15] Independence from subject area/context makes possible a temporal separation of power formation and the exercise of power,[16] and makes initiatives easier.

The media-code itself therefore consists of symbolically generalized rules about the possible combination of other symbols which guide the process of selections for experiencing or acting. Included in the truth-code, for example, are general rules of logic, the current concept of truth, criteria for the acceptability of methods, but not the theories and individual insights which are offered as being possibly true in particular cases. Likewise, included in the power-code is the symbolization of the power sources, of limitations on power, etc., but not the particular selections of the power-holder, his wishes, his orders. The code itself can then outlive changes in particular subject areas and can be stabilized, relatively speaking, independently of them.

The differentiation and augmentation of the media function depends very significantly on the degree of abstraction at which this multi-level situation can be installed. An important step towards differentiating the levels is making the medium *impersonal*. According to the degree to which this succeeds, the act of transmission no longer depends on the person making the selection, but only on the conditions of the code. The person who knows certain truths, or who has power, is then only one factor in the ability to anticipate choices of subject area and reductions, but is not a formative factor in truth or power itself. Under these circumstances, distinguishing between the position and the person, and relating the power to the position not the person, has been of decisive significance for the power-code.[17] If this distinction is assured, it is, in the framework of a power-code, possible also for power-holders to be chosen and in certain instances interchanged, because they appear as combining in one person all possibilities for the selection of choices.

The plurality of levels brings about the advantages of generalization without having to pay for them with uncertainty or by sacrificing the possibility of concrete realization. Posts can be filled. At the same time as differentiation at the symbolic levels, a secondary problem arises – namely the question of whether and to what extent difficulties of communication can be transformed into code problems and transposed to that level.[18] There are then critical thresholds in interaction which generate meta-communication about power or even a formulation of the power question. A wealth of secondary strategies is related to this. These include avoiding the possibility of infringements being noticed (or even merely the possibility of this being possible),[19] bypassing conflicts, keeping silent about them or rendering them harmless.[20] They can be achieved through avoiding the formation of binding precedents in cases where the power-holder withdraws, or preserving forms of deference if insubordination occurs on a given matter, etc. The conditions for the multiplicity of symbolic levels, above all the separation of position and person, presuppose the existence of organization, which implies that the results of this and the resulting strategies can best be studied in organizational milieus.

3. If one accepts that a distinction between media-code and the subject area of communication can be achieved,[21] one comes to the question of whether and how the code *can steer the change of subject area.* Differentiating between the two levels of meaning is only justified if the code does not lay down concretely what should be ordered. The code, like language itself, also remains abstract in the sense that it does not establish a sequence according to which communication about a subject area is to take place. On the other hand, it cannot be completely indifferent to the boundaries placed around possible subjects. It defines the conditions for possible subjects which can be dealt with under this particular code, and the question is to what extent such 'conditions of possibility' at the same time take on a regulating function, giving a rough direction to the communication process.

In the case of the truth-code we would have at this point to deal with the difficult question of whether and exactly how the change of theory orientates towards truth; whether the truth-code, for example, contains criteria according to which old theories can be exchanged for new, for better or for worse. In the case of power, the medium's action-reference allows the problem to be more sharply outlined with the help of institutional organization. When there is a pre-existing organization the distinction between position and person, which we have already dealt with, can be built directly into the power-code. There is the possibility, at least, of the interchange of decision-making premises of a personal, task-oriented or organizational type, because of an orientation towards unchanged structures.[22] In so far as the mechanism for defining organizational positions fails, this form of codifying change in a subject area is also called into question. This applies especially to top positions in the political system. Even here, however, there are examples of well-institutionalized solutions to our sample problems which show that political power can be achieved only if the power-holder at the same time subjects himself to conditions involving a change in political subject areas, or even to his very person.

4. Our next concern is with the formation of *action chains*. By this we mean an ordering of power processes, which brings more than two parties together so that A has power over B, B power over C, and C power over D, etc., until the chain terminates with one party who, for his part, has no one below himself. One finds corresponding features in other media – for example chains of exchange via money,[23] chains of established truths or untruths as a basis for further investigation in the sciences,[24] or even chains of growing selectivity in love that are forced by the structural relationship between two people to run back into themselves. Power serves as a catalyst for the construction of action chains. If power can be taken for granted at several points, there arises, so to speak, a temptation to form chain combinations in which the selection of one action leads to those of others or anticipates them as consequences of the completion of the former selection. More frequently than was the case with the chance coincidence of interests, it results in the formation of extensive action chains which prove worthwhile because of the gains which combinations yield.

Raising the performance level in this way requires the medium to become specific. It is not something which can be looked for in any kind of combination, which could run in any direction at all, since, in the final analysis, everyone has influence over somebody. Even a mere causal relationship between the power sources cannot suffice. We want to talk of chains only when, and in so far as, A can arrange not only any of B's actions but specifically his exercise of power, i.e. when A has at his disposal B's power over C. Therefore, a chain does not exist if the king can command the general, if the latter can give his wife orders and she her servants, who, likewise because of their position, are able to tyrannize their neighbours. But a chain only exists if and in so far as the power-holder can intervene in the chain.

Accordingly, the defining characteristic of chain formation is the *reflexivity* of the power process, i.e. the possibility of using it on itself. Comparison with other reflexive processes[25] shows that this process structure is on the one hand built upon a series of assumptions, and on the other is capable of a wide range of effects. It assumes a sufficiently generalized, functional definition of the identity of the process, which is used on itself – for otherwise what does 'itself' mean? Thus one only finds reflexive mechanisms in systems which possess sufficiently clear limits and which can make their processes functionally specific. For example if political power becomes reflexive, this demands a corresponding degree of differentiation in the hierarchical structures with a sufficient amount of role separation.[26] If reflexivity is also extended to the *most senior* power-holder, making him part of a power chain and thus exposing him to being overpowered, the political system has to be more strongly differentiated and political power has to be more clearly specified.[27] As a precondition of increase, of extensiveness, range, and of capacity for intervention, therefore, chain formation demands and also creates barriers against the functional and systemic use of power. However, it does not obstruct the creation of power which turns back along the chain itself, the reciprocal power of subordinates over their supervisor, the supervisor over his minister, the minister over his party.[28] One probable structural characteristic of power stretched out in chain form is to create counter-flowing power, since the power of the system exceeds the potential selection capacity of a single power-holder and the ability of middle links in the chain to intervene serves them as a personal source of power. In this way power-codes are divided into 'formal' and 'informal', and the greatest agglomeration of formal/informal powers will be found at key points below the very top.

The formation of chains has the function of making more power available than one power-holder can exercise – to make all power available, in the borderline case of political elections, to those who cannot exercise it at all. Chain formation thus makes possible increases in power which go beyond the selection capacity of the individual power-holder. The artificiality of such an increase in power is reflected in the demands it imposes on the power-code; for example, it cannot be realized without binary schematization (see Chapter 6), without distinguishing between power-code and power-themes and between the position and the person. At the same time the risks of breaking the chain and of obstructing it grow through reciprocally formed counter-power, and this too gives rise to demands on the code, especially in the area of the division between formal and informal power.

5. Differentiation into formal and informal power is an undisputed fact of considerable significance, but in the present formulation, from a theoretical point of view, it is not very productive. A comparison with other communication media suggests that this problem has a more general significance. We will term it the concept of the *extra code*.

Such extra codes are formed if, with increasing complexity in society, communication media have to satisfy increasing demand for the transmission of selections. Then, alongside the actual communication codes, which have to be abstracted and specified, extra codes arise running counter to them which, while having *opposite* properties, are able to fulfil virtually the *same function*. In the scientific system, for example, processes of communication and information-processing rest not only on officially recognized criteria of truth but, in addition, very considerably on reputation.[29] Intimate relationships are not orientated only to the code of love but also form a concrete history of interwoven personal histories, which can to a greater or lesser extent be substituted for the code. Money is in itself so complex that sub-currencies are normally not needed, but they do appear in times of crisis, especially in times of inflation – for instance in the form of moving into foreign currencies, gold, cigarettes, property and land, which, for better or worse, take over part of the function of the money-code. The relationship between formal and informal power is only another instance of this general situation.

Extra codes always have three characteristics which connect with one another, namely: (1) greater concreteness and dependence on context; (2) a lesser capacity for social legitimation, and so also less 'presentability'; and, therefore, (3) for their functioning within the system, dependence, in special circumstances, on sensitivity, knowledge of the milieu, knowledge of history, trust and (!) mistrust, which are not shared in their environment.[30] All this applies also to informal power, the emergence of which is dependent on organizational conditions of work and co-operation. Informal power can and must always carry *one* part of the code-functions. On this basis it can take on *more* functions in exceptional circumstances up to the final point at which formal power serves only as a facade justifying the decisions to its environment. The separation and simultaneous use of main code and extra code therefore assumes a sufficient differentiation in the system and a separation of internal and external media usage.

6. Successful communication media can achieve only the form and selection capacity of a code if they institute a *binary schematism* which pre-structures the possible operations by assigning them paired values. Value pairing is a precondition for the formation of symbolically generalized codes, because only in this form can universalism and specification be combined. In other words, only then can *every* relevant item have another *concrete* item unequivocally assigned to it. For example, if truth is to be more than a shared construction of reality, it has to be structured by a paired-value logic. The possibility of science depends on this – science in the sense of a chain (in principle infinite) of progressive operations with selectivity involved in each connection. In the code of love the demand for exclusivity and its institutionalization in marriage have the same function.[31] In the case of the money-code, property (including freedom in the sense of the right, in economic terms, to dispose of one's own labour power) fulfils the function of a definite separation of property and non-property as an assumption for guiding expectations in economic calculations and transactions.[32] Property can only be institutionalized with the help of the binary schematism of right/no-right. There is the same dependence on the legal system in the case of power. 'From its very

nature' power is diffuse and unevenly distributed. It can only be brought into a clear either/or situation with the help of differentiation between lawful and unlawful power.

Contrary to appearances, binary schemas serve not only to separate but also to unite opposites. They facilitate the shift from one definition of the situation to its opposite by requiring no more than a negation, the admittance of which can be regulated in the system – a technique of paradoxical integration. There is a closer connection between truth and untruth than between truth and love, for instance. Above all, such a principle of binary integration can be abstracted, made specific and universal, while the connections between different media-codes (truth/love, power/money) would have to be regulated much more concretely and in terms much more specific to each situation, because neither exclusion nor interconnection can be asserted as being of general validity.

Binary paradigms serve as components of a medium-code to differentiate societal subsystems. They facilitate negations and bring them into line with a specific schematization and thereby make possible a system-specific operation of relevant functions which have a universal societal status.[33] At the same time, however, such schematizations, like some other code elements, have and maintain something artificial and problematical. As such, they must be imposed (ignoring the question of how – and among whom – property/non-property, right/no right, love/hate, truth/untruth are then distributed).[34] On the other hand they have functions which they cannot give up, so that a mere protest against binary paradigms – for instance in love or in relation to property – must remain ideological unless equivalents are developed for the medium itself or for the function of binary schematization. The problem lies in the *presumptive completeness* of the scheme, in the claim to construct the totality of the possible by means of a dichotomy.[35] The degree of institutionalization of a communication medium can be recognized, among other things, by how far the imposition of its binary schematization is recognized independently of the concrete distribution of opportunity. If and in so far as such is the case, developments occur within and with the help of the binary scheme – such as the transformation of truth into untruth, of what is declared lawful into what is declared unlawful.

This can all be formulated independently of the particular features of the power-code. The theory of media relieves power theory of problems that are not specific to it. To this extent Sorel's distinction between force and violence[36] as the exercise of power by or against the rightful power-holder is in this respect not a power-related problem. At the same time, however, the comparison does illuminate particular characteristics of the power-code. The imposition of the schematic arrangement into lawful and unlawful power means that a normative form is needed, since in this medium we are concerned on both sides with action which is attributable. It supports itself by counter-factual expectations and comprehends uncertainly and inexactly the reality of power. Even unlawful power *is power* – and, in fact, in a different sense to the one in which untruth is truth. It is real power which must always be taken into account by the lawful power-holder, and not simply a possibility, whose arrival one can await with curiosity and an interest to learn, while possessing the possibility of negating it.

At the same time, this means that the relationship between power and law is more insecurely formulated than the relationship between truth and logic. Distributions of power can tend to endanger the legal order, and, *because it is action-related, this tendency presses towards a decision,* towards an approximation of the legal situation matching the power situation. A change of theories, on the other hand, hardly ever occurs on the basis of a discrepancy between truth and logic.[37] In the context of knowledge one even can put up with truths (such as the truth, which goes back to Aristotle's idea of the incapacity of truth where future contingencies are concerned) that contradict the binary schematism of logic, without these insights hampering the operative function of binary truth and logic.

Differentiation between different media and different binary schematizations leads to complex interdependencies, since the binary paradigms will not let themselves be brought together. The action of increasing one medium has a diffuse effect on the others. Sometimes there are structurally significant connections. In this way constitutional peace guaranteed by power makes it possible to increase possibilities of having *or not having property.* And, as even Locke realized, property, for its part, is a precondition of justice *or injustice.* Thus in this relationship between the media of power and money the operation of one medium increases *the disjunction of the other.* It is the complex tension resulting from this – and not, for instance, the naive assumption that property-owners possess power – which characterizes the 'political economy' of bourgeois society. And, to return to the subject of power, this results in certain demands on the code and on the degree of necessary power which today tends to lead to a repoliticizing of economic questions and thereby to a de-differentiation of society in this respect.

A final contribution to the problem of binary schematization concerns the extent of its realization. It is likely that all binary paradigms have their own rules of evasion. It would be fascinating, but impracticable here, to examine this question in the context of truth (logic), love (marriage) and money (property). In the context of power (law), it is at this point that the phenomenon of the emergence in power chains of reciprocal counter-power through the differentiation between formal and informal power should come into consideration. The binary scheme lawful/unlawful is only applicable to formal power, which is in fact defined thereby. But, as we know, informal power may well become the greater power without subjecting itself to this schematization. Law itself – as appropriate or inappropriate definition of the situation – is turned on or turned off in interactions internal to the system. The schematism of lawful/unlawful power is then directed by a second, system-internal schematization into formal/informal power, which can be used only by the involved participants. This complication takes for granted an operative distinction between system and environment which the participants themselves can recognize.

7. Rules of evasion are needed only when and in so far as a code with binary schematization claims to possess *universal relevance*. With this attribute, which we have already mentioned briefly, we come up against a further characteristic function of differentiated media-codes. We shall make use of the term universalism in accordance with Parsons' usage, if it is understood that meaning-references are only realized according to general criteria and independent of the characteristics of the particular participant in any one situation.[38] Accordingly, a universalistic code develops for power, indeed not without power-holders and power-subjects, but without dependence on their respective qualities, realized through generally assignable conditions.

In the case of power – in comparison, for example, with the cases of money or of truth – this condition is particularly hard to fulfil. For where power is concerned, of course, the selections are attributed to the participants as decisions. Nevertheless, even power cannot be institutionalized in complex societies without a universalistic code. Universally applicable symbols, which can be deployed whatever the particular situation, are preconditions for the emergence of expectations concerning as yet unknown or not yet constituted situations and for the elaboration of related grounds for action. Without a primarily universalistic orientation, it is impossible to form chains, to have a sufficiently wide-ranging attitude to an open future and to have high social mobility with constantly changing participants.

The consequence of this is that there are demands on the symbols of the power-code. For example, they must be able to be quoted by anyone, whenever a situation arises in which power must be taken into consideration. They exclude the use of power on a whim, which is not related to the situation or the particular decision, but rather is intended as a useful strategy, possibly operating as part of a chain, which relies on relieving the pressure brought about through expectations. In such circumstances power can be symbolized better, for example, as 'decision' rather than as 'will'. Functional specification and conditional programming – connections which can be tied together by 'in so far as' and 'whenever' formulations – are particularly suitable for articulating a universalistic power claim. At the same time they make it clear that power which must be claimed for unknown situations and be guaranteed in advance is in no way absolute or unlimited power. The legal stabilization of power is one – but not the only – basis for universalistic specifiability.[39] We shall come back later to the significance which accumulating and monopolizing physical force achieves in this context.

These briefly outlined functions suggest a normative, legal and moral bond between the power-holder and his power which, as such, has structural consequences and which can be observed from the early days of advanced civilizations onwards, particularly in the Near East and then in Europe. Power-holders are to use their power for the good, to uphold the law, to protect the poor. The other side of this coin is that opportunism and adapting oneself to the situation must then be sacrificed. Consistency constraints are built into the chain of the power-holder's own conduct (see point 4 in the previous chapter). The myth of legitimation increases the consequences of the exercise of power. If one has started a project, it is very hard, from a normative viewpoint, to abandon it. Each engagement reduces the freedom of the power-holder, who is caught up in consequential obligations. If pronouncing on any appeal made to him has the force of law, he must be careful about showing favour. In spite of all precautions and tactical readiness for inconsistency, it is, in such initial structural conditions, probable that the normative, moralistic dimensions of power, and the frequency of its actual exercise, will increase reciprocally. In such conditions politics gains functional primacy in the societal system.

Of particular importance and relevance are the problems which result if media-codes combine the functions of binary schemas containing built-in preferences (for truths, lawfulness, love, property) with a claim to universalistic validity. This combination in itself has consequences for the code, for if a binary paradigm is imposed on it, the inappropriate alternative within the paradigm cannot be enforced *at the same time*. Such a code must then guarantee for *everyone* the *possibility* of experiencing, or acting according to, the preferred code alternative. It must be possible for everyone to experience truth, to exercise legitimate power or to have it exercised for him, to acquire property, to love or be loved. This possibility is at least guaranteed by excluding its impossibility. For these reasons alone, the principle of internal consistency belongs to the truth-code as well as to the power-code. Furthermore, this excludes certain features of the content of code-symbols – such as the definition of truth as a secret of God, or of law as a set of secret formulae to be used by complainants. Property must then either be communal or be attainable by everyone. Finally, this use of the media-code can legitimize wishes or demands which, in a more concrete fashion, impinge upon the availability of the preferred alternatives, for instance through reformist policies for simplifying and publicizing the law, the division of property, the abolition of unemployment, etc.

8. If it happens that the power-code is linked with the binary schematism of legality/illegality and this link is made universally relevant, there are wide-ranging consequences for the degree to which power is technicalized, i.e. its availability made relatively context-free. In situations in which none of the participants, from their own power resources, definitely has power over the others, it is then still possible to refer to an

existing power differential, based on a distant power-holder and mediated through law. The person who in that situation is in the right then has the power also to mobilize power. He does not have to rely on the 'help' of those around him – which is, as we know, a not very reliable mechanism in highly differentiated societies[40] – but has at his disposal a direct line to the power-holder, which he can activate according to previously established rules. This presupposes the existence of the 'rule of law' in the code, asserting that law is a necessary and – equally important – a sufficient reason for exercising state power. Using this assumption, which of course depicts only a highly improbable and always imperfectly functioning achievement, power sources of a localized nature can to a certain extent be removed from society and concentrated in a subsystem. Society's political system takes over the creation, administration and control of power for society.

The law, however, not only guarantees those without power a share in social power; it also arranges the co-operation of different power sources, above all the co-operation of economic, political and military power.[41] With the help of the legal/illegal dichotomy it is possible to format those communications which link several power-holders to chains in which one can make use of the power of another. If we accept an idea of Stinchcombe's,[42] that such formatted possibilities of recourse to the power reserves of others show one's power to be legitimate, then we can see that the law as power-code creates legitimacy *structurally* (and without it being bound to particular values or even the convictions of the power-subject). Legitimacy is then no more than the formation of contingencies within the sphere of power.[43]

At this stage we are not yet concerned with the consequences for society of such an achievement, but with certain demands on the power-code which arise in connection with it. For this we must refer back to our analysis of how power is constituted (see point 2 in the previous chapter). As we have seen, power depends on a combination of alternatives as well as on the fact that the power-holder forms *conditional* links between combinations of alternatives through *contingent* decision-making. Given this initial situation, it is important for the functioning of the communication medium to assume that power-subjects be convinced of this *as a possibility and hold themselves in readiness*. In other words the contingency of power must convert into a reliably predictable practice and must be made predictable, without thereby losing its characteristic of contingency. The power-code has to formulate jointly the motivation and the 'credibility' of the motivation of the power-holder.[44]

This gives rise to a special problem because readiness to engage one's power resources effectively, for instance by exercising physical force, constitutes an avoidance alternative for the power-holder too. The communication of power conveys the message that the power-holder would rather not realize his avoidance alternative, but is prepared to do so. Negated intention must be made plausible. Research in social psychology, game theory and the theory of deterrence in international relations in particular, has been concerned with the problem of the power-holder's credibility, which is regarded as a significant precondition for power.[45] If there is no credibility, or insufficient information on this matter, a dangerous testing of power ensues, a trying out of readiness, which often causes irreversible developments towards a realization of the avoidance alternatives.

In relatively simple system conditions, the power-code can symbolize credibility simply through strength, perhaps supported by occasional demonstrations of strength. In highly complex, highly differentiated systems this means of symbolically performing undifferentiated strength breaks down.

Credibility has to be secured in a different way. In its place come the legal schematization and technization of power. The conditional linking of the alternatives is, once more, conditionally programmed by law itself. Its contingency is regulated and thereby made calculable. At least the power-code takes over the function of representing that this is the case. This does not solve the problem of the credibility of will and strength; rather, it becomes obsolete, and another problem takes its place, namely the problem of information in the programmed power apparatus. The power-subject will now no longer speculate about the power-holder's not being ready to use his supplies of power but will speculate on the power-holder's not being informed about reasons for such action.[46] This opens up other 'rules of evasion' which do not possess the tendency to unleash an open power struggle and which are thus more compatible with peace.

9. *Problems of consistency* arise as a result of the symbolic generalization of the power-code (e.g. because binary schemas facilitate negation and thereby a wholesale handling of facts). Power can thus only be increased if it is guaranteed that it will not itself be constantly discredited. This is really a condition for the formation of expectations about conduct. Even in relation to the power-holders' selections themselves, a thematic line must make the coherence of their negations recognizable. In addition, on the level of the symbolic code, the consistency of power, as such, becomes a problem and needs symbolic control through the code itself.

This is particularly relevant in two respects – in the dividing up of unified power among a multiplicity of power-holders, in other words in chain formations, and in the fluctuation of power relationships resulting from a change in the power-forming situation and a change in preferences in the way that power is exercised. The power-code itself can only offer somewhat precarious solutions to both problems in the form of reductions in more rational terms. The code responds to the first problem by accepting a *hierarchically transitive ordering* of the conditions of power. This permits any number of power-holders each to find out for certain who is the superordinate and who the subordinate and thus who has more power. Hierarchy avoids the need to measure power, and, especially, efforts to clarify unclear conditions.[47] A power-code can react to the second problem of the fluctuation of power relationships with the premise of *zero-sum conditions*. This assumes that a given amount of power is available, so that every alteration involves a redistribution. Power accruing to one person must be taken from someone else. In cases of easily recognizable lines of conflict, especially party formations, these premises allow a swift survey of the consequences of power changes. It can be formalized in the form of voting arrangements, which express power in terms of votes.

The principles of hierarchy and of zero-sum are relevant in opposite conditions. In so far as conflicts arise about a change of power, the hierarchy principle breaks down, since it takes for granted that the conflicts can be resolved on the basis of the existing power distribution. The principle of zero-sum, on the other hand, assumes its value as a framework for orientation arising only as a consequence of conflicts about the distribution of power. Logically the two principles are not mutually exclusive. If they are used side by side, an organizational division between the two becomes necessary to deal with the question of whether, and in which interaction combinations, conflicts about changes of power are to be accounted for.

Let us emphasize, however, that both the hierarchy principle as well as the zero-sum principle are possible parts of a power-*code*, not premises for a power *theory*.[48] Rather, power theory must be in a position to investigate the functioning, the conditions for use, and, especially, the precarious, more or less fictive character of such code-elements. It must show itself free of the premises in question in order to analyse them as abstractions from their objective reality.[49]

10. It is becoming clear that a theory of power cannot be bound by the normative rules of the power-code itself, if one goes beyond the previously discussed reductions (symbol formation, binary schematism, principles of hierarchy and zero-sum principle) by asking *for easier ways of calculating*. A communication medium may not overstretch the participants' capacity for information-processing. This is also of significance for all communication media and this too is a variable, whose development changes according to the type of medium and the complexity of the social situation in which it is functioning.

In all media some of the problems of information-processing are taken out of the process of verbal communication and left to perception. Not only love but power too makes itself visible. Symbols of hierarchy, along with symbolically intended acts of violence, and not least the personal appearance, the presence, of the greatest power-holder in the interaction, all help in this.

Information problems are in terms of content closely connected with two further questions – the form of motivation and the attribution of the selection. There are codes such as love and money which solve the problem of motivation partly by selecting already motivated partners – with correspondingly high demands on information in the selection of partners. The same applies to power, if one first has to look for durable combinations of alternatives. This is difficult because partners ready to subject themselves to power are unlikely to object to presenting themselves as partners who are ready to love, or ready to buy, or interested in truth. Thus, many technically possible power combinations fail due to excessive demands for information. The demand for information decreases in respect of those means of power, such as physical force, which are, to a great degree, independent of motivation structures, or with regard to organized power, which rest on previously and generally established submission and thus also, so far as it goes, (!) operate independently of motive.

This solution to the motivation problem is backed up by a corresponding solution to the problem of attribution. One needs motives only when action is imputed.[50] In the case of an action motivated by power, the selection, although carried out by both parties, tends to be attributed to the power-holder alone, because the power-subject does not appear to have motives which can be recognized as his own. Admittedly this does not have to be the case. For example, not every exercise of power frees the power-subject from criminal responsibility. A power-code, however, must take account of this *tendency* to shift attribution and can legalize and formalize it by giving the power-subject, for example, the possibility of being 'officially' compelled and thereby relieving himself of responsibility.[51] In extremely power-specific codes, such as the military, this even occurs without the assistance of the subordinate; the officer takes responsibility for an unclear order.

11. If the generalized codes of communication media have to cover and combine a multiplicity of such functions, the probability that the code itself will attract attention and be presented in articulated symbols and rules of conduct increases, along with the level of demand and fulfilment. This is particularly necessary when the code takes the form of norms which also have to be valid when conduct runs counter to the facts and thus has to rely upon the way the norms are formulated. But how can the code itself address the subject-matter if the very content of that subject-matter is always open to the possibility of negation?

All communication pre-requires a level of taken-for-granted understanding that cannot be negated. This level, at which negation cannot occur, has to change according to the type of communication process, and its readiness to address its subject-matter. In the older European tradition, the verbal formula of perfection was available for such taken-for-granted understandings.[52] It introduced, for example, the form of political ordering of human life as the 'most glorious' community.[53] The concept of perfection points on the one hand to the possibility of augmentation, and on the other sets a boundary to it. As a form of reality, perfection itself can be increased to the *ens perfectissimum* (God as the most perfect being), where the relatively imperfect finds at once its reason for existing and the grounds for its own critique. With the help of this logic of perfection, the aspects of a code, preserved from negation, could be formulated in a way which also catered for the use of negations in the codified processes. Participation in perfect truth implied the possibility of error, participation in perfect power, the acceptance of limitations.

This logic of perfection obviously failed for many reasons, among them the purely religious reason of the speculative expansion of the increased potential for negation.[54] In the field of the power-code the discussion about sovereignty which arose in the late Middle Ages may have operated as a trigger, by defining – still in the style of the logic of perfection – the sovereign commonwealth as *civitas superiorem non recognoscens* (the sovereign/ independent city).[55] No matter how the actual causes occurred, whether more French or more Italian sources first inspired the discussion, this does give greater freedom for addressing the subject-matter and greater potential for negation within the power-code, until finally addressing the topic of the code itself becomes contingent and appears otherwise than what it is.

The problems which this raises must be encompassed in the power-code through new possibilities for negation, for how else is one to be able to communicate about the code, to question, explain or change it? It is usual for this question to be answered with the concept of legitimacy.

In the end, it is held, power has to be legitimized, and in this context legitimacy is defined by means of value consensus. A satisfactory explanation of what is meant by this has not, however, been reached. One possible way of making it more precise would lie in the idea that communications about the code of a medium must always be directed through *another* medium.[56] For systems theory, this would mean that [symbolic generalized] media systems lose their autonomy in respect of their *most important* symbols and are thereby most sensitive to the environment. According to Parsons, one should envisage the structure formed by communication media as being hierarchical.[57] This then gets into difficulties with the question of how communication can still take place about the code of the highest medium in the hierarchy. One is thus forced into the inconsistent position of abandoning the principle of the extraneous steering of the highest media symbols in the highest medium. According to this, every society would need ultimate foundations, noncontingent in themselves, by means of which contingency and changeability can be limited and controlled. However, this contradicts the phenomenologically demonstrable peculiarities of meaningful orientation, of which a reference to other possibilities is an inescapable part. Aside from this, such a concept of the absorption of contingency via the highest principles clashes badly with the historical evidence about past intellectual experiences, such as those focused on the notion of perfection.

A theory which tried to solve the problem of code-thematization by exploring the *media- and system-specific opportunism* would look fundamentally different. For example, if the power-code receives its secondary coding from law and it is therefore possible for the highest power-holder to do wrong and even the weakest of the weak to be in the right – and, in cases of argument, to be capable of maintaining that right – the question of the precedence of power or law *must be reflected in the system, while nevertheless remaining structurally unresolved*. Of course secondary codification does not mean that the preference choices of power and right and of powerlessness and no right are made to coincide completely – that would not only be a political utopia but also a structural flaw – but it does mean that the disjunctions power/powerlessness and lawful/unlawful are related to one another. In this structure, problems of closure must be decided differently in each case and thus may be solved only in an opportunistic way.[58] So it is structurally important that long-term identifications are avoided and that decisions, whether taken according to subject-matter or by implication, do not lead to a situation where the power-holder is always in the right. To be legally justified (*legibus solutus*) is the most which can be granted to him.[59] This is in no way to recommend recourse to ultimately irrational decisions and/or to recommend an existing status quo.[60] Rather, in the face of a code which is becoming contingent, one is concerned with providing supports to orientation, learning and decision-making which are plausible vis-à-vis the concrete situations prestructured by the code itself. In individual cases one must differentiate between the opportunism of the practical everyday world, its discussion in scientific terms, and the opportunistic procedure of scientific analysis itself.

A further consequence of that secondary codification is that the problem of closure (in older European terms, perfection) of the power-code can no longer be articulated in moral terms. Morality associates code-symbols with conditions in which people can mutually respect one another. But when two disjunctions have to be related to one another without entirely overlapping, when, in other words, the highest power-holder has to be someone who can do wrong, the glow of his glory can no longer be portrayed in a unitary formula of perfection which is at the same time subject to qualification. The moral demand on the power-holder to do no wrong remains intact but it loses its relevance for societal structure. It no longer designates at the same time the nature of the society and the real perfection of power, but becomes a matter of 'mere morality', for which an autonomous grounding must be sought in the subjectivity of consciousness.

It is symptomatic of the conditions in very complex power and societal orderings that fully developed bourgeois society does not use a media hierarchy to give political direction (i.e. it does not legitimize politics by reference to truth), but that it has formed for this purpose a new sort of political code with a high affinity to opportunism, namely the dichotomy between *progressive* and *conservative*. This binary paradigm fulfils the strict prerequisites for a code in the sense outlined above[61] – it can be suitably used to attach its opposite to any particular political theme. In so far as it becomes a matter of politics, anything in existence can become a topic propounded from progressive, reformist points of view, and vice versa, any proposal for change can be countered by questioning the reasons for it and by arguing for what already exists. The code does not contain within itself anything to obstruct either change or preservation. It is formal, and for precisely that reason can be used both universally and in ways quite specific to certain subject-matter. The (binary) code effects a patently forced doubling of political reality; it is part and parcel of the structure of political subject-matter; it has become a condition under which topics become politicized. If any topic emerges, progressive and conservative forces also emerge, no matter how they proceed to arm themselves ideologically from history's catalogue of slogans.[62]

It is no coincidence that bourgeois society uses a scheme to codify politics in which time functions so as to generate and direct structure. It could also be shown how and why this political code, with its temporal structure, pushes back the neutral schematization of law.[63] But these questions cannot be pursued here, interesting as they are.[64] For our purposes we must simply remember that this particular political code is compatible with opportunism, thanks to its formal nature and thanks to its temporality, and thereby saves society from being tied to a fixed media-hierarchy.[65]

Within the framework of this political code, other codes may be rendered problematic. We can suggest a few further prerequisites for making codes problematic in this way, even though there is very little directly relevant research available, namely: (1) sufficient security on the level of simple interaction systems in relation to the ability to continue the interaction;[66] (2) temporary, satisfactory equivalents for code-functions in the structure and in the comprehension of the environment by interaction systems, e.g. convincing common situation-definitions in obvious crisis situations; (3) the availability of extra codes in the same medium which can take over part of the functions of the problematicized code-symbols and, in addition, can temporarily function as a substitute, e.g. reputation in conjunction with truth, informal power with formal power, family background and interconnected personal histories with love;[67] and (4) the very complex assumptions about the ability to learn which allow the problematicized components of the code to be replaced by promptly available alternatives.

On the basis of the foregoing discussion on legitimacy, I differ from much current opinion in seeing the problem of legitimacy neither as one of establishing a sufficient (even a logically valid) *justification* for the power-code, nor *actually accepting* it solely on the basis of a mixture of consensus and force. I see it rather as a problem of the *structures and processes which make the code possible and control it as it becomes contingent*. Justification and acceptance are only aspects (and in scientific terms inadequately formulated aspects) of this general problem of contingency control. Into this abstract formula old problems become integrated,[68] while the emphasis on and search for the formulation of follow-up problems are cancelled. The question of how it is possible to maintain differentiations in the face of high code-contingency comes to the fore., i.e. how does one prevent all communication problems always turning into code problems, and, on the other hand, how does one stop the differentiation between the various media-codes breaking down and power having to base itself on truth, or love, or money?

Notes

1 See Holm (1969) and compare the definition on p. 278: 'The power of A over B is the ability of A to be able to attach negative values to the actions of B.'
2 This leads to difficulties which we wished to avoid in the choice of the concept of power. See Holm (1969), p. 282. As a critique of the methodological simplifications in this view, cf. also Krysmanski (1971), pp. 65ff.
3 Cf. Douglas (1966), especially pp. 94ff.
4 Cf. Parsons (1951), pp. 10f.; also Parsons et al. (1953), pp. 41f.
5 See the concept of the state of conditional readiness in MacKay (1972), pp. 12f.
6 Cf. Eigen (1971), pp. 492ff., on molecular systems with abilities to give complementary instruction.
7 Cf. Schmidt (1973) on this and on the limits to negation possibilities which can be linguistically articulated.
8 See pp. 161ff.
9 I am deliberately using the past form in order to say that the expression of power puts the partner into a position of having to have another history, namely one which gives his goals a sharpness of selection with distinctive front-line positions.
10 See, for more detail on this, pp. 155ff.
11 See Bachelard (1938, 1940).
12 Cf. Günther (1959, 1967). Also Heil (1971/2) on the lack of solutions to the coding problems in systems theory.
13 The same phenomena are of functional importance in other communication media. It is completely unthinkable that all operating truths and all truths that have a need for co-ordination with other truths should always be transmitted by communication. In the case of love a deep feeling of mutual understanding is based precisely on the absence of any need to use the crude methods of linguistic communication (to this extent, very problematically, Berger and Kellner (1965)). And a challenge to communicate can even be a sign of crisis. Equally, successful order in the communication medium of money rests to a great extent on calculations which are only in borderline cases checked explicitly by using tests on the market, questions about prices, etc. In all these cases a differentiation of code-symbols and of themes is assumed and interest centres on their reduction. We will return to this in the text.
14 On this see Mechanic (1962); Rushing (1962); Kahn et al. (1964), pp. 198ff., from the milieu of organizations. Cf. also Walter (1966). My conjecture is that modern tendencies towards a style of leadership which is prepared to show

understanding, which is permissive and which provides for participation results from the fact that the power of the superior cannot do any more than this anyway; or to put it another way: that increases in power by taking pressure off the communication process are necessary, but assume a certain dividing up of the power-increment. More detail on this later.

15 The significance of such topic-independence is well illustrated in a counterexample – in a system such as a university or faculty which, as it were, neutralizes any strong personalizing of power by using fluctuations resulting from changes in subjects; it cannot, however, also be directed by means of power or, from a power viewpoint, be approached from outside. Cf. the excellent analyses of Bucher (1970). In every case the university, as an organization specializing in truth and education, seems to need some neutralizing of power. Today that dynamic and consensual stalemate of power is being increasingly replaced by a stalemate of power arising from group conflict, where an 'inner circle' of individuals who are still interested in what happens exercise actual power.

16 This separation seems to be more important in the case of power than in the case of money. One can collect money from others and convince them with the help of the money collected that the money had to be collected in the first place, for there is credit. The equivalent in the case of power would be bluffing with power resources which are only created by means of the bluff.

17 One of the important reasons for the political failure of the Chinese theoreticians and royal advisers who were called legists seems to have been the lack of a separation of the office and person of the ruler. This had the result that a highly abstract and demoralized theory and practice of power became bound concretely to particular ruling personalities and stood and fell with them. Cf. Vandermeersch (1965), especially pp. 175ff. Contemporary reflections give the impression that as a result of this an excessive amount of mental effort had to be expended in keeping the ruler under observation. See, for example, Han Fei Tzu (1964), and also Bünger (1946).

18 On this, see pp. 161ff.

19 As one example among many, see Bensman and Gerver (1963).

20 This could relate to what Evan (1965) ascertained, i.e. that more open conflicts can be observed in higher ranks.

21 Thus power no longer exists in the commands – as little as love in acts of love, truth in words or sentences, money in coins.

22 Cf. Luhmann (1971a), pp. 188ff., pp. 207f.; Grunow (1972), especially pp. 18ff.

23 Blain (1971) uses this example to try to develop an alternative to Parsons' model of communication media as exchange.

24 On this Bachelard (1938).

25 See Luhmann (1970), pp. 92–112.

26 Smith (1960) is interesting on a borderline case of this.

27 This emerges clearly at a point which is critical in this context – in the arrangement of political elections which, it is true, may ensure a change in the greatest power-holders, but *for just that reason, are based on a differentiated role structure so that the political voter is hardly in a position to convert his interests, relating to other roles, into political power.*

28 There are contributions on this which are worth reading in Smith (1960), pp. 27ff.; on the power-theory problems of reciprocal power, cf. Wrong (1968), pp. 673ff.

29 See also Luhmann (1970), pp. 232–52.

30 It is worth noting that in the case of truth/reputation the relevance for external relationships seems to be reversed: while in the societal environment of the scientific system reputation is explicable as scientific authority, the same does not hold for real theoretical standards and methodological criteria for finding out truth.

31 This comparison cannot be elaborated here, but one possible misunderstanding should be avoided. The binary schema of the love relationship does not consist in the duality of the partners but in the fact that the public world is duplicated by the private world in which all events must be evaluated over again with respect to what they mean for the experience of the partner. Besides, the fact that it concerns only one partner at a time (there being only two in total) makes it much more possible to do this unambiguously. Thus the duality of partners laid down in the love/marriage code is a rule only for duplication, not the duality itself. The duplication can only then be attained according to that symbolic instruction. That means that it may fail.

32 See also Luhmann (1974b), pp. 60ff.

33 In connection with this see pp. 154ff.

34 Cf. Kelley (1958); Weinrich (1967).

35 This is an ancient problem of reality construction in archaic societies; in later societies it is, as it were, delegated to the individual media in the course of continuing differentiation, and thus attains a more rational and more easily specifiable, although all the more improbable, formulation. On older forms see for example Massart (1957); Yalman (1962); Leach (1964). A more recent version of the same problem is found in the Arrow theorem, which is concerned with the very restrictive conditions under which a large number of complex views can be expressed in a yes/no decision. Cf. Arrow (1963).

36 Cf. Sorel (1936).

37 Cf. Kuhn (1967).

38 Cf. Parsons et al. (1953), pp. 45ff., p. 81; Parsons (1969). Cf. also Blau (1962).

39 This is so because in law very widely universalistic orientations developed very early, so as to guarantee that legal conflicts could be resolved according to previously established criteria without depending on concrete characteristic and situation-definitions by the participants.

40 For a survey of research and for further references see Macaulay and Berkowitz (1970).

41 The power of the *educator* (in the family and in school) appears to be non-linkable, because it is difficult to legislate for it. The task of bringing up children also runs into difficulties with (as always subject to legal conditions) reference to external power sources. No matter how much it is based on the power of sanction, it cannot be strengthened by it. And it is equally difficult to domesticate the power of the educator through laws and to tie it down to political or legal controls. A noteworthy case-study of this problem is Rubington (1965).

42 See Stinchcombe (1968), pp. 150f., pp. 158ff. A similar idea is to be found in Popitz (1968) in the notion that 'basic legitimacy' has its starting point in the 'mutual recognition of the privileged'. A comparison between these two analyses by Popitz and Stinchcombe, by the way, makes one aware that the same phenomenon on the level of interaction systems, with which Popitz is dealing, is much more problematical on the level of functionally differentiated societal systems, where, according to conditions, it integrates very different types of power sources.

43 We return to these questions again on pp. 134ff.

44 Cf. pp. 147ff.

45 Cf. the survey of research in Tedeschi (1970).

46 While this was being written, according to reports in the *Frankfurter Allgemeine Zeitung* (of 12 August 1972), politicians of all parties had distanced themselves from a legal search instigated by the Public Prosecutor of the editorial offices of a magazine; even Germany's Chancellor publicly cast doubt on the action of the Public Prosecutor. This discredits the law as a sufficient cause for the exercise of power. And the question arises, on what other code 'Mr Brandt' (Germany's chancellor at that time) would wish to base his credibility as power-holder. On the recognition of his good intentions or on the fact of superior physical force? Both answers would be regressive; they would point to a social and political situation which had just been overcome by codifying political power in the constitutional state.

47 Cf. Rammstedt (1973) on the development of hierarchies out of relationships of force.

48 Cf. Luhmann (1969b), pp. 160ff., for a critique of corresponding theoretical premises. While the hierarchy-critique is common, Parsons in particular drew attention to the problem of premises of zero-sum; see (1963a), pp. 250ff., and (1963b), pp. 59ff. Cf. also Lammers (1967), and with reference to processes of exchange and exploitation between the centre and the periphery, see Jessop (1969).

49 I would – in contradiction to the views of Habermas and others – stick to the programme of making the theory of communication media independent of the normative codes of these media, even in the case of the communication medium of truth. Here, this takes the special form of referring media theory back onto its own object. The media theory, for which, as we have seen, even logic and freedom from contradiction are primarily attributes of the truth-code, will then have to test itself on its own knowledge and on its own ability to be true. Cf. Habermas and Luhmann (1971), pp. 221ff., pp. 342ff.

50 This view of course only applies in the context of the concept of motive accepted on p. 147.

51 In bureaucratic organizations there are rituals worked out to deal with this. For these reasons, power-codes which are formed against the general tendency and, for instance, attach to the subordinate the right and duty of and thus also the responsibility for refusing to obey illegal orders, must account with difficulty for the execution of orders. For example in the military context, it would normally never occur to a subordinate that the choice of whether to carry out a command was up to him personally. And the burden of information involved

in testing in *all* command situations, whether this might *exceptionally* be the case, would be so great that a corresponding shift of responsibility would seem to offer little chance of success. Nevertheless even illusory elements of this type may fulfil specifiable functions in a power-code. Cf. Rostek (1971).

52 Cf. Lovejoy (1936). For the contexts of perfection and negation see also Burke (1961), especially pp. 283ff.

53 κυριωτάτη in Aristotle, Pol. (1252a) 5; principalissimum in Aquinas (1942), p. 1.

54 Thus the gradual displacement of the *ens quo maius cogitari nequit* (Anselm) by the *ens infinitum* (Duns Scotus) in the late Middle Ages had consequences for the scientific recognition of the real infiniteness of the world without touching on attributes pertaining to God.

55 Cf. Calasso (1951); von der Heydte (1952); Quaritsch (1970), pp. 80ff.

56 One of the best-known examples of this is Kelsen's doctrine of the *basic norm*, if one understands this as a hypothesis in the theory of *knowledge*, which aims to ground the lawful exercise of *power*. Cf. for example Kelsen (1960). Another version of this is Jürgen Habermas's well-known idea that all power should be discursively questioned about its own justification.

57 Cf. for instance, Parsons (1964b). According to Parsons, the medium of power is controlled in social systems by the medium of influence and that in turn by the medium of value commitments. For details see Parsons (1963b) and (1968).

58 See for one example among many, Bünger (1946), pp. 27f., pp. 66ff.; or the fragment from Paulus in Digests: 32, 23: 'Ex imperfecto testamento legata vel fidei commissa imperatorem vindicare *inverecundum* est: *decet* enim tantae maiestati servare leges, quibus ipse solutus esse videtur' (my emphasis, NL).

59 See Esmein (1913); Krause (1952), pp. 531f.; Tierney (1962–3) for the origins and for the medieval usage of this formulation, from the Digests (D I, 3, 31). It originally meant no more than a concretely conceived privilege of personal dispensation – e.g. from police regulations of buildings.

60 As Lipp (1972) among others feared. Rainer Baum also asked questions along these lines (orally).

61 Cf. pp. 144ff.

62 On the creation and development of political topics, see also Luhmann (1971a), pp. 9–34.

63 There are relevant considerations on this in my lecture: Luhmann (1974a).

64 See Luhmann (1974c) for a detailed analysis.

65 Here, in the secondary political codification of power, as previously in its secondary legal codification, we can observe tendencies towards a naive direct association of preferences, which are then, significantly, given not a basis in the structure of the system, but a moral basis. Thus, the postulate that power should be progressive (and not conservative), according to the logic of the political code, invokes the antithesis that power should be conservative (and not progressive).

66 This is the basis for the supposedly high fluctuation of norms in primitive societies. For the supporting of the validity of norms by interaction consensus,

cf. also Luhmann (1972b), Vol. 1, p. 39, p. 149; Vol. 2, pp. 267ff., for further reference.

67 Cf. pp. 150f.

68 To this extent I believe it is justifiable to continue to use the concept of legitimacy or legitimation. See Luhmann (1969a).

4

Power and Physical Force

Power is constituted through the distribution of preferences for alternatives and depends, therefore, as regards content, on such combinations of preferences. In the last chapter we made do with this statement so that we could then turn our attention to general code problems. Now we must take this point up once more with a view to clarifying the relationship between power and physical force.

As far as the assumption of a given range of alternatives and of a given order of preferences is concerned, power is associated with other social system structures. Power is not a completely self-sufficient complex, but is dependent on other factors for the conditions which make it possible, as well as for its level of demand and need. As has often been observed, it varies mainly according to the type and extent of the differentiation in the societal system and according to the division of labour in individual organizational systems.[1] Very different power typologies can be constructed from this in accordance with the type of alternatives which can be preferred or withdrawn. However, this is a possibility which cannot be explored in more detail in the present essay; yet, in general, it can be taken that both the need for and possibility of power increase as a result of the increased interdependence which is the consequence of differentiation – although not always in a straightforward usable form. One cannot assume that societal development automatically produces power in the form that it needs or that power simultaneously occurs, as a by-product of social differentiation, as if of its own accord, and is then available to compensate for higher complexity and higher contingency in possibilities for action. Against this, it could be said that power which is based on structurally formatted dependencies fragments with increasing differentiation and becomes fundamentally specific and rigid, e.g. the power of the maintenance worker over production workers paid on a piece-rate system.[2] For this reason the structural dependencies of power formation demand suitable flexibility in the construction of power itself. This should not automatically mean that the power-holder will have at his disposal a corresponding increase in the freedom to act. If power increases in possibility and in necessity with system differentiation, this principle governing increase remains dependent on suitable generalizations in the power-code itself. That is, it must be possible to select power bases which do *not* depend exclusively on social differentiation but which can be used more universally. *Physical force* functions in this way as a power base at the societal level.

We shall first refer back to the observation reached above[3] that power is annulled by the current exercise of physical force, e.g. by bodily impositions. That is true, at least, for the situation in which this happens. *Nemo ad praecise factum cogi potest* (No one can be compelled to do something), goes the old saying, applied to legal judgments. Physical coercion can thus not simply be understood as the 'last resort' on a scale of increasing pressures. Rather it has a much more general meaning in relation to the symbolically generalized power-code in that it mediates the relationship of the symbolic to the organic level *and does so without involving other, non-political function systems, such as the economy or the family*. In this way it becomes possible to differentiate power which is specifically political – always with the proviso that the power itself does not 'degenerate' into physical coercion.

As was the case with code problems relating to the communication medium of power, we can profit here too from analyses at the level of a general theory of communication media. No communication medium can consist solely of a series of generalized symbols, such as a list of signs. All those involved in the communication process are subject to common conditions and limits of selectivity on the basis of their physio-organic existence – in other words, on the basis of conditions of compatibility with other levels in the formation of the system. Since these conditions are the same for any participant, we can talk of symbiotic conditions and label whatever regulates the relationship between symbolic and symbiotic levels as *symbiotic mechanisms*.[4] All communication media form symbiotic mechanisms – depending on the degree of differentiation, of generalization, and of specification of their code under varying conditions. On the one hand there are *common* symbiotic bases for all communication media, such as conditions and limitations on the organic capacity for information-processing,[5] and, in addition, specific, context-dependent mechanisms, which are each *particularly* relevant only to an *individual* communication medium (although they are, of course, assumed by all). In the case of truth, *perception* becomes particularly relevant, as does *sexuality* in the case of love. The money-code relies on the fact *of paying out to satisfy needs*, and power has a specific relationship to *physical coercion*.

The same problems are repeated despite these different types of symbiotic mechanisms. In all cases the following applies:

1. The symbiotic relationship *cannot be ignored*. In questions of truth one cannot simply disregard what is being perceived, just as in questions of power one cannot simply ignore where the superior ability to exercise physical force is located. The relationship to the symbiotic level, therefore, also has to be accounted for in the code.

2. Put positively, symbiotic mechanisms offer a sort of *security* for media-guided processes with which they find themselves matched.[6] This security becomes all the more important, the higher the selectivity of the regulated experience/act on both sides and the more insecurely the selection comes about. If much is feasible, the sooner one has to know what it is that one should be aware of; if anyone could marry anyone else, sexuality would become more important as a basis and proof of love.

3. Moreover it is a consistent characteristic that the locating and conditioning of the symbiotic mechanisms in organic systems allows them to achieve an *unspecific* effect on the higher level of the processes of meaning formation. There, they are undetermined and function relatively structure-free – it is precisely here that their higher-level function lies. There are, it is true, limitations inherent in the organic perceptual apparatus, but they do not apply to the content of perception. One cannot achieve everything by means of physical force but one can make things happen relatively free of preconditions. Of course, this quality cannot be taken for granted, but is in its turn dependent on the symbolic processes, which give it its form, for in the natural lifeworld there is to begin with no pure physical force, no context-free perception, no libido as such seeking a partner. It is a function of the media-code at the outset to give a symbiotic mechanism freedom, so that the fact that it is not anchored to the symbolic level and is independent from specific meaning-structures can be exploited. And this performance varies, as was indicated above, according to the increasing claims of differentiation, generalization and specification in the media.

4. Since many organic systems become involved in media-guided communication processes, the media-code must see to it that these organisms and their psychic systems do not take on a life of their own and that they operate jointly via the indirect route of socially meaningful communication relationships. This occurs by means of *banning self-gratification*. In the case of love/sexuality this relationship is obvious. Truth, also, cannot rely on the purely subjective evidence of experience – either in the process of perception or in a sort of intuitive apprehension of meaning. And power would hardly be able to fulfil its social ordering functions, so as to transfer selections and get beyond mere force, if anyone could use violence at any time. It is also self-evident that property and money first gain meaning and function from lack of economic self-sufficiency, though only to the

extent that the code does not refer back to normative prohibitions but to the conditions for behavioural advantages.

5. Symbiotic mechanisms will therefore receive a specialist communication function, on fixed organic bases, just through symbolically generalized codes. With increasing demand comes *dependence on organization* as an addition to this. Then specialized social systems reappear again behind the organic processes as a supposed last link. Money manages to satisfy needs only by means of organized trade. Scientifically meaningful observations can for the most part only be approached by means of organized preparation. If the superiority of physical force over any other possible form of force is to be guaranteed reliably in one geographical territory, it assumes that resources have been amassed and mobilized. At that point this superiority no longer provides ultimate security but requires organization of decisions about its deployment and that this organization is certain. Sexuality alone is no longer a secure basis for love, i.e. a proof of love, but itself demands a further guarantee – in the products of the pharmaceutical industry. Safety chains of this type offer greater certainty in the face of greater uncertainty, precisely because they are formed so heterogeneously that all the links do not break at the same time.

These points of comparison with other symbiotic mechanisms form the structure of a theory of physical force. Nevertheless we must not stop at merely forming an analogy, for then functional analysis would degenerate into a merely classificatory exercise. Its distinctive concern with the equivalence of different forms demands that we go further than this and relate the characteristics of physical force to the characteristics of the power-code and to its function for a specified interaction situation.

Exercised against people intentionally, physical violence[7] has a bearing upon the action-oriented medium of power[8] in that it *eliminates action through action* and thereby *excludes a communicative transmission of reduced decision-making premises*. Given these properties, physical violence cannot be power, but it forms the inescapable borderline case of an *avoidance alternative* constituting power. In this situation the characteristics of symbiotic mechanisms sketched out above come into operation. The possibility of the use of violence *cannot be ignored* by the person affected; it offers the superior a *high degree of security* in pursuing his goals; *it can be applied almost universally*, as it is a means which is not bound to particular ends or to particular situations or to particular motives of the persons affected. Finally, since it is a matter of relatively simple act, *it is easily organized* and thus can be *centralized*, as long as self-gratification is excluded. In addition to this, physical force displays that property of *asymmetrical ordering* of relative preferences which is essential to the formation of power. It is less unwelcome to the superior than to the inferior.[9] Apart from this, the exercise of physical force forms the culmination of a conflict in which it is impossible to avoid a decision – either one party or the other must win. This results in the formation of a binary orientation-schema which in itself anticipates the outcome of the conflict. When in use as an avoidance alternative in societal contexts, this schema is supplemented, for positively selected alternatives, by a further schema, that of lawful and unlawful. Thus the double nature of the power-code, which consists of strength/weakness and lawful/unlawful, lies in the doubling of negative and positive combinations of alternatives. This constitutes power. This all gives rise to demands for the compatibility of strength and lawfulness and at the same time to the realization that strength and lawfulness are not identical. The discussion about 'might is right', which has recurred since the days of the Sophists, is based on a much too simple theory of power.

Because all these properties coincide, physical force achieves an exceptional position in the formation of power. In the combination of these features physical force is not superseded by any other avoidance alternative. At the same time, this combination of advantages remains limited to being used as an avoidance alternative. Thus it is and remains of a power-specific nature, and cannot, therefore, symbiotically form the basis for other types of media such as truth or love. Herein lies one inherent limitation of power based on physical force, namely, although it can be utilized almost universally, it cannot exploit such attained 'surplus value' directly in order to gain ground in other media areas.

Against the background of these considerations, the significance of all these efforts to keep violence in the status of an avoidance alternative becomes clear. This can happen, for example, in the demonstration of impressive strength which it would be insane to challenge. A functional equivalent for this is the civil (*bürgerliche*) technique of temporalizing violence. This technique, in conjunction with the differentiation between dual time horizons, is possible in two ways – by shifting into the past and by shifting into the future, i.e. into horizons which are not current, but which do, in each case, relate to the present. Physical force is put in place as the *beginning* of the system, which leads to the selection of rules, whose function, rationality and legitimacy render them independent of past, initial conditions.[10] At the same time physical force is portrayed as a *future* event, the inception of which can at present be avoided, since the conditions for its release are known. Both temporal references are based on the effective regulation of the present power-stance, i.e. on the secondary coding of power by means of law. They replace mere omnipresence of physical force which, through the presence of a regulated present, is now compatible with the time-horizon of a different kind of, but no longer current, past or future.

Solutions possessing such a degree of structural elaboration are, of course, historically conditioned and dependent on many factors. They presuppose not only a guaranteed monopoly on making decisions about physical force, but, in addition, also assume a sufficiently complex relationship between the societal system and time. If future and past are to appear as different types of present, the differences between modes of time must be used from more than just a power-oriented viewpoint for the reconstruction of social complexity – a possibility which was first realized in the bourgeois society of the eighteenth and nineteenth centuries.

We now turn to two further areas of consideration which relate to system formation and generalization. Power based on physical force is characterized by a *relatively simple*, decision-driven orientation principle which is at the same time *compatible* with *greater complexity*. Such an orientation principle, if it coincides with a discontinuity between *system and environment*, can give rise to the construction of highly complex systems by means of the cumulative effect of simple steps.[11] Power-transmitted reductions (of complexity) can be selected on the basis of superiority in physical force in such a way that they open up new sources of power, for example by forming chains. In this way a system of contingent complexity can arise from simple conditions, whose successful ordering makes it largely independent of the preconditions for its inception.

Through such a course – which is by no means inevitable – the genetic conditions and control conditions of power become differentiated. In a genetic sense and in the sense of non-negatable minimal conditions, the system is based on physical force, but it is not thereafter to be controlled through physical force. The rationalization of its complexity becomes a problem. The rise of the modern, sovereign state based on the monopoly of decision-making about the use of physical force, and its inflation to a level of complexity which can hardly be controlled, is the most significant example of such a development on the general societal level. At the same time, this power theory explains the way this situation is conducive to revolution, that is, to recourse to violence in order to modify an uncontrollably complex system by means of regressive progression.

We find a similar break in the path towards escalation if we consider the problem of the *generalization* of power on the basis of physical force. Communication media are structured in too complex a fashion for it to be possible to increase their functioning on a linear scale. An increase in the disposition over the instruments of physical force only concerns one particular, albeit important, avoidance alternative. The increase quickly reaches saturation point, after which it no longer produces greater certainty, let alone more power. Further gains in power are then no longer dependent on the increased probability of victory in a physical struggle, or on a lessening of the burdens one carries with such a struggle in prospect. But such gains are accounted for on structurally different grounds, which we have dealt with in terms of claims on a symbolically generalized code of power. Then the generalization of the symbolic code no longer takes the form only of a universal device which can be used for almost any purposes. Rather, it is general on a higher level, in that it is able to combine very different types of resources and to focus them on selectivity in very different types of situational contexts.[12] For this reason the most generalized instance of power does not hand a power-holder complete choice within a very large range of alternatives (he cannot himself reduce so much complexity), but, like money, it is able to encompass the greatest possible variety, by determining others' decision-making premises. And for this reason too the bottleneck does not lie in having the instruments of power at one's disposal but in the extent to which highly complex decision-making contexts are subject to rational control.

If increases in power do not go beyond relatively elementary thresholds, they give power in a *non-arbitrary, and non-arbitrary executable*, form, because they co-constitute counter-power. We have established this, inter alia, in the analysis of chain formation, but it always applies when the power-subject can cause the power-holder to focus on the conditions and defined situations in which he can exercise power. Even the ability to call forth physical force is an example of this. Conditions for increase are dependent on limitations. It is for this reason only that a theory of power can exist in relation to superior power also.

As the upshot of all these reflections on the theme of physical force, it has to be borne in mind that the widespread idea of an opposition or a one-dimensional polarity, existing between legitimacy and physical force, or between consensus and coercion,[13] is misleading. This idea seems to be concerned with a bourgeois construction which parallels the problem of situating the exercise of physical force in the present, which we have just dealt with. Such a concept is part of the power-code itself, is therefore a prescription for conduct, and suggests that the power-holder should always strive for consensus before using physical force. Such a statement is much too simple for a theory of power and, above all, as a conceptual instrument for the analysis of the relationship between generalizations and the compatibility/incompatibility of media symbols and symbiotic mechanisms.

Neither legitimacy nor physical force arises without the mediation of symbolic processes. The concepts characterize neither a simple opposition nor the dual poles of a single dimension, such that one might say: the more physical force, the less legitimacy, and vice versa. Rather, symbolic interdependencies exist in the sense that regulations of the relationship at the symbiotic level – i.e. at the organic side of social co-existence – have to reckon with the requirements of the relevant communication medium. The interplay of both is necessary for the processing of contingencies, and the preconditions for this combined action can vary as they evolve. Above all they depend on the differentiation of a specifically political power mechanism and on its universal accessibility throughout society.

In the following discussion we shall take up again this theme of the variability of societal-structural claims on power and physical force, this time from the point of view of the technique of power.

Notes

1 Cf. Mey (1972). The best analysis for organization systems is Dubin (1963).

2 On this example cf. Crozier (1963), pp. 142ff., pp. 203ff. Cf. also Elias (1970), pp. 701f., pp. 96ff., for the general problem of the neutralization of centralized power through growing interdependencies.

3 See p. 122.

4 More detail on this in Luhmann (1974d).

5 One can, for example, conjecture that the continuing importance of binary schemas is symbiotically caused, perhaps by a physiological distinction between pleasure/non-pleasure, and perhaps also has its basis in the threshold between short-term and long-term memory. At any rate recent research indicates that if the stream of experience is interrupted, this threshold normally retains no more than two pieces of information in long-term memory. Cf. Simon (1969), pp. 39f. If this supposition should be confirmed, it will at the same time become possible to explain that and why, under these initial conditions, it is advantageous, on the *symbolic* level, to give one of these two pieces of information the highly generalized form of a *negation*, in other words to schematize binarily in this specific sense.

6 In this context Parsons speaks of 'real assets', Deutsch of damage control. Both see in this a precondition for exceeding this guaranteed base through processes of symbolic generalization. Cf. Parsons (1963a) and Deutsch (1969), pp. 184ff.

7 We will limit ourselves to this case of violence against people. We would also include in this violence exercised using material arrangements which hinder people in their freedom to do as they like with their bodies, such as locking people in rooms into which they had entered of their own free will. Other cases of violence used against things, such as wilful destruction, only serve to build up power if they have a symbolic significance and give notice of readiness to use force against people too – for instance against people who want to defend their belongings.

8 This association should, of course, not be considered as exclusive. It by no means explains all actual occurrences of physical violence. Rather, this has many more and different functions and causes – of an expressive or of a helping nature, for example, such as in the treatment of the sick or in rescuing people who are drowning, and perhaps also functions of an educative nature, etc. Fanon (1961), pp. 29ff., for example argues in this way, on a *socio*-political level, using an aggregation of *mental* effects. Thus, acts of violence by the oppressed would increase group consciousness. This may be so – it still, however, says little about the possibilities and limitations of the politically organized aggregation of such effects, and also little about the complexity ('lucidity') of such a consciousness.

9 In Chapter 2, Note 11 above, on provocation, we already noted that this asymmetry in avoidance alternatives can be precarious and in certain circumstances can be subverted. If this possibility is used, a certain type of compulsion can also be exercised against superior force, namely by compelling the actual use

of violence. Such a strategy of provoking the exercise of violence can, in some cases, be successful politically, namely when the power-holder cannot politically afford the recourse to violence as a basis for power.

10 With reference to Kant, cf. Spaemann (1972).

11 Cf. Simon (1969) for the parallel area of data-processing. For the case of power itself one can use the analyses by Popitz (1968).

12 Cf. also Lehman (1969) on these special demands on 'macro-sociological' power.

13 Cf. for example Schermerhorn (1961), pp. 36ff.; Partridge (1963), pp. 110ff.; Buckley (1967), pp. 176ff.; or for further bibliographical references, Walter (1964).

5

Lifeworld and Technique

In the preceding chapters we have discussed the power mechanism in a highly specialized form as a differentiated communication medium. We bore in mind that there are several different types of communication media. Even taking them all together, the area which they affect would not cover everything which, in a very broad sense, one could call influence. All media are developed and earmarked for specific constellations of interactions, in other words for particular problem situations. They always presuppose an actual human co-existence, i.e. they assume a social 'lifeworld'.

Since Husserl[1] it has often been noted that the co-existence of people in daily interactions proceeds on the basis of a taken-for-granted certainty about the world (Husserl uses the slightly more abstract term world-certainty) unproblematically or, in any case, unproblematized. Disturbances remain the exception. The foundations of human co-existence and the conditions for its continuance normally do not need to be considered; actions do not need to be justified; motives do not need to be expressly obtained and displayed. Problematizings or applications are never excluded and always remain a possibility, but this non-actualized possibility usually already suffices as a basis for interaction. If no one takes it up, everything is in order.

This basic condition of the lifeworld nature of everyday life cannot be removed. It is based on the narrow limitations of the ability to process experience consciously. One cannot regard cultural progress, the increase in technical or normative conditions, dependencies or regimentations, or a phenomenological programme for refurbishing all meaningful achievements of creative subjectivity as if they were a process of gradually converting the unconscious into the conscious, of gradually substituting rationality for naivety. Neither development nor enlightenment can be understood as the simple substitution of better for worse. The lifeworld remains pre-conscious, as having the status of a horizon of non-actualized possibilities. Improvements in capacities for order are thus only possible as improvements in the formulated *and* non-formulated, problematized *and* non-problematized, premises of meaning in social communication.

Given these preconditions, such improvements take on the form of techniques. We see the essence of the technical – again following Husserl, but without going along with his dismissal of the technical from the standpoint of transcendental thought[2] – in relieving the processes of experiencing and acting from the burden of perceiving, formulating and explaining all the references to meaning that they entail.

In borderline cases technique takes the form of making the processing of information automatic and calculable, of operating with idealized entities without at the same time having to consider their extensive meaningful implications. Technicalization enables the selective processing of very complex situations and thereby the reorganizing of those possibilities which remain compatible with the limits of consciousness and the status of the world as lifeworld.

This concept of technique has a much broader sociological foundation than the concept of machine technology. Hence, it is also firstly much more loosely defined, as far as correlations with other variables in the societal structure are concerned. It does not carry the immediate suggestion that the way work is organized, environment control, conditions for production, the state of the economy, and class domination are primary factors in social change, although it does not exclude such factors. It thereby attains a comprehensiveness which is adequate for the societal system as a whole. It can be assumed that more advanced stages in the technicalization of society have a direct bearing on all function subsystems.

Taking this general concept of technique as a basis, one can then show the differentiation of communication media and in particular the differentiation of power as a manifestation of technique. The technical in the structure of communication media is based on the characteristics found in binary codes; they schematize any number of processes at the start; they regulate the sequences of their operation and they strengthen their selectivity, by forming chains, beyond what individual participants can oversee and be responsible for. Of equal importance is the possibility of symbolizing possibilities in such a way that the selection process can react not just to what is actually there, but also to what is possible and real in its possibility of being something different. Codification and symbolization take the pressure off consciousness and thereby increase its ability to orient towards contingencies.[3] All this, like the technicalization of the lifeworld in general, only becomes meaningful and possible under specified evolutionary preconditions.

The construction of complex systems is accelerated by a sort of self-catalysis wherever sufficiently specific media-codes having these functions can be assumed. For a system with an environment varying at *random*, the orientation around relatively *simple* rules – and, in social communication, acceptable rules – leads to the construction of increasingly

complex structures.[4] Simplicity and chance are relatively modest preconditions for the construction of complexity. For this reason these preconditions of existence do not contain any guarantee whatever that the system
will maintain itself, let alone be capable of self-regulating. Problems of
maintenance and of continual adaptation loom very large as follow-up
problems from technical developments, and thus demand that special
sorts of techniques be used on the basis of the level of complexity already
achieved. This obviously also applies today to political or administrative
systems constructed with power.

The analyses which follow are meant as a contribution, using the
example of power, to clarifying both the relationship between the lifeworld and technique and the conditions under which that relationship
develops. The general theory of communication media helps transfer
a theme more commonly examined with reference to science to the
practical arenas of power/law/politics. The capacity for increase of the
power-code, its effects in abstracting, idealizing and schematizing, its
reductions and short cuts to orientation are here paralleled by other types
of technicalization – for instance in the realms of logic or finance. At one
and the same time they are conceived of as 'deviations' from the basic
phenomena of social life, as 'normalized improbabilities', and as structures which always assume that influence normally does not have to be
based implicitly or explicitly on power, but can be exercised with ease
and practised as determined by the situation, without making it essential
and without having much depend on it. Power presupposes that not too
many problems which can be solved only by power will arise; in the same
way that, within communication regulated by power, it must be assumed
that not too many communication problems will turn into code problems.

Proceeding from these assumptions, in the chapters which follow we
will deal with the following subjects:

1. How can influence mediated through meaning be generalized in the
context of transmitting action-reductions, and what selective effect do
conditions of differentiation and technicalization have on the form of the
generalization of influence? (Chapter 6)

2. What risks appear as side-effects of achievements which are improbable in terms of evolution and lifeworld, and what forms of risk-absorption
correspond to them? (Chapter 7)

3. What is the relationship between the technicalization of the communication medium of power and the increasing differentiation through
evolution between different levels of system formation (society, organization, interaction) and in what sense is power a specifically societal phenomenon, and in what sense does it remain so? (Chapter 8)

Notes

1 In this context Husserl's (1954) treatment of the problem remains within the area of the communication medium of truth. His works only give a few criteria for a phenomenology of practice.
2 Cf. Husserl (1954). On this also Blumenberg (1963).
3 If we could, together with Blumenberg (1972), imagine a lifeworld completely without contingencies, we could even say that technique constitutes contingency in the first place. In that case, obviously, the phenomenology itself, to the extent that it is looking for truth according to logical premises, must be understood as technique.
4 On this see Simon (1969), pp. 1ff.

6

The Generalization of Influence

In general, and without further qualification, we wish to define influence as the transmission of reduction-achievements.[1] As a basis for different selection-possibilities, influence assumes a mutual orientation around a meaning that is always constituted in terms of a temporal, factual and social dimension.[2] Reference to experiencing at other times, to other circumstances of experiencing, and to others who experience, cannot be eliminated from experienced meaning, although in certain respects it may be negated or put in parenthesis by abstraction. Thus, meaning may also be generalized in these three directions. Meaning is generalized to the extent that it can be made independent of differences in each dimension, i.e. independent of when something is experienced, of what is experienced, and of who does the experiencing. Adequate generalization of meaning is a precondition for the relatively context-free and situation-free use of meaningful content and thus for any sort of technicalization. The most important instrument of generalization is language.[3]

We will now apply this general approach to the special case of influence sought in order to trigger not merely experience, but action. First of all we should try to find generalizations for the motivation of the person who is to be induced to carry out a certain act. He experiences his situation and his options meaningfully and contingently. Accepting influence is for him selection. For this he needs motives. Like all meaning these motives can be generalized in terms of their temporal, factual and social dimensions. In the case of temporal generalization, time differences are neutralized – *ego* accepts the influence because he has already accepted influence previously, because there is a history whose continuation seems obvious.[4] In the case of factual generalization, fact- or case-related differences are neutralized – *ego* accepts the influence because he has also accepted influence in different circumstances and because he transfers to someone else the task of taking on the content of the communication. In the case of social generalization, social differences are neutralized – *ego* accepts influence because others accept it too. In order to be able to label these types of generalization clearly we will call temporally generalized influence *authority*, circumstance-generalized influence *reputation*, and socially generalized *leadership* influence.[5] While authority, reputation and leadership may differ in direction, they offer completely compatible generalized motives for the acceptance of influence.[6] Authority, reputation and leadership are relatively 'natural' forms of motive generalization. This means that their origins and their development into predictable structures are already to be observed in simple interaction systems,[7] i.e. they can take place relatively free of preconditions. They can be increased in the direction of higher generalization. Here as elsewhere such increases are not necessarily possible at any given point, as they all have their own conditions of compatibility and their own consequences. We must put together at least a brief survey of such considerations, so as to be in a position to outline the specific function of the communication medium of power – or as we can now put it, the function of the technicalization of the transmission of reduction – in relation to the limits of the generalization of influence under 'natural' conditions.

Authority is created on the basis of a differentiation of probabilities as a result of previous action. If influential communications have, for whatever reasons, always been successful, there emerge expectations which strengthen this probability, facilitate new attempts, and make rejection more difficult.[8] After a period of untroubled acceptance, rejection causes surprise, disappointment, unforeseeable consequences and thus requires special reasons. And, vice versa, authority does not need to be justified initially. One could say that it is based on tradition, but does not need to invoke tradition.[9]

Reputation is based on the assumption that reasons for the correctness of the influenced action can be given.[10] The factual generalization of influence is also that direction of generalization which lies closest to cognitive mechanisms. Thus, even scientific theory could use the concept of reputation to designate a possible substitute for truth.[11] In this case generalized motivation comes about because a general ability to explain and develop arguments is accepted or transferred from proven cases to others in a *relatively uncritical* way.[12]

Here too, the basis of the relationship is a *possibility* – the simple possibility of further inquiries and queries, which, however, is not exercised. This possibility contains an element of indeterminacy – to be more explicit, it lacks the necessity of complete determination – and this factor underpins the act of generalizing. Thus, to the extent that reasons for certain actions are clearly and generally recognized, reputation decreases. In this context it is often said that to make relationships in industry based more on objective circumstance would lead to the breaking down of the hierarchical structure.[13]

Leadership is based – and here we are referring back to research on group theory – on increasing willingness to follow, as based on the experience that others are also following; in other words, it is based on imitation. Some, then, accept influence because others are doing so and the latter accept influence because the former do so. Where influence over several people is possible and expectable the leader can choose whom to influence and, in addition, he gains options which in turn become an orienting factor for others. The leader becomes independent of concrete conditions of obedience which a given individual could demand of him. The individual relinquishes possibilities which he himself possesses and, should he object, he has to incite the group against the leader. And likewise the leader has to concern himself with maintaining the climate of the group – however illusory it may be – in other words, with keeping up the understanding that the group will accept him as leader and that the dissident will isolate himself.

Temporal, factual and social generalizations of this type share certain common assumptions. As a condition of the possibility of forming expectations, they postulate something distinctive and thereby a certain centralization of the system's meaning-structure through significant themes, for example, objectives, or through significant roles. One must refer the expected influence to something which can be specified; one must be able to locate it within the system.[14] This inevitably links up with the construction of more complex structures which we must understand as non-arbitrary imperatives on a higher level.

Such a build-up of structure in combination with thematic and/ or role-oriented foci cannot cope with total specification from either a dimensional or a functional viewpoint. No leader can rely exclusively on the social aspect of a mutual understanding about expectations; he will always have to make the claim of having proved himself, to rely on his reputation for having made successful and correct decisions in a certain area. That he has proved himself cannot be verified without reference to topics and people. In other words, even generalizations relating to time cannot bring about the creation of authority entirely without reference to reputation, and this will tend towards social generalization as soon as communication about it takes place. The opinions and willingness of others to follow will count above all where what is right is not immediately and clearly obvious. There may be emphases one way or another among these considerations, but the reconstruction of solely analytical differences between various dimensions of meaning in the reality of social systems is neither necessary nor possible.

This entails limits not only on generalizing and abstracting influence relations, but, at the same time, on the functional differentiation of social systems. Despite all the interest in the 'principles' of social life, generalizing about motives being available at different points in time cannot be entirely separated from the factual background of the system and its multifarious concrete commitments. With all the conceptual abstraction and highly developed verbal skill it involves, reputation always retains a link with available knowledge. In short, generalizations in the different dimensions of meaning presuppose one another.[15] On this basis, situations brought about according to only one of these aspects can be achieved only to a limited extent and are always risky. It is more difficult to achieve a higher potential for combinations which support generalization of motive, and freedom of disposition and re-disposition, if no account is taken of given contexts.

However, influence on actions becomes less dependent on these initial conditions of generalization of motive because of the differentiation of a particular communication medium, i.e. power. Power can become independent of particular motivational preconditions to a greater extent than influence in general is able to. It relies on the combination of preferences outlined above (see Chapter 2, point 2), particularly if it can fall back on superior physical power. Such a combination can be standardized. It can be made independent of earlier validation and tradition and thus also of its connection with themes, persons, role-types or contexts with which such kinds of validation were connected. It can also be made immune to an appraisal of other people's willingness to follow, as long as this does not itself become a power factor. So it is more compatible with a change in communication topics and with a turnover in power-holders, in other words, with greater mobility within the system. These are all preconditions for social recognition of the *contingency* of influence – in other words, for the fact that obedient people accept a reduction by others of their potential for action, although this has come about merely *through decision*.

The differentiation of a power-code thus makes the processes of influence to some extent independent of the all too concrete, historical, sources of their temporal, factual and social generalization. Thus the processes of influence can be endowed with increased selectivity and be used in an innovative way in respect of or against very different kinds of situation. But greater mobility and freedom from the context of the process of transmission are at first only *possibilities* which can be achieved by means of power. Differentiation, symbolic generalization, and specification of the communication medium are conditions for those possibilities. In this, nothing has been said about further preconditions under which corresponding action-contexts are realized, or even only made probable. The whole spectrum of conditions for the realization of concrete happenings is naturally very complex and cannot be outlined without concentrating on particular historical situations. Power alone is in no way a sufficient condition for its self-realization (i.e. as if it would be up to its force to force itself). The power of power cannot be attributed once more to power. Rather it needs fundamental analysis from the point of view of evolution theory and systems theory, if one wishes to explain on what societal-structural conditions the development and institutionalization of more abstract, more effective media-codes depend.[16]

These considerations can now be referred to the relationship between the lifeworld and technique. This technical dimension of power cancels out certain limitations on the generalization of expectation based on the lifeworld. It opens up possibilities which reach beyond this and provides, thereby, greater freedom of choice within the system. In this way the selectivity of power decisions increases at the same time, and so, ultimately, the selectivity of the power-code itself. It is no coincidence that *politically* constructed societies were the first to experience *contingency* and treat it as problematical.[17]

In those times, contingency was conceived of and dealt with in religious terms.[18] One example from more recent times will make the contours of our problem still clearer. As one may deduce from the mathematical understanding of the world implicit in the natural sciences and in machine technology, higher selectivity and contingency in technical achievements in no way mean chance, uncertainty, will or arbitrary choice in experiencing and acting.[19] On the contrary, they mean increasing dependence on conditions and on limitations. For the same reasons increases in power also lead to problems in the theory, organization and techniques of decision-making and thus more conditions can be raised, more limitations built up, and more consideration demanded. The lists of sins committed by those in power have always been longer than those of the common man; however, it was not believed that it was possible to dispense justice in relation to these lists.[20] Nevertheless, one can remove the moral side of this problem and formulate it more abstractly as a spiral in the mutual increase of possibilities and limitations. In this conception the greater rationality of a greater degree of power does not consist in being bound to seek what is good (in a strenuous but still problematic way), but in the fact that more possibilities can be subjected to more limitations. Rationality lies in this *relationship*, not in particular results. To increase it makes more abstract decision-making criteria necessary and applicable. This brings us to the technical character of power and its rationality. In this sense the technical character of power can then be conceived of as democracy and be normalized and reformulated in moral terms in the premises of its construction. The presupposition for this is that the limitations on power are integrated into the conditions of compatibility with the structure of society.[21]

Notes

1 For this type of broad concept of influence as a basis for typological differentiations, cf. for example Raven (1965); Cartwright and Zander (1968). In addition a survey of recent research into social psychology in the United States can be found in Tedeschi (1972).
2 For more detail on this and what follows see Luhmann (1971b).
3 It may be characteristic of this instrument that temporal and social generaliza-

tions can occur more easily and be taken much further than factual generalizations. In everyday and taken-for-granted communication exchanges they can, to a great extent, disappear from the arena of conscious attention. Words can mean something independent of who is using them and when they are used, but against this, they are not to the same extent independent of what their content means. Correspondingly, language makes possible a complete dissociation of the speaker and the moment of the utterance from the social and temporal contents about which he is speaking, but, on the other hand, it is not possible to dissociate completely opinion and signification without the interaction system, which is using the language, collapsing in confusion.

4 Adams and Romney (1959, and in more detail also in 1962), suggest a theory of influence on a behaviourist basis, developed particularly from this viewpoint of temporal generalization (generalized reinforcement).

5 This terminology is being introduced for purposes of definition and without claiming conceptual consistency with other research which uses these terms. The agreement must thus be examined in each case independent of the terminology. In *Funktionen und Folgenformaler Organisation* (1964), pp. 123ff., I myself suggested the designation power (instead of authority), authority (instead of reputation), and leadership. The cause for the redefinition lies in the further development of the theory of communication media. There are analyses of the history of the concept in particular for *auctoritas*/authority. Cf. now Veit et al. (1971), and Rabe (1972), each of which have further bibliographical references.

6 In Dahl (1957) we find a similar distinction with a quite different intention, namely in respect to measurable dimensions of power. From five variables which in Dahl's opinion define the concept of power, he selects three which concern the subordinate as relevant for comparison. The three variables are: scope of power (= factual and thematic range), number of comparable respondents (= the social dimension abstracted into a mere number of subordinates), and change in probabilities (= the temporal dimension of the readiness to accept, conceived however not in terms of permanence but as change). Similarly also Kaplan (1964), pp. 13ff.

7 As in Luhmann (1972c).

8 Cf. Maruyama (1963) for the general cybernetic theory of the probability of reinforcement of deviation.

9 Since Karl Mannheim (1927) this distinction between unreflected and reflected traditionalism has appeared in many examinations of the problem of tradition.

10 In this sense Friedrich (1958) defined authority as capacity for reasoned elaboration. By this he does not mean a purely subjective capability, but the quality of a communication which also communicates a corresponding anticipation. In this it depends less on the ability itself than on the presumption of the ability and on its being overestimated. In research in social psychology the cognitive connections between the type of reputation and influence on opinions have been particularly emphasized since Asch (1948). One also finds the characteristics of a communicant who heightens his ability to convince brought together under the misleading designation 'ethos'. Cf. Andersen and Clevenger (1963). Other inquiries appear under terms such as expertness,

competence, credibility. Cf. for example Hovland et al. (1953), pp. 19ff.; Hollander (1960); Aronson and Golden (1962); Aronson et al. (1963).

11 Cf. Luhmann (1970), pp. 232–52.

12 Even this moment of unexamined, uncritical acceptance appears for the most part in discussions of the concept of authority. Thus, even in Lewis (1849), especially pp. 6f., on the basis of an old tradition connected with the difference between opinion and knowledge (and in terms of social theory this means the differentiating of knowledge from the lifeworld).

13 See for instance Weltz (1964), pp. 27ff.

14 With reference to leadership, group research, on the other hand, has emphasized that role centralization cannot be taken for granted from the functional viewpoint, and that leadership can also be diffusely distributed in the system. Cf. for example Paterson (1955), pp. 117ff.; Thibaut and Kelley (1959), pp. 283ff.; Shelley (1960); French and Snyder (1959). See also the critical remarks by Janda (1960), especially pp. 351f.

15 For the function of law as a guarantee for such a congruence of generalizations in the context of normative expectations, cf. Luhmann (1972b), especially Vol. I, pp. 27ff.

16 I am thinking of the research studies by Eisenstadt (1963) which are, however, very crude both theoretically and empirically. Cf. also Fried (1967) and Sigrist (1967).

17 Cf. Luhmann (1973a).

18 On this see Luhmann (1972d).

19 To this extent Claessens' (1965) formulation that rationality is discretion is misleading. To be more exact one should say: greater rationality is greater contingency of choice under more limitations on its being exercised. It is higher discretion which is able to bear more limitations, or, with reference to the medium of money, used as an example by Claessens: greater rationality is achieved because money's greater freedom of employment makes it possible to take into consideration more aspects of the limitation on employment.

20 Cf. Aristotle, Pol. III, 4.

21 These brief remarks are explained in more detail in Luhmann (1971a), pp. 35–45. Cf. also Luhmann (1965) and (1973b).

7

Risks of Power

More developed forms of the institutionalization of media-codes are conceivable only if the selective achievements of media-guided processes (if not the selection achievements of the code itself) are socially visible. In order to deduce that other people accept matters for code-specific reasons, one has to be able to know, or at least to suspect, that selections do actually take place. This applies above all to differentiated communication media which no longer represent simply a shared reality.

Conscious risks increase with increasing consciousness of selection. In the first place they are conceived in general terms, at the level of the processes of selection and transmission, as risks of making mistakes. In this conception of the problem, the solution lies in imposing standards of correct selection. This applies equally to all media – with vast differences in the type of rules about prudence, morals, dogmatisms and organizational and institutional provisions which are thought out and recommended in order to counteract the danger. In the particular case of power, one fears misuse by its holder. As soon as centralized power becomes visible and operational, the problem of tyrants, who use power despotically and arbitrarily, arises. Political theory counters this with an institutionally bound ethic. In this conception the problem of the risk of differentiated power is formulated as structurally dependent and must be solved according to the individual circumstances of each case.

Since its early days the bourgeois society of the modern era has been conscious that its conditions have developed beyond this definition of danger, and beyond these remedies. The reasons for this are complex and cannot be analysed here in detail. They lie in the societal inter-systemic relationships of politics with other social systems, in the increasing generalization of political goals and of other formulae for consensus, as well as in the societally necessary increases in power. Furthermore, they culminate around the subject-matter in the debate about sovereignty. After these changes, the bourgeois revolution, when it finally came to be expressed as a political matter, did not construct any of the usual

correctives for particular cases of power misuse, and this was also completely clear to the conscious minds of those engaged in the revolution.

It is less clear what concept of the risks of power could now replace
the old, easily understood, and 'law-minded' concept of misuse framed
in terms of morality. This concept has not become obsolete but rather
appears in technically enlarged dimensions, in a century which surpasses
all others in the extent and efficiency of the misuse of power. But even the
helplessness of the old remedies for the misuse of power, beginning with
the right to resistance, gives food for thought. And it is equally clear that
merely generalizing old ideas about misuse and suppression – as in the
concepts of 'structural violence', of the 'ruling class' or, quite naively, in
the notion of capitalists or plutocrats creaming off surplus value – does
not deal with the reality but only serves as a stimulant for aggression.
Syndromes of imagination of this kind cannot be tested against the ability
of its concepts to open up new ideas. They are only a blind reflection of
the power relations themselves (and thus one aspect of the risk involved),
in so far as there are at a societal level increasing interdependencies of
power potentials, which can be presented only through abstract ideas or
politically resonant and responsive mystifications.[1] One further point –
the simple 'continuation' of the theme of revolution in the sense of Hegel's
prognosis[2] gives one food for thought – above all concerning the urgent
needs inherent in making a higher degree of power compatible with
unstable political relationships. But, by connecting itself to a historical
theme, this prognosis does not contain a sufficiently differentiated analysis of the risk problem. Now, does the theory of communication media
take us any further?

In order to reach a more general formulation of the problem, we must
first clarify the connections with the theory of evolution. In the evolutionary process the more likely event usually asserts itself because it happens
more often and can be reproduced more quickly. The unlikely event, if
you like, must be introduced and be maintained counter to this tendency
(or as scientists would have it – counter to the tendency towards entropy).
Evolution equals the creation of improbabilities – or, if one so wishes to
put it, normalizes the improbable. This always involves, among other
things, a time problem, in other words a balancing-out of the temporal
advantages of the probable, e.g. in organic evolution by means of catalysis
or by controlling the speed of reproduction. Susceptibility to accidents
increases alongside this. If the relatively probable has to compete with the
relatively improbable for chances to reproduce, time acquires structure in
the sense that it is no longer equally probable and no longer a matter of
indifference when something happens, and time acquires irreversibility,
in the sense that lost opportunities do not recur (as long as there is no
structural guarantee that in rare cases repetition can be assured).

In a very general sense, then, evolution implies increasing the rate of
independence for the speed at which things move, differential scarcities of

time and risks which are conditioned by, and increase reciprocally with, the remedies which relate to them. The differentiation of special roles and, in the last resort, of special symbolic codes for the use of power, represents on the one side an answer to these. On the other side lies a growth, concentration and specification of risk at one point in time. Differentiation is an answer, making society independent of the chance success of a transmission of decisions, in so far as it works as an accelerator and as a controller of a point in time.[3] Thus the risk is concentrated in a different form which is more visible and to that extent also more controllable in the power-holder's selection-practice. It shifts from the temporal dimension into questions of factual accuracy, of success and of social consensus. This problem situation gets labelled the 'tyrant-complex' and lends itself to traditionally handed-down descriptions. This has always been a danger of too much power, but more recently the danger of 'too little power' has also become recognizable. As a result of this, new types of risks of loss of function, obvious ineffectiveness and the disintegration of power become even more apparent.

The starting point for this problem is a need for decision-making which increases rapidly as society develops, but which cannot be met by corresponding decisions and their transmission. The capacity for resolution has increased so much relative to natural constants of any type (i.e. those of an 'external nature' as well as of an 'internal nature'), that almost every selection is presumed to be a decision or be traceable back to decisions. However, because obviously this burden of decision-making cannot be borne at one point alone, indeed cannot even be controlled from one point, the organization of decisions and thereby the transmission of power in a chain formation becomes a problem. Although we know next to nothing about the relationship between cognitive complexity and the other power structures in organizations – and this is an important field for future organizational research – it is obvious that, in dealing with this problem from the perspective of a theory of society, there are limits to decision-making capacity which themselves become power sources, in two respects: (1) as power to obstruct in power chains which can achieve nothing, which can take responsibility for nothing but which can prevent much from happening;[4] and (2) as power not to take decisions at the relevant junctures.[5] Under these given conditions, therefore, cases where power transfers negative decision achievements become more probable and cases where power transfers positive decision achievements become less probable.[6]

A second point connects closely with this. It concerns the appearance of time problems in the context of the exercise of power, i.e. precisely that aspect set out in the first of the evolutionary advantages of differentiating out power. Here too symptoms of overloading become evident. Tempo, synchronization and timeliness become problems in the exercise of power and distort its preferences.[7] In cases of greater interdependency of societal processes which have different individual time rhythms, a power-holder, when deciding a programme, is usually not also in a position to control the synchronization of this with other processes. A succession of events can be predicted, linear sequences can be reproduced, but in more complex cases the fact that other essential elements to the process are simultaneously present defies any programme and constantly forces delays.[8] In this way time becomes a disruptive factor, an intangible resistance. It is not the toughness of the material, or stubborn mentalities, which makes it impossible, but the clock and the calendar. Along the same lines we find that the increase of power in the political system is closely connected with the possibility of changes in the occupancy of at least the top positions, with the result that the thinking in time-frames has a temporal effect that dominates not only the exercise of power, but also on the selection of what can be done and what can happen within a term of office.[9]

In relation to the factual and temporal dimension, it seems that the power available in political systems is no longer capable of dealing with what is required for carrying out the operations of decision-making and transmission. It is not surprising that even where the social dimension is concerned, tensions and crisis symptoms manifest themselves.[10] Translated into the terminology set out in Chapter 5, this means that politically constituted power as a unified technical substitute for authority, reputation and leadership begins to fail. However, given the stage of development society has reached, a return to more 'natural' bases for the generalization of influence for the central functions of society cannot really be considered. Instead, technical substitutes for power develop – for instance in the form of the self-mystification of leaders or in intimations of success which impress the masses.

We will not go further into the question of whether this sort of manifestation really reveals deficiencies. Such a verdict cannot be derived simply from the fact that something better is imaginable. It could only be justified by an encompassing analysis of society and justification of the assessment dimensions and standards for comparison. We are a long way from this. At this juncture we are only dealing with the evolutionary risks of power and here we are interested in the question of whether, along with this chronic lagging behind of structurally anchored expectations, there is not a new sort of risk to power, namely the risk that it will become visible that power does not realize its own possibilities.

It is likely that one of the generally ascertainable risks of differentiated communication media is that, along with the degree of their symbolic articulation and the degree of consciousness of selection, the discrepancy between the possible and the actual also increases and, in one way or another, comes to influence attitudes. The symbolic elements of the media-codes can encompass very diverse situations and heterogeneous motives. They are, therefore, highly generalized and in this function use idealizations and fictions – such as the concept of absolute intersubjective certainty in relationships, the concept of sovereignty, or the idea of a feeling of love being directed at one particular person, yet remaining completely free of constraints in the way one loves the other.[11] The disappointments which then occur belong to the *structural* (and not only to the *interactional*) risks of differentiated communication media and they too have to be controlled by means of their symbolic codes or extra codes.

Accordingly, one can say that all communication media have in common this differentiation, generalization and functional specification which serve to increase the discrepancy between the possible and the actual. This applies not only to the sense of increasing selectivity in the processes, but also in the structural creation of exaggerated expectations and claims on the capabilities of the corresponding communication systems, which, in fact, cannot be fulfilled. In an economic context the much discussed revolution of disproportionately rising expectations is a good example of this. These discrepancies can also be conceived of as cases of complexity, as differences between the complexity of the possible and that of the actual. They are, as such, a real factor which feeds back into the conditions of possibility, and leads, for example, to code-symbols being discounted, or becoming transformed into ideologies, or being used in a purely opportunistic fashion.

This intermediate consideration highlights the normality of such risks. They are not abnormal developments. But this says little about conditions for stabilization. On the one hand these could lie in the development of suitable *attitudes*, on the other in a translation of the problem into *crisis techniques*. Lastly, they could find expression in the controllability of the *inflation* or *deflation* of *power*.

We must now deal briefly with the question of compatible attitudes, because virtually nothing is known about this subject. It is an important area of research for political psychology. There are attitudes such as fatalism or apathy which serve particularly to forestall disappointments. Concerning other attitudes, it can be expected that in cases of high contingency and limited opportunity for the realization of evident possibilities, a different reorientation takes place – for instance a shift from internal to external attribution, with consequences in the area of motivating performance.[12] Further possibilities for adaptation do not lie in socialization processes but in selection processes, which move people with dispositions compatible with problem settings into decision-making positions. In all these respects the degree of research is insufficient for any sort of reasoned verdict. But at least the theoretical and empirical instruments necessary to research such attitudes need no further clarification.

In the case of crisis techniques, additional problems appear, i.e. a lack of clarity in both conceptual and theoretical contexts.[13] It is best initially to conceive of crises in a purely formal way from a temporal perspective as a phase in the process carrying exceptional dangers and, as a consequence of this, exceptional possibilities. The complexity of the possible is then not attributed simultaneously to the system but is illustrated on the time axis as a sequence of differences – between, on the one hand, normal situations with little power and with remote possibilities, which for the time being are not really possible, and, on the other, crisis situations in which situational specific power and power relating to a particular subject-matter can be activated, and to which temporally limited special conditions of structural compatibility apply. In this way advantages in temporal differentiation can be gained by suspending accepted premises of conduct.

There are indications that crises develop where power and/or insight is lacking. Since these indications relate to organized social systems,[14] they cannot simply be transferred without amendment to the societal level of analysis.[15] The processes of obstructing power – or rather of filtering power which can be used only negatively – which have been described are, however, organizational phenomena. It can be assumed that it is on this level – whether in the realm of cognitive complexity or in the realm of power – that one must look also for those obstructions which give rise to developments of the kind which produce crises. Moreover, there have been initial investigations of whether crises alter the power situation in organizations.[16] One must first devise instruments for dealing with crises which are specific to organizations in order to cope with demands in the context of the societal functions of power.

Crisis techniques do not mean trying to prevent or delay a crisis in the societal system which, as Marxists understand it, is inevitable anyway. Rather we mean the differentiation in terms of time of the risks of power by including crises in a sort of power-planning. Emergency laws show a formalized pattern for this. This pattern can be reproduced in the political process with less difficulty and in a smaller format.[17] Similarly, organizations are aware of 'management by exception'. This pattern can be extended into the political sphere in the sense of an exceptional activation of the political resources of power. In this type of anticipated and calculated crisis, the risk of greater power is paid for by certain restrictions in the decision-making process, by time pressure, by the short-term nature of desired effects and by dependence on drastic, widely politicized problems, thus with less ability in planning.[18] Above all, however, such a mechanism works in a highly selective way in those possible subject areas with which it can concern itself, for by no means all suffering is organizational and capable of being treated as a crisis.

A third variation on the risk problem – again more strongly related to communication media theory – is *inflationary trends*. It was Talcott Parsons who suggested that the concepts of inflation/deflation could be transferred from money theory to power theory and, finally, to the general theory of communication media.[19] However, it is not clear how these concepts should be abstracted, so that they can be applied in this context. Inflation has the effect of exaggerating the risk of generalization with the danger of devaluing the tools available for motivation. On the other hand, deflation has the effect of not exploiting the opportunities for generalization, with the disadvantage that possibilities of transmission remain unused. Accordingly, in the case of power, a practice of communication which worked with empty or only rarely backed-up threats would stimulate inflation, for example the 'criminalization' of areas of conduct in which violations, in fact, cannot be pursued for reasons of penal policy.[20] Similarly in money matters, 'slight' inflation seems to be a possible risk strategy which, however, does have the disadvantage of being anticipated by the persons affected and can be exploited for their own purposes. This then results in a more or less extreme splitting apart of the code-symbols on the one hand and of the distribution of roles and disposition of resources on the other, with the result that media differentiation cannot be maintained on either level.[21]

Notes

1 See Elias (1970), pp. 70ff., pp. 96ff. Cf. also the view of the bourgeois revolution as removing the old balance between 'centre' and 'periphery' with the result that politics became ideologized and susceptible to protest, in Eisenstadt (1971), Introduction to Chapters 9–12, pp. 317ff.

2 Cf. Ritter (1957).

3 This politically won independence from chance in a highly developed society was a leading idea in ancient Chinese political philosophy, which is called legistic. Cf. Duyvendak (1928), especially the Introduction, pp. 109ff.

4 On this cf. pp. 149f., for the formation of reciprocal power in power chains, and in more detail pp. 210ff.

5 Cf. Bachrach and Baratz (1962 and 1963).

6 One cannot in any way conclude from this that the status quo would remain and that society would be prevented from changing. Rapid social change is in progress anyway; it is neither possible nor sensible to stop it. The only possible question is whether it can be guided in the form of the exercise of power, or ever.

7 Cf. Luhmann (1971a), pp. 143–64.

8 More exact analyses would have to start here, namely with the question of whether the reproducibility of solutions to problems demands an arrangement into linear sequences. Should this conjecture be confirmed, it would present a detectable limitation on what can be transmitted via power to more or less automatic, intervention-free reproduction.

9 Cf. also Luhmann (1973b), pp. 12ff.

10 This is shown first of all in the fact that the question about the 'legitimation of political domination' is posed quite baldly (and not as a question of the legitimacy of a ruler); and it emerges today increasingly in the fact that this question is no longer asked, but that the answer to it is presumed to be negative. An opinion poll among members of the Federal German civil service, for example, has shown that 62 per cent of those asked (in the youngest group as much as 71

per cent) are not prepared to let their political superiors exercise political influence over their opinions. Cf. Luhmann and Mayntz (1973), pp. 337ff. Although these figures do not give any definite conclusion about actual submissiveness, they do show how far the basis of political leadership has been eroded and, as the same investigation shows, *this occurs today no longer only because a functional equivalent is available in the formal legal nature of the power to give orders.*

11 In terms of their conceptual history, all these code-symbols have medieval roots which cannot really be severed. They were first formulated within a logic of perfection as something which could not be increased further, as the final point in a progressive increase, and took from this a concretely visible reference to order.

12 For the case of the career risk see Luhmann (1973c).

13 At present interest in conceptual clarifications is being shown mainly by late Marxist observers of late capitalism, e.g. Habermas (1973).

14 Cf. particularly Crozier (1963); Sofer (1961); Baum (1961), pp. 70ff.; Guest (1962).

15 Bucher (1970) is also very interesting as an analysis of the extent to which their power arrangements made the universities previously unresponsive to the student revolts.

16 Habermas (1973) chooses perhaps too rigid a starting point for the analysis of society as a whole in the concept of 'organization principles' which determine types. Cf. Mulder et al. (1971).

17 Similarly Scharpf (1971), pp. 27f.

18 Cf. Vickers (1965), pp. 197ff., on 'desperate decisions'.

19 Cf. Parsons (1963a); also (1968), pp. 153ff. Baldwin (1971a), pp. 608ff., also, despite his otherwise very sceptical attitude to the money/power comparison, sees here a proposition which could be developed. Similarly Mayhew (1971), p. 143.

20 Warnings concerning this have been sounded for a long time in the context of discussions of law-making. Cf. for example Montesquieu (1941), p. 95.

21 On this see Baum (1976), who links the definition of the concepts of inflation and deflation to this finding.

8

Power's Relevance to Society

Symbolically generalized communication media are comparable to language in having a necessary system of reference, that is, society. They are concerned with problems relevant to society at large; they regulate combinations which are possible in society at any time and at any place. They cannot be restricted and isolated into subsystems, for instance in the sense that, say, truth has an exclusive role to play in science or that power has an exclusive role to play in politics. There are combinations in the context of doubly contingent selectivity which cannot be eliminated from the horizon of possibilities of human interaction. Wherever people communicate with one another, or even only consider this possibility, selection transmission in one form or another becomes probable. (The opposite view would be a good sociological definition of entropy.) Wherever people communicate with one another, it is probable that they will orientate themselves around the possibility of mutual disadvantage and, in so doing, influence one another. Power is a universal factor of the lifeworld and for societal existence.

Thus, all communication media, in so far as they can be differentiated at all, are societal institutions. Even truth, even money and even love are in this sense omnipresent. Participating in them, whether positively or negatively, is a necessity of existence. Evolutionary changes in such codes thus always affect the fortunate and the unfortunate simultaneously – those who can love and those who get to know through new types of symbols that they cannot love; those who have property and money and those who do not. Code-change can, indeed, to some extent, lead to a new distribution of opportunities, but the 'inner logic' of the code, the non-arbitrary nature of the arrangement of symbols, usually stops innovation from leading to radical redistribution. It can never be that all non-property-owners become property-owners, because this would mean that everyone owns everything, in other words everyone would own nothing. The structure of all media-codes makes 'revolutions' impossible.[1] It individualizes and operationalizes all processes of movement. Codes are catalysts for historical and self-substituting orderings. In this sense they are also elements in the formation of that system which is society.

These statements also apply to the relationship between the lifeworld and technique and are to be examined here from that viewpoint. It is against the background of the lifeworld's societal universality that the differentiation of power, its augmentation, and its functional specification become a problem. This differentiation demands the development of new political systems of reference, specializing in the formation and management of power. In late ancient societies these are primarily the usurpation and growth of durable power relatively independent of subject content in particular centres of civilization, without it ever being possible to bring together and integrate all power within the political system. To the extent that a political system becomes differentiated, it shows that it finds that other power – in the first instance that of other societies, other political systems, but also that of land-ownership and later, above all, financial power – exists outside it.

The differentiation of political power by using a power-specific media-code made possible in the course of historical development – the shift from primitive societies to high cultures – has since that time become one of those evolutionary achievements which cannot really be reversed. It completely revolutionized the position of power in society – the visibility of power, its symbolism (including the need for legitimation), the way it functions, its range. Thus it concerns not only a process of specification, narrowing down and restriction to a part of what is available. The formation of political power is relevant not only to politics; it changes society as a whole. With the formation of specialist political systems able to base themselves on permanently superior physical force, a certain systemization and specification of purpose – and thus also a more complex dependence on decision-making for the application of power – can be achieved, but not a complete monopolization of power in the hands of the 'state'. This does not just mean that one must reckon with power being exercised *against* politically legitimized decisions which are put under social pressure, if not quite threatened with violence, because of attempts to influence decisions over power. A further and perhaps greater problem concerns the volume of societal power which arises and remains *outside* any connection with the political system – primarily and especially power within the family ('despotism' in the strict sense) and the power of the priests, then power in the economy (mainly the recently much discussed power of property-owners) and also, not least, nowadays, power exercised in the education system which is used as a means of allocating status. All these phenomena raise the question of the *limits to which power can be politicized*.[2]

Firstly, one must realize that there are parallel developments in other media areas and subsystems which limit the use of negative sanctions and make possible the differentiation between positive and negative sanctions. It is not possible within the love code to threaten to withdraw love. The threat already equals that withdrawal and so affords no power. In economic matters, power, i.e. the power of the person who possesses scarce resources, is neutralized by money – one can buy them from him. It is only a question of one's own resources and of calculating rationally how much to offer. In comparison with the redistribution in late primitive societies of scarce goods in the 'larger household' of society, a monetary economy makes it possible to distinguish clearly between positive stimulation and negative sanction, and thus to distinguish between the corresponding forms of influence.

This observation makes it clear, on the one hand, how much politics has again, particularly today, usurped distributional functions and in so doing even uses money to neutralize counter-power. It makes clear, on the other hand, the remnants of power in society which cannot be politicized. It should be noted that we are concerned all the time with power in a strict sense, not with the fact that fathers, priests, property-owners or educators exercise influence in the execution of their functions.[3] Those functions put into their hands the means of threat and sanction which they can use as a basis for power, but which also, if communicated via structural expectations, can work by means of anticipation and can thus unleash functionally diffuse effects. So the problem regarding the *structure of society* does not in any way lie simply in occasionally overcoming the ruling upper echelons of the political system – societies have usually survived that well, because social power, as a threat to the political system, must of course change itself into political power. The problem lies elsewhere – in not being able to eliminate power from non-political interactions, in limiting the functional specification of *other* areas of society to purely personal love, rational production and pure exchange, and purely educational work. Hence, the self-assertion of the political system is not the only long-term political problem in relation to sources of power which exist throughout wider society. There is also the problem of keeping the functional specification of different systems as *being different*.

This twofold problem situation of, on the one hand, the possible threat to the political system and, on the other, the functional diffusion of social power and the limits to its becoming politicized, is itself subject to social change. The acuteness and extent of the problems depend on other factors and change with them. Functional interdependencies and stratification structures are of especial significance. Increasing interdependencies multiply the power sources in society which cannot be politically controlled (which does not automatically mean that manifestations of power might be politically uncontrollable). In cases of high interdependency, withdrawal, slowing down, or even merely unwillingness to co-operate – little readiness to make sacrifices in order to provide contributions for which there may be a need elsewhere – become a major source of power which neither has recourse to physical force nor can be countered by threats of physical force. Indeed, the generalizability, independence of control over subject areas and capacity of such power to make threats remain only within limits. Hence no political opposition can develop out of the interdependency of those contributions that have been provided. But that is precisely the problem. For any question of this power itself coming forward and claiming to rule is excluded. At best it remains politically parasitic in that it attempts to profit from a political system which is still functioning, yet in so doing undermines its ability to function. At the same time such power tends to undermine the functioning of its own immediate area of concern by imposing upon interactions which are taking place there a transcending position around questions of power, while always assuming that this ability to function will be maintained.

In older types of societal formation, interdependencies are limited and controlled in important ways by means of stratification into families, status and roles. According to the social stratum to which a person belonged, there was for each one a point of view over and above every functional specification to which behavioural rules of a type specific to the stratum could attach themselves. It also contained non-political, interactionally effective power-controls, above all in the higher strata, where the microcosm of a society based on personal acquaintance could be reproduced within a wider society.

The extremely high interdependencies of modern society, however, can no longer be neutralized in this way – either in strata-specific contact systems of face-to-face interactions, or, in particular, on the level of status and roles. Thus it has become possible to reject stratification as a principle also in ideological terms. The question of functional equivalences remains unsolved in that the problem cannot be simply superseded by lessening the need for integration in modern society. This question remains open as far as our special problem of non-politicizable power is concerned. It would appear that at present two main possible solutions compete with one another. Both gain increasing significance with the reduced importance of social stratification in bourgeois society and both already clearly show symptoms of overloading – namely 'juridification' and 'democratization'. In one case we are concerned with exporting political power into interactional contexts far removed from politics, in the other with imitating politics in areas far removed from politics.

While in earlier societal systems, interactionally motivated legal disputes were the mainspring for politicization in particular situations,[4] after political systems had been differentiated and after the legal system had become positivized, the legal framework has, vice versa, become a means for generalizing and extending politics. In the form of law, political power can, as it were, be conserved and kept available for those who themselves neither act politically nor have power of their own available. Thus, a legal contract must above all be conceived of as an instrument for putting unprogrammed political power into the service of non-political (private) purposes.[5] The fatal distinction between private and public law has obscured this connection between all law and politics, although private law in particular was originally *ius civilis*, in other words, political law. Accordingly, discussion about the constitutional state takes place almost entirely with reference to public law. Yet the legal control of political violence itself is just as important as the legal form attached to interactions between private parties.

Expressed in the form of law, political power, as was shown above (Chapter 3, point 6), becomes schematized in a binary form. In this way it can be *reproduced in simplified form without repeating the conditions for its reproduction.* To make use of this schematic, no regeneration of political power is necessary; it suffices if it exists somewhere and can be called upon. In this way it can be exported to non-political interaction contexts without politicizing them. However, such schematization not only affords relief to the process of reproduction. At the same time, it eases the transfer of media-guided motives over boundaries between systems and over very heterogeneous interaction fields, and thereby makes communication media compatible with higher functional differentiation in society.[6]

To the extent that social control is mediated by law and guaranteed by remote power-holders, interaction systems can be freed from concretely binding, and thus much more rigid, forms of social control on a face-to-face basis. Thus law makes relatively unconsidered action possible in highly specified functional contexts. Interaction systems may then be assigned more or less to exclusively specific subsystems of society. In the market, things are only bought and sold; there is no longer any place for gossiping, for looking for a love-partner or preparing for the next political election.

The significance of law for the nascent bourgeois society of modern times must be appreciated against this theoretical background. First, only recent research and international comparisons show how little this expansion of politically controlling law into society can be taken for granted (it remains equally obvious that every society carries out necessary functions in the form of law).[7] Neither the binary schematization of conflict situations into lawful/unlawful, nor reference made to remote, politically instituted, decision-making power, can be universally guaranteed. Even morality very often gets in the way of such legal relations, and it seems that a progressive industrialization does not necessarily depend on it. Instead, it is possible for society to have recourse to stratification structures which have not yet been broken down in order to mediate between differentiation and integration. Thus, it is hardly possibly to reach any judgement about the future of the rule of law as a solution for mediating between politics and society.

At present more attention is being directed to solving the same problem of the difference between society at large and political force by means of a sort of localized politics specific to small systems.[8] Under normatively intended postulates, like democracy, participation or co-determination, all types of organizational systems in all societal functional contexts, be they schools, mines, prisons or parish churches, are being confronted with claims from all and sundry for participation in the exercise of power. Thus the difference in level between societal systems and individual organizations as well as the differentiation between the functional domains of society become undermined ideologically. We are back to the lifeworld universality of the phenomenon of power. Obviously it is impossible to undo the differentiation of the political system or even just to carry on small-scale politics everywhere in the same way as large-scale politics. What appears to happen is that influence related to status and functions in organization gains visibility and becomes ensnared in a web of communications and meta-communications dealing with questions of power. One can foresee that this will increase the power of veto which is anyway typical of organizations. Taking this route, there is less prospect here than anywhere else of altering society through interactions which use the communication medium of power. The weaknesses of power in the context of societal evolution are today obvious. They are due to the complexity of the system of world society. Ultimately these are reflected in – but do not let themselves be eliminated by – the attempt to replace communication through power with communication about power.

Notes

1 It would be worth considering whether the moral-code is different. Moral-codes are based on the disjunction between respect and non-respect. At least one radical suggestion about respecting the non-respected is known – that of Jesus of Nazareth. But even here it remains unclear whether this amounts to a simple inversion of the moral or to a revocation of it. In any case since that time revolutions have been styled as moral events, because a revolution in the moral can at least be imagined.
2 On this see also Heller (1933).
3 For the rest, it is already an unjustified analogy to politics to speak of the family father, the property-owner, the educator in terms of a dominating role. In the present-day family (and by analogy in other cases), for example, the child who uses coercion may present a greater problem in comparison with the notoriously weak 'visiting father'. Cf. Patterson and Reid (1970). To preview the following discussion, let us add that a child's ability to coerce may be politically and legally more difficult to control than that of the parents.
4 Moore (1972) gives a good outline in this context.
5 'Such rational-legal instruments as contract permit actors to bring the power of the established state to bear upon their private affairs', states Mayhew (1971), p. 37, with reference to Max Weber.
6 Other examples are the use of logically schematized knowledge outside the context of its creation and independent of the conditions and interests of the

research; or using property on the basis of the binary scheme of possessing/not possessing independent of the context of acquisition.

7 Cf. van der Sprenkel (1962), e.g. p. 71; Cohn (1965); Hahm (1967); Kawashima (1968); Rokumoto (1972, 1973); Gessner (1974).

8 From the now overwhelming body of literature, cf. Naschold (1969) and particularly on this Oberndörfer (1971).

9

Organized Power

If, in the first instance, power must be viewed as universal for the whole of society, it is necessary for the theory of power to take the system being referred to (i.e. the reference system), in this case society, as the foundation. In other words, the starting point must be the functions of power for the societal system as whole. The system referred to does not change in any way if politics and law are included in the perspective, for the political system and the legal system are subsystems of society, differentiated according to social functions. Their differentiation and functional specification alter society itself, changing the possibilities and conditions of compatibility of all societal subsystems, and are thus an aspect of societal evolution. However, when analysing the functions and structures of a symbolically generalized power-code we frequently came up against follow-up problems which can no longer be properly dealt with within the scope of this system reference. This applies, for example, to the formation of long power chains in which consistency of subject-matter is nevertheless controllable, to the creation of counter-power in these chains, and to the problems we have already mentioned concerning the potential for information-processing and the limitations on rational decision-making. A suitable treatment of these questions demands a change of system reference, an analysis which would include the special structural conditions in organized social systems.

The choice of reference system for the purpose of scientific analysis is, of course, one option in the context of the process of research, one aspect of the choice of and limits surrounding the subject-matter. As can be seen in the question of societal media-code, the code itself takes for granted the existence of a different type of system, i.e. organizations.

The possibilities for reinforcing and transmitting selectivity leave an imprint in the symbolical structure of the communication medium and can be exhausted only if, within society, not only subsystems of the societal system but other additional types of systems, have also been formed – namely organizations. The symbolism which serves general societal functions presupposes a difference between, and an interdependence among, several possibilities for system formation. The use of more limited possibilities for system formation is a precondition for the realization of emerging society-wide possibilities. At the same time, the differentiation and specification of specialized communication media create catalysts for system formations in the form of organizations concerned, in particular, with property and political power backed by force.

What can be gained from organization does not result from bringing new communication media to bear, but from a particular process in system formation. Organization systems are formed if it can be presumed that a decision can be made about joining and leaving the system and if rules can be developed for taking this decision. This assumption can also be formulated in connection with the problem of contingency. Organization presupposes that the role of membership in the system is contingent, i.e. that a non-member could become a member but also that members could become non-members, in other words, that there is a recruitment pool of possible members and that it is possible for members themselves to leave or be dismissed. This is one area of contingency. The other lies in the rules which constitute the role of the member and the rules which are designed to determine conduct in organizations. These rules too are defined contingently; they are positive in the sense that they are based on decisions and are, through this mode of validity, in regard to origin or their changeability, or by a comparison with systems in the environment, seen as contingent. These two areas of contingency can now support one another and foster one another to the extent that both become prominent and distinctive. Increasing the contingent improbability of rules for membership, and of rule following in membership roles, relates to the contingency of the job market. It increases and limits the possibilities for the selective recruitment and dismissal of personnel. Vice versa, role mobility can develop only if contingently attainable role configurations stay available and can be kept unchanged independently of who fills them. The relationship between these two areas of variation – of joining or leaving and of rules – is thus not contingent, or is less contingent than these two areas: rules and members can be changed, but only so long as there is a concern for maintaining the ability to relate rules to members and members to rules. In this sense, one can characterize the organization mechanism in terms of the systematizing of relationships – themselves not contingent or less contingent – between contingencies. Its rationality is based on the relation-making of relations. In this, relating contingencies works self-selectively on its own possibilities, for even arbitrary selections could not be combined arbitrarily.[1]

Consequently, organization is a particular way of creating systems by increasing and reducing contingencies. This principle is carried into organizational systems and is formulated by means of identifying 'jobs' in the sense of employment positions. Each job indicates a point which links contingent programmes of conduct (= conditions for the correctness of conduct), and contingent communication relationships with, in each case, one contingent person. It is only the identity of the job which lets these different aspects emerge as contingent. At the same time, this identity, as point of reference for making connections, reduces the arbitrariness of these contingencies, since not every person and not every communication network is suited to every duty. Thus, under increasingly restrictive conditions, contingency can be specified with an increasing improbability attached to it. Thereby a more or less non-contingent construction arises from linking up elements which could all be different. In the case of a high complexity of the contingent, its relation-making and its intercontingency serve to reduce complexity. While scholasticism still held the simple as necessary and therefore claimed combination as contingency[2] and thus maintained '*Ex multis contingentibus non potest fieri unum necessarium*' (It is not possible for one necessity to emerge from many contingencies),[3] we today would tend to deplore the cumbersomeness of organizations and the inflexibility of obsolete structures, in other words we would lament that contingency has become necessary.

It is not possible here even to sketch out a theory of organization on this basis. In the context of a theory of power, however, we must consider some of its implications for the formation and elimination of power in organizations. It goes without saying that the construction of organizations changes what is societally possible precisely in the area where power is involved. The power-code established across society as a whole, in a variety of ways, points to this possibility of making new power combinations possible, and of restraining them, by means of organization. Centralizing the distribution of power bases and engaging power as a catalyst in the formation of organization brings this possibility into play. At the same time it would be unrealistic to view organizational systems merely as an instrumental apparatus, as the lengthened arm of the power-holder.[4] This is again only a replication of the symbolic self-presentation of the power-code, not an empirically satisfactory power theory. In reality the relationship between the societal medium and the organization as a type of system is much more complex.

1. We will start this analysis with the thesis that shifting to a different level and a different principle of system formation makes it possible, at the same time, to *convert* the communication medium in a way which would otherwise not be permitted at the wider society level. By 'conversion' is meant that having at one's disposal those possibilities of influence which accord to the preconditions of one medium can be used to gain influence which accords to the conditions of another medium. For example, changing knowledge into power through the ability to identify and determine truths which increase the potential for threats, or changing influence based on property or money into influence based on power.

A societal system which in any way differentiates and distinctively symbolizes several communication media must always ensure also that these media cannot be transmuted into one another at will, for that would discredit the symbolism of the media and destroy the distinction between them. Thus there exist sure and effective barriers to the direct sale of truths or of love or of power.[5] Of course money, to cite just this single example, is not without influence over the production of truths. The person who can finance research can also direct the choice of subject-matter. Nevertheless there is no direct payment in terms of true or untrue statements, let alone a correlation such that money can be directly exchanged for truth without the mediation of the specific code of the other media. Such direct equivalences are excluded in that truths are problematized and have to pass through the particular controls of a special code. In calculating the financing of research, considerations about the relationship between expenditure and returns do arise but they remain limited to their own evaluation-context. They cannot be expanded into arguments for or against the truth of particular propositions. Thus typical finance for research *organizations* covers the research needs and associated resource costs but is not concerned with the content of (true or untrue) propositions, i.e. they do not interfere directly with the binary schematism of the other medium.

This example already shows us the type of solution we are interested in – direct confrontation between media, their respective values and behavioural directives, and their amalgamation can be avoided by changing the system reference and by shifting the problem of conversion onto the level of organizations. One does not finance truths but organizations which more or less successfully concern themselves with exploring and ascertaining truths or untruths. *Mutatis mutandis*, a similar situation results with the conversion of property and money into power.

On the level of societal subsystems such as the economy and politics there are initially important normative barriers to the direct convertibility of money and power. Political influence ought not to depend on the wealth of the individual, and, in today's society, does in fact depend less on this than in the case of its historical predecessors.[6] The opportunity to determine the content of laws is not auctioned to the highest bidder. Similarly the reverse holds true – constitutional provisions against expropriation prevent political power from acting so as to be directly profitable in itself or even from enriching its holders.[7] Below such barriers, however they are deployed, the medium of the economy can make organizations attractive, or even deploy property ownership, safeguarded by law, in land or other assets simply to bring about the elementary conditions necessary for organized work to be possible.[8] In this function the medium of the economy is also called capital. Organizations formed with capital (based on a division into property/non-property) then define conditions for joining and leaving and for subjection to authority, and thus constitute autonomous power. This applies to state as well as to private bureaucracies.

It is usual to suspect and to maintain that this is how undeserved power accrues to the property-owner. This can be so.[9] This anxiety itself, for its part, reflects the barriers to convertibility laid down in the media's code. Meanwhile, within organizations, a peculiar logic of social structures comes into play which changes the conditions in which barriers to convertibility are necessary. If money is a general means of imparting attractiveness to a system, it cannot – or can only to a very limited extent – also be a means to ad hoc motivation. The switch from money to power must to a greater or lesser extent be achieved all in one go. Yet this is just what prevents code-amalgamation from occurring. Moreover, in constructing complex, organized power-systems one very quickly reaches the ultimate limits to the possibility of concentrating power in the hands of one or more property-owner. From then on the power situation in the organization becomes a problem which can no longer be solved by direct recourse to economic criteria for the management of one's own property ownership. The property-owner then possesses favoured access to positions in the organization from which power can be exercised according to *their* own (not *his* own!) conditions. The limitations of these opportunities are known through numerous investigations into the problems of recruiting successors in family businesses.[10] From an economic viewpoint it becomes irrational to couple the occupancy of posts to owning property and therefore to the coincidence of combining ownership and capability in one person. The owner retains his potential to threaten, that is, the possibility of withdrawing his funds from the business. But here, from the point of view of the technique of power, he is at a disadvantage in comparison with a person who is already committed and has renounced liquidity.[11] Hence, for potential opponents, the possibility arises of exploiting the owner, since his power to liquidate is too great, compared to that which can be exercised within the organization.

These few remarks must suffice to show how the transmuting of money into power can be accomplished with the help of the complexity of organizational systems without any frustrating amalgamation of the codes. The genetic newly formed power link between property and money is thus less problematical. On the other hand, the differentiation between societal systems and organizational social systems which makes this possible has the effect at the same time of uncoupling organizational power from the political power formed in the societal system, and, in the long term, this could become the greater problem.[12]

2. While formal organizational power rests on the competence to give official directives, whose recognition is a condition of membership and which can then be sanctioned by dismissal, actual power in organizations depends far more on influence on careers. Thus, it does not depend so much on the arrangement regarding membership as on the arrangement regarding appointments to positions – on those decisional faculties which the (German) civil service calls '*Personalhoheit*' (exclusive competence in

the area of human resources). In order to be able to use short and concise terms we will speak of organizational power and personnel power.

In both the power basis is the same, that is, arrangements over contingency, over 'yes' and 'no' in relation to desired roles. This becomes a power basis to the extent that interests, incumbencies or expectations develop, whose removal or disregard can function as an avoidance alternative. Nevertheless the two types of power differ from one another in important respects. Organizational power relates to the membership as a whole, personnel power to the characteristics of a job, which one occupies and desires to occupy. If membership is at all attractive, it can be, and usually is, broadly advantageous over a whole range of different types of jobs and working conditions.[13]

Thus the question of remaining in the system does not arise on each change in appointments and especially not on every occasion of 'being passed over' when posts are assigned. Correspondingly, only very rarely does withdrawal of membership rights for disciplinary reasons seriously come into question and one can protect oneself against this without much trouble, by fulfilling minimal demands and not being openly rebellious. In order to make one's way up in the system, on the other hand, much more is necessary, and personnel power can be brought to bear on anyone who has such desires.

This difference is connected with the fact that organizational power is to a much greater degree sensitive to cyclical conditions. In business recessions, the danger of dismissal grows, and with it the readiness to conform to norms and to be excessively obedient. An economy with full employment has the opposite effect. Personnel power remains relatively untouched by such ups and downs, because there is always a shortage of attractive jobs. Organizational systems which, because of the economic situation or, in the case of state and church organizations, because of legal guarantees of tenure, have at their disposal only a small degree of organizational power, must, therefore, be able to fall back on personnel power to a greater extent or, otherwise, more or less give up influencing their personnel by the use of power. Accordingly, the limits of organizational power lie in the shortage of usable personnel, while the limits of personnel power lie in the shortage of attractive jobs in the organizational system. The sanction of organizational power, dismissal, occurs very seldom; it is clearly shown to be a negative avoidance alternative for both sides. It always has an official character. Sanctioning through personnel power occurs more frequently according to the mobility in the system but in a less obvious form. In it circumstantial considerations are mixed with positive and negative sanctions. It may consist simply in preferring other applicants for the job and may only appear as a negative sanction to those who are rejected. It is based more on anticipation and the attribution of intentions. For the power-holder, therefore, it does not need to be an alternative to be avoided. All the same he will not be able to optimize simultaneously in his appointments policy an emphasis on qualifications, on the management of incentives and on the use of sanctioning power, because in each individual case this would demand separate decisions. The 'costs' of this avoidance alternative become significant not so much in individual cases as in a functional aggregating and the rationalizing of such an approach.[14]

Finally, reference to the formal rulebook of the organizational system is correspondingly different. Organizational power, with its own contingency, serves to stabilize these contingent rules. It has an official character. Against this, personnel power tends to be weakened if tied to formal rules for the occupation of jobs, to criteria, to job analyses or standardized personnel evaluations. It uses reference to such rules rather as a camouflage, as an excuse or as a possible way of making one person's negative treatment appear as another person's positive treatment. The fact that such a possibility almost always exists also counters the establishment in law of constraints over personnel power in the form of an entitlement to challenge personnel decisions.

Precisely because of these structural differences, one possibility of increasing power is contained in a combination of organizational and personnel power. Both forms of power are ultimately unified in the hierarchy of superiors. Even if competence over decisions about personnel is taken away from the immediate superior, who alone can operate personnel power effectively,[15] he retains considerable influence over these decisions, for example in personnel evaluation, and this suffices as a source of power.[16]

Recent tendencies to reform and rationalize personnel matters in large organizations affect personnel power less through separating off than through systematization and complication. In this mixture, decisions about personnel, so rationalized that they lose that predictability necessary for them to be used in a power context, occur only in a situation where several previous decisions about job evaluation and personnel judgements about appointments and individuals coincide. Manipulating the system then becomes too difficult even for superiors, and subordinates realize that it is not clear how positive or negative attitudes held by the superior will affect the subordinate's career. The system gains transparency on the level of criteria, but at the same time loses transparency on the level of decision-making. With sufficient refinement of sensitivity the power of control over membership shifts not only to exercise control over the occupancy of jobs, but, to a greater extent still, over points of evaluation which could potentially become relevant to careers. But the question is whether the constellation of alternatives on which power rests will produce so highly refined a sensitivity, so deep a focus of interest.

3. However, it could be that important power sources become too complicated for the practical possibilities open to a superior. Similar tendencies arise in the case of power decisions themselves. We have already

touched several times on a situation which typifies organized power. It makes possible chain formations of some considerable length and with a considerable amount of branching, and very quickly overstrains the capacity for information handling and the possibilities of control[17] by any single power-holder. We are then no longer faced with the case which classical power theory counts on, that is, that power *meets* with pre-existing countervailing power and stimulates resistance. Rather, in organizations power *generates countervailing power*.

Excessive strain on the power-holder in organizations can, in other words, always be exploited by others as their own source of power, if his position does not leave him with the pleasure of acting or not acting. One can not only withhold information from him and thus protect oneself from him, one can also count on his seeking consensus, because he relies on 'co-operation' and decisions about 'free' consensus or dissent. To the extent that this is the case in a bureaucratic context, a penultimate option, i.e. the possibility of getting one's way through orders, makes itself available, before the final avoidance alternative of dismissal or resignation. This too contributes to power, if one keeps it in the background and uses it as little as possible. In order to avoid making explicit orders the superior then would prefer to drop relatively unimportant goals, while, on the other hand, subordinates skilfully avoid bringing him to a point where he needs to issue an order.[18]

If one does not relate these points to increases in production, as research in organizational sociology does,[19] but rather to increases in power, one can then ask whose power really profits from increasing reciprocities. How do power opportunities between superiors and subordinates change under such conditions, if the complexity of their possible relationships increases? Obviously the ability of the superior to absorb complexity is narrowly limited. Since precisely this is the source of the subordinate's power, one must suppose that each increase in complexity alters the power relationship in favour of the subordinate, with the result that the more complex an organizational system, the less susceptible it is to leadership.

Of course, limitations on the capacity of the superior stand in opposition to those on the capacity of the subordinate. If the former lacks awareness, the latter lacks communication. The power accruing to subordinates accrues to them individually or, at most, in cliques. It results from situations, and remains dependent on personal initiative and sufficient prior understanding. Initially, at any rate, it cannot result in a simple reversal, in the subordinates taking over power, because structurally their power rests on their position as subordinates and on the relative impotence of their over-powerful superiors. Of course, individual subordinates can try to become superiors by renouncing the power of their previous positions, but they cannot behave like a horse trying to climb into the saddle. If this is so, there would have to be tendencies for the power of the subordinate to collectivize, to systematize, domesticate and legitimize the power of the subordinates. And this is in fact the case. It is put to the subordinates more and more that it is good for them to exercise their power collectively, to select representatives, to constitute committees which become involved in making decisions. Nowadays this idea is being sold with the help of slogans such as participation or collective decision-making – hand in hand with the suggestion of false consciousness. Thus 'emancipation' becomes management's last trick, denying the difference between superior and subordinate and thus taking away the subordinate's power basis. Under the pretence of equalizing power,[20] this simply reorganizes the power which the subordinates on the whole already possess.

It is impossible to predict whether and how this can succeed.[21] There is some support for the view that the power of the subordinates, if organized formally as a collectivity, cannot possibly absorb their informal power, but also cannot strengthen it. Rather, it has to be exercised independently of informal power and under completely different conditions (e.g. greater transparency, less elasticity,[22] greater potential for conflict, greater exposure to external influences). In this way the power situation once more becomes more complex and independent of its subject-matter simply through organization. It is not suggested that these bodies gain much influence and much reputation for having power,[23] but some subordinates could increase their direct influence over their superiors by being members of such bodies and at one and the same time being able to use their voting potential as an avoidance alternative vis-à-vis their superiors. On the other hand, this road also leads to the point where it is no longer worth influencing the superior because he no longer has any power.

Even before the 'wave of democratization' in relation to organizations, Mary Parker Follett[24] had supplied the following statement: 'The division of power is not the thing to be considered, but that method of organization which will generate power.'[25] Somewhat later, after the world economic crisis, an idea arose in the context of another medium, other than the medium of the economy, that demand for growth must be a priority because one could solve problems of distribution with its help, but not vice versa.[26] Acknowledging this argument, Parsons then again insisted that power theory give up its zero-sum assumption and the relativization of distribution issues to variable amounts of power.[27] Once these questions have been posed, albeit much too sweepingly, it is impossible either to return to the notion that one could, without loss, take over the power of others gradually step by step within the organization or believe that the separation of powers (legislature, executive and judiciary) is sufficient to safeguard power from being wielded in arbitrary fashion. Our own analysis, tailored more specifically to organizations, has added the view that the conservation of a superior's impotent superiority is a precondition for the subordinate's power. Accordingly, if one must see amounts of power as variable and if increasing power creates countervailing power, the key to the problem must lie in a greater differentiation and specification of power sources and power communications, which would prevent reciprocal power potentials cancelling one another out.[28] Or, to put it another way – how, with the help of the selection mechanism of an organization, can the asymmetrical structure of power communications be maintained even in cases of reciprocal power?

Current organizational knowledge has no answer to this. No doubt a simple copy of the separation of powers model (legislature, executive and judiciary) would make things too easy. This model has the specific function of differentiating between the legal and illegal use of power, in order to permit the former and block the latter. This would not suffice, however, because power internal to an organization in particular cannot be subjected to sufficient legal constraint. Just as unsatisfactory are suggestions about the mutual increase in influence which have been developed in the context of the 'human relations' movement, namely chains of increasing influence which turn in on themselves, in which *alter* accepts greater influence from *ego* because *ego* accepts greater influence from *alter*.[29] This may be a perfectly realistic possibility even for organization systems, but it is hardly compatible with reliance on negative sanctions and avoidance alternatives and would be more a case of love than a case of power.[30] At any rate there is a strong emotional, social and local colouring to these suggestions, thus leaving open the question of how far increases in reciprocal influences, achieved in this way, are available for purposes of adapting the system to the environment and how long they would survive changes in the personnel structure.

This result seems to be conditioned by the simple fact that power sources, but not the subject content of power, can be sharply differentiated in organizations; that, in other words, power is formed on different power bases, but cannot be satisfactorily separated out by subject-matter. The power of a superior, whether organizational power, personnel power or ultimately personnel evaluation power, finds itself confronted with the power of inferiors, which is based on quite different avoidance alternatives. On the other hand, it follows from the functional division of labour in large organizations that superiors and subordinates have to co-operate in different subject areas within relatively narrow boundaries. They have few opportunities to delimit zones of interest so that the superior has more influence over one project and the subordinate over another, and in such a way that mutual respect for the zones of influence is motivated by bargaining. The interdependencies and centralized responsibilities within one differentiated area of activity are in general too high for that.[31] Even in universities and faculties in which very different areas of power such as examinations, appointment policies, curriculum planning, budgetary administration, political manifestations, etc., can be clearly discerned, agreements about zones and areas of tolerance between power groups do not seem to come about. In the face of the diversity of types of organizations one cannot formulate an indisputably true statement about them. Rather a power increase within an organization would tend to come up against the dilemma that the differentiation of power sources cannot be matched by a differentiation of the subject-matter of power, so that there is no leeway for balancing the power out. Interdependency within the system is too high merely for an accumulation of different types of power.

4. Together with these considerations and with increasing awareness of the power position of subordinates, a further problem arises which cannot be adequately encapsulated by limiting one's view to the power gap and to the equalization of power between superiors and subordinates, to the dismantling of political domination and to democratization within organizations. This is the problem of the *power relationships between subordinates*. If, in organizations, potential power shifts to a greater extent onto subordinates, the way they regulate their relationship with one another becomes all the more important. An increase in the power of the subordinates will spur them on to test out their power on one another. The superior gains a new function as a moderator in the power struggles of subordinates.[32] He then not only finds himself confronted with differences of opinion and the sensitivities of his subordinates but also with power differentials between them, based on structure or cliques which he cannot get rid of as such and in which he is one factor among others. The participation incumbent on the superior then has to take on the function of mediating in arguments and of equalizing power among the subordinates simultaneously – and the question is whether participation of that kind is suited to this function.

There is hardly any research into the components of power in the decision-making processes of large bureaucracies. The judgements of experts, however, help bring out the significance of how questions are formulated, and at the same time give the impression that a mainly negatively directed power of defence and obstruction prevails.[33] An overall 'yes' thus results as a sum total of the unwillingness to say 'no'. This effect would tend to be augmented by a policy of increasing the influence exercised by participation and interaction on the basis of personal proximity, by the capacity for concrete knowledge about the milieu, and by readiness to be sympathetic. From the perspective of a societal theory of power, such a development appears to be a far-reaching renunciation of the technicity of power as discussed above (Chapter 5) and of the formation of power chains which can respond to initiatives all down the line – and this in particular in the context of organizations! A most interesting study in the field of community politics in a US metropolitan city[34] shows how this reduction of power to mere veto power, caused by organizational decentralization, can be compensated for by means of informal arrangements and of diffuse structures for political influence, with the result that within such informal arrangements power then becomes once more politically calculable and controllable. Power develops, so to speak, in spite of organization. In this informal system of political influence, overcoming the difficulties which result from the formal structure ranks among the 'political costs' which may – but do not necessarily – prevent an action from taking place. Politics then thrives on this and at the same time suffers from the fact that power has reached the stage of sacrificing technical efficiency.

One must not underestimate the current effect of doctrine and of modes of thought on events in and research on organizations – especially concerning topics relating to power. A highly developed sensitivity to power which is based on and so legitimized by ideology prevents any exploration of the limits of the possible in practice and in scientific study.[35] In this too there are no independent foundations for empirical certainty. Notwithstanding this, it is possible to proceed from the fact that the findings of analysis indicate intrinsic barriers to increasing power in and through organizations. The barriers will become more detectable if one increases the interdependence of decisions in organizations and changes over from conditional programming to goal-directed programming. Power then acts less and less as a mechanism for transferring selections. This is not to deny that it is still possible to live among the ruins of excessively large organizations, particularly on the lower floors.

Faced with this power deficiency, the 'human relations' movement can be characterized as a search for other sources and forms of influence. However, one cannot sufficiently compensate for the shortcomings and limited achievements of a highly technical instrument like formal power with forms of communication and interaction which are less technical, more concretely focused, and more context-dependent. It will never be possible to create out of aggregations of influence, arising from intensified interaction, an equivalent for the organizational and societal achievements of technicalized, context-free, applicable and innovatively initiated power. The error of the 'human relations' movement lay in collapsing different levels of system formation and this error is faithfully repeated in the amalgamation of participation and democracy. If our conjecture that this will not work is correct, it becomes relatively unimportant whether it will be in the interests of control or in the interests of emancipation that it will not work.

Techniques can only be complete through techniques. Here we must think mainly of more or less developed techniques for quantification, data-processing and for statistical data-aggregation and control which can begin with measuring output, but also include demand and performance. With their help the informational resources of organization management can be improved. But this is not all. The connection between decisions about direction and mechanisms of selection transmission is loosened. The changes may relate to the production programme, to the organization of positions or to the personnel system with its criteria for aptitude, achievement and remuneration. For those affected, the changes bear no direct relation to their own previous conduct or to events occurring elsewhere. Rather they result from highly aggregated data. They do not result by way of sanction, which is not even threatened, and in no way do they take a form of avoidance alternative, whereby one holds back from putting into effect, if at all possible. They alter the parameters and decision-making premises for future action within the system as a result of levels of aspiration and actual states of affairs. Of course decisions concerning the system's policy contribute to the definition and assessment of such bases for judgement. Automatic control will never become logical automatism. More than ever we withhold any judgement about the 'rationality' of such forms of guidance. What the relevant technologies can achieve and learn cannot yet be assessed sociologically as they constitute unknown quantities so far as their societal significance is concerned. Nevertheless, possibilities do emerge at this point for reconstructing organizational power as the purely formal power of defining conditions of membership and of domesticating them in their own rule contexts. This would involve differentiating more clearly between the small world of interaction and the large world of organization, and playing the appropriate power game within each.

Notes

1 The model for this argument is to be found in Kant's theory of morality and law as conditions for the co-existence of the freedom of different subjects.

2 Thus Joannes Duns Scotus, *Ordinatio* I, dist. 39.

3 Thomas Aquinas, *Summa contra Gentiles* III, Chapter 86.

4 This view is found explicitly in Max Weber's amalgamation of the concepts of domination and administrative staff, domination and administration, domination and organization. See Weber (1948), pp. 29f., pp. 607ff. But one finds similar simplifications even in more recent analyses, for instance when Stinchcombe (1968), pp. 149ff., judges power channels in organizations from the point of view of chains of obedience and the penetration of the power-holder over intended effects on the action of the last link in the chain. For critical analyses, cf. especially Bendix (1945) and Schluchter (1972).

5 We must also note that money, as a medium specialized for exchange, is least sensitive to conversions and that barriers to protect the other media have to be institutionalized. As far as money is concerned there are initially no reasons why power or love or truth should not also be marketable. This shows that social systems with higher media differentiation at the same time tend to develop a functional primacy for economy. All the same, a closer analysis would very quickly show that any monetary influence over the difference between truth and untruth would destroy the basis for the monetary system itself.

6 We are, of course, here not disputing that there is a correlation between the economic situation and political participation of people, and above all we do not dispute that division into social classes demands such a correlation. At the same time, however, the code symbolism directed against convertibility is so heavily institutionalized that even scientists become angry about such correlations and call for counter measures, instead of taking them as a sign of order and enjoying them.

7 On this see also Luhmann (1973b), pp. 14ff.

8 Cf. particularly Commons (1932).

9 We cannot and, at this stage, do not wish to go into the extensive discussion of the problem of the actual power of property-owners within their 'own' organizational system. For a recent introduction to this problem see Pondy (1970).

10 See, as one such example, Sofer (1961).

11 Cf. under general power theory points of view, Abramson et al. (1958).

12 Analyses of the political problems of 'late capitalism' also point (unintentionally) in this direction; in these analyses the dimension 'private' remains characteristically pale and undeveloped, while the political indisposability of privately constituted organizational power becomes clearly pronounced. Cf. for example Offe (1972). The question is then whether this can differ in publicly constituted organizational power, if and as long as the motivation for joining and leaving is here also conditioned by money or by security defined by money.

13 Cf. Barnard (1938), pp. 139ff.; Simon (1957), pp. 71ff.

14 Cf. on this the differentiation between selection function and stimulation function in the promotion system – the negative power of sanction recedes as being politically unmentionable (?) – in Mayntz (1973).

15 Blau (1956), pp. 64ff., makes suggestions in this direction which aim at a lessening of power. On the other hand see Myers and Turnbull (1956). Cf. also Haritz (1974), pp. 24ff.

16 If personnel assessment is used as a power-spending avoidance alternative, this of course means that negative judgements must be avoided and must just be kept back as a possibility. This function of assessment, however, leads to distortion favouring positive assessments. Empirical research results are compatible with this, when they show that superiors are considered positively as critics (cf. Luhmann and Mayntz (1973), p. 224; Moths and Wulf-Mathies (1973), pp. 33f.) and that superiors give more positive personnel assessments than subordinates. Cf. Kamano et al. (1966).

17 'Control possibilities' can also be examined as limitations on the ability to express power through personal intervention, through being present, through participation in interaction systems. For such 'limits to personal power' see Bannester (1969), pp. 382f.

18 Research in organizational sociology partly leans towards explicitly recommending a tolerant, considerate style of leadership. Cf. inter alia Roethlisberger and Dickson (1939), pp. 449ff.; Gouldner (1954); Blau (1955), especially pp. 28ff., 167ff.; Blau and Scott (1962), pp. 140ff.; Schwartz (1964). Critical voices have, however, pointed out the uncertainty of these maxims; thus Dubin

(1961), especially pp. 403ff. Cf. also Dubin (1965), and empirical research (Kahn et al. (1964), pp. 161ff.) which shows that, with such a multiplication of reciprocities, life, at any rate, does not become easier but that tension and conflict increase.

19 Naschold (1969) and Hondrich (1972) also argue in this primarily economic perspective with further reference to 'increase in performance'.

20 See the criticism of Strauss (1963).

21 See Lammers' (1967) juxtaposing of direct (legitimate) and indirect (collectively organized) participation. An empirical comparison of the two forms of the power of subordinates would be extraordinarily difficult, especially if the extent of their interdependence is still unclarified and could vary with the constellation of persons involved.

22 'Elasticity' here is meant to relate to the problem discussed above of the power-holder's own decision chains. Collectivities have greater difficulty than individuals in revoking their opinions in moralized power questions; because of this they forget more quickly, especially in cases of high turnover in personnel.

23 Thus, for example, the influence of the human resources committee on matters in the public service is given a low estimation, and it is more frequently low, the higher the ranking. Cf. the results of this in Luhmann and Mayntz (1973) p. 226, pp. 253f. The result is particularly impressive if one compares it with the influence which is attached to their own superiors. See Luhmann and Mayntz (1973), pp. 223ff.

24 In a lecture on 'power' (January 1925). See Follett (1941), p. 111.

25 Cf. Schelsky's (1973) assessment of the results.

26 See especially Kaldor (1939) and Hicks (1939).

27 See above, Chapter 3, Note 47.

28 Cf. van Doorn (1962/3), especially pp. 161ff.; also the social-psychological research on tendencies in norm formation in reciprocal power situations quoted above (Chapter 1, Note 18).

29 For a critique of the zero-sum premise on the basis of such ideas, cf. for example Likert (1961), especially pp. 55ff., pp. 179ff.; Tannenbaum (1962), especially pp. 247ff.; Smith and Ari (1964).

30 On this see also Wolfe (1959), p. 100.

31 Suggested solutions along the lines of delimiting zones of influence appear occasionally in the literature. But is it pure chance that to make themselves plausible they employ examples from family life? Cf. for example Strauss (1963), pp. 59f.

32 The earlier idea of the superior as mediator in arguments when subordinates were in conflict (cf. for example Schmidt and Tannenbaum (1960)) proceeded from the higher power of the superior and limited itself accordingly to working out tactical recommendations in cases of conflict between the subordinates. The increasing Balkanization of organization and the approaching state in which there is no longer any work but only intrigue and fighting, brings quite different problems onto the scene.

33 See for example Dalton (1959); Sayre and Kaufman (1960), especially pp. 709ff.; Burns (1961); Gournay (1964); Zald (1970); Bosetzky (1972); or the critique of

'negative co-ordination' (which makes implicit reference to power problems) in Mayntz and Scharpf (1973); also Scharpf (1973), pp. 47ff.

34 Banfield (1961).

35 The experiment by Milgram (1965) has become famous precisely as an exception to this rule.

References

Abramson, E., Cutler, H. A., Kautz, R. W. and Mendelson, M. (1958) Social power and commitment: a theoretical statement. *American Sociological Review* 23, 15–22.

Adams, J. S. and Romney, A. K. (1959) A functional analysis of authority. *Psychological Review* 66, 234–51, revised under the title: The determinants of authority interactions, in N. F. Washburne (ed.), *Decisions, Values and Groups*, Vol. 2. Oxford, 1962, 227–56.

Andersen, K. and Clevenger, T. Jr. (1963) A summary of experimental research in ethos. *Speech Monographs* 30, 59–78, reprinted in K. Sereno and C. D. Mortensen (eds), *Foundations of Communication Theory*. New York, Evanston and London, 1970, 197–221.

Aquinas, T. (1863) *Summa contra Gentiles*. Paris.

Aquinas, T. (1942) *Aristotelis libri octo politicorum cum Commentariis*. Rome.

Arbeitsgruppe Bielefelder Soziologen (ed.) (1973) *Alltagswissen, Interaktion und gesellschaftliche Wirklichkeit*. 2 Vols. Reinbek.

Aristotle (1957) *Politica*. Ed. W. D. Ross. Oxford.

Aronson, E. and Golden, B. W. (1962) The effect of relevant and irrelevant aspects of communicator credibility on opinion change. *Journal of Personality* 30, 135–46.

Aronson, E., Turner, J. A. and Carlsmith, J. M. (1963) Communicator credibility and communication discrepancy as determinants of opinion change. *Journal of Abnormal and Social Psychology* 67, 31–6.

Arrow, K. J. (1963) *Social Choice and Individual Values*. 2nd edition. New York.

Asch, S. E. (1948) The doctrine of suggestion, prestige and imitation in social psychology. *Psychological Review* 55, 250–76.

Bachelard, G. (1938) *La Formation de l'esprit scientifique. Contribution à une psychanalyse de la connaissance objective*. Paris.

Bachelard, G. (1940) *La philosophie du non: Essai d'une philosophie du nouvel esprit scientifique*, Paris.

Bachrach, P. and Baratz, M. S. (1962) Two faces of power. *American Political Science Review* 56, 947–52.

Bachrach, P. and Baratz, M. S. (1963) Decisions and nondecisions: an analytical framework. *American Political Science Review* 57, 632–42.

Bachrach, P. and Baratz, M. S. (1970) *Power and Poverty: Theory and Practice.* New York.

Baldwin, D. A. (1971a) Money and power. *Journal of Politics* 33, 578–614.

Baldwin, D. A. (1971b) The power of positive sanctions. *World Politics* 24, 19–38.

Baldwin, D. A. (1971c) The costs of power. *Journal of Conflict of Resolution* 15, 145–55.

Banfield, E. C. (1961) *Political Influence.* New York.

Bannester, E. M. (1969) Sociodynamics: an integrative theorem of power, authority, interfluence and love. *American Sociological Review* 34, 374–93.

Barnard, C. I. (1938) *The Functions of the Executive.* Cambridge, MA.

Baum, B. H. (1961) *Decentralization of Authority in a Bureaucracy.* Englewood Cliffs, NJ.

Baum, R. C. (1976) On societal media dynamics: an exploration. In: J. J. Loubser, R. C. Baum, A. Effrat and V. Lidz (eds), *Explorations in General Theory in the Social Sciences.* New York.

Bendix, R. (1945) Bureaucracy and the problem of power. *Public Administration Review* 5, 194–209, reprinted in R. K. Merton, A. P. Gray, B. Hockey and H. C. Selvin (eds), *Reader in Bureaucracy*, Glencoe, IL, 1952.

Bensman, J. and Gerver, I. (1963) Crime and punishment in the factory: the function of deviance in maintaining the social system. *American Sociological Review* 28, 588–93.

Berger, P. L. and Kellner, H. (1965) Die Ehe und die Konstruktion der Wirklichkeit: Eine Abhandlung zur Mikrosoziologie des Wissens. *Soziale Welt* 16, 220–35.

Berger, P. L. and Luckmann, T. (1969) *The Social Construction of Reality: An Essay in the Sociology of Knowledge.* New York.

Blain, R. R. (1971) An alternative to Parsons's four function paradigm as a basis for developing general sociological theory. *American Sociological Review* 36, 678–92.

Blau, P. M. (1955) *The Dynamics of Bureaucracy.* Chicago.

Blau, P. M. (1956) *Bureaucracy in Modern Society.* New York.

Blau, P. M. (1962) Operationalizing a conceptual scheme: the universalism-particularism pattern variable. *American Sociological Review* 27, 159–69.

Blau, P. M. (1964) *Exchange and Power in Social Life.* New York.

Blau, P. M. and Scott, W. R. (1962) *Formal Organizations: A Comparative Approach.* San Francisco.

Blum, A. F. and McHugh, P. (1971) The social ascription of motives. *American Sociological Review* 36, 98–109.

Blumenberg, H. (1963) *Lebenswelt und Technisierung unter den Aspekten der Phänomenologie.* Turin.

Blumenberg, H. (1972) The life-world and the concept of reality. In: L. Embree (ed.), *Life World and Consciousness.* Evanston, IL, 425–44.

Bonoma, T. V., Tedeschi, J. T. and Lindskold, S. (1972) A note regarding an expected value model of social power. *Behavioral Science* 17, 221–8.

Bosetzky, H. (1972) Die instrumentelle Funktion der Beförderung. *Verwaltungsarchiv* 63, 372–84.

Bucher, R. (1970) Social process and power in a medical school. In: M. N. Zald (ed.), *Power in Organizations*. Nashville, TN, 3–48.

Buckley, W. (1967) *Sociology and Modern Systems Theory*. Englewood Cliffs, NJ.

Bünger, P. (1946) *Quellen zur Rechtsgeschichte der T'ang Zeit*. Peking.

Burke, K. (1961) *The Rhetoric of Religion*. Boston.

Burns, T. (1954) The direction of activity and communication in a departmental executive group. *Human Relations* 7, 73–97.

Burns, T. (1961) Micropolitics: mechanisms of institutional change. *Administrative Science Quarterly* 6, 257–81.

Calasso, F. (1951) *I glossatori e la teoria della sovranità: studio di diritto comune pubblico*. Milan.

Carlsmith, J. M. and Aronson, E. (1963) Some hedonic consequences of the confirmation and disconfirmation of expectancies. *Journal of Abnormal and Social Psychology* 66, 151–6.

Cartwright, D. and Zander, A. (1968) Power and influence groups. Introduction to *Group Dynamics: Research and Theory*. 3rd edition. New York, Evanston and London, 215–35.

Chazel, F. (1964) Réflexions sur la conception parsonienne du pouvoir et de l'influence. *Revue française de Sociologie* 5, 387–401.

Chenney, J., Harford, T. and Solomon, L. (1972) The effects of communicating threats and promises upon the bargaining process. *Journal of Conflict Resolution* 16, 99–107.

Claessens, D. (1965) Rationalität revidiert. *Kölner Zeitschrift für Soziologie und Sozialpsychologie* 17, 465–76, reprinted in Claessens, *Angst. Furcht und gesellschaftlicher Druck, und andere Aufsätze*, Dortmund, 1966, 116–24.

Clark, K. B. (1965) Problems of power and social change: toward a relevant social psychology. *Journal of Social Issues* 21:3, 4–20.

Clausen, L. (1972) Tausch. *Jahrbuch für Sozialwissenschaft* 23, 1–15.

Cohn, B. S. (1965) Anthropological notes on disputes and law in India. *American Anthropologist* 67, II, No. 6, 82–122.

Commons, J. R. (1932) *Legal Foundations of Capitalism*. New York.

Coser, L. A. (1967) *Continuities in the Study of Social Conflict*. New York.

Crozier, M. (1963) *Phénomène bureaucratique*. Paris.

Dahl, R. A. (1957) The concept of power. *Behavioral Science* 2, 201–15.

Dahl, R. A. (1968) Power. In: *Encyclopaedia of the Social Sciences*, Vol. 12. New York, 405–15.

Dalton, M. (1959) *Men Who Manage*. New York and London.

Danzger, M. H. (1964) Community power structure: problems and continuities. *American Sociological Review* 29, 707–17.

Deutsch, K. W. (1969) *Politische Kybernetik: Modelle und Perspektiven*. Freiburg im Breisgau.

Doorn, J. A. A. van (1962/3) Sociology and the problem of power. *Sociologia Neerlandica* 1, 3–51.

Douglas, M. (1966) *Purity and Pollution: An Analysis of the Concepts of Pollution and Taboo*. London.

Dubin, R. (1961) Psyche, sensitivity, and social structure. In: R. Tannenbaum, I. Weschler and F. Massarik (eds), *Leadership and Organization*. New York, 401–15.

Dubin, R. (1963) Power, function, and organization. *The Pacific Sociological Review* 6, 16–24.

Dubin, R. (1965) Supervision and productivity: empirical findings and theoretical considerations. In: Dubin et al. *Leadership and Productivity: Some Facts of Industrial Life*. San Francisco, 1–50.

Duyvendak, J. J. L. (1928) *The Book of Lord Shang: Classic of the Chinese School of Law*. London.

Eigen, M. (1971) Self-organization of matter and the evolution of biological macro-molecules. *Die Naturwissenschaften* 58, 465–523.

Eisenstadt, S. N. (1963) *The Political Systems of Empires*. New York and London.

Eisenstadt, S. N. (ed.) (1971) *Political Sociology: A Reader*. New York and London.

Elias, N. (1970) *What is Sociology?* London.

Emerson, M. (1962) Power dependence relations. *American Sociological Review* 27, 31–41.

Esmein, A. (1913) La maxime Princeps legibus solutus est dans l'ancien droit public français. In: Paul Vinogradoff (ed.), *Essays in Legal History*. Oxford, 102–14.

Evan, W. M. (1965) Superior–subordinate conflict in research organizations. *Administrative Science Quarterly* 10, 52–64.

Fanon, F. (1961) *Les Damnés de la Terre*. Paris.

Fisher, R. (1969) *International Conflict for Beginners*. New York, Evanston and London.

Follett, M. P. (1941) Power. In: H. C. Metcalf and L. Urwick (eds), *Dynamic Administration: The Collected Papers of Mary Parker Follett*. London and Southampton, 95–116.

French, J. R. P. and Snyder, R. (1959) Leadership and interpersonal power. In: D. Cartwright (ed.), *Studies in Social Power*. Ann Arbor, 118–49.

Fried, M. H. (1967) *The Evolution of Political Society*. New York.

Friedrich, C. J. (1941) *Constitutional Government and Democracy*. Boston.

Friedrich, C. J. (1958) Authority, reason, and discretion. In: *Authority (Nomos I)*. Cambridge, MA, 28–48.

Friedrich, C. J. (1963) *Man and His Government*. New York.

Gamson, W. A. (1968) *Power and Discontent*. Homewood, IL.

Garfinkel, M. and Sacks, H. (1970) On formal structures of practical actions. In: J. C. McKinney and E. A. Tiryakian (eds), *Theoretical Sociology: Perspectives and Developments*. New York, 327–66.

Gessner, V. (1974) *Recht und Konflikt: Eine soziologische Untersuchung privatrechtlicher Konflikte in Mexiko*. Tübingen.

Giddens, A. (1968) 'Power' in the recent writings of Talcott Parsons. *Sociology* 2, 257–72.

Goodman, N. (1965) *Fact, Fiction, and Forecast*. 2nd edition. Indianapolis.

Goody, J. (1973) Evolution and communication. *British Journal of Sociology* 24, 1–12.

Goody, J. and Watt, I. (1963) The consequences of literacy. *Comparative Studies in Society and History* 5, 304–45.

Gouldner, A. W. (1954) *Patterns of Industrial Bureaucracy*. Glencoe, IL.

Gouldner, A. W. (1971) *The Coming Crisis of Western Sociology*. London.

Gournay, B. (1964) Un groupe dirigeant de la société française: les grands fonctionnaires. *Revue Française de Science Politique* 14, 215–42.

Grunow, D. (1972) *Ausbildung und Sozialisation im Rahmen organisationstheoretischer Personalplanung*. Stuttgart.

Günther, G. (1959) *Idee und Grundriss einer nicht-Aristotelischen Logik*, Vol. I. Hamburg.

Günther, G. (1967) *Logik, Zeit, Emanation und Evolution*. Opladen.

Guest, R. H. (1962) *Organizational Change: The Effects of Successful Leadership*. Homewood, IL.

Guzmán, G., Borda, O. F. and Luna, E. U. (1962) *La Violencia en Colombia: Estudio de un proceso social*. Bogota.

Habermas, J. (1973) *Legitimation Crisis*. London.

Habermas, J. and Luhmann, N. (1971) *Theorie der Gesellschaft oder Sozialtechnologie – Was leistet die Systemforschung?* Frankfurt.

Hahm, P. (1967) *The Korean Political Tradition and Law*. Seoul.

Han Fei Tzu (1964) *Basic Writings*, translated by Burton Watson. New York and London.

Haritz, J. (1974) *Personalbeurteilung in der Öffentlichen Verwaltung* (doctoral dissertation). Bielefeld.

Harsanyi, J. C. (1962a) Measurement of social power, opportunity costs and the theory of two-person bargaining games. *Behavioral Science* 1, 67–80.

Harsanyi, J. C. (1962b) Measurement of social power in n-person reciprocal power situations. *Behavioral Science* 7, 81–91.

Heil, P. (1971/2) *Komplexität, Planung und Demokratie: Sozialwissenschaftliche Planungstheorien als Mittel der Komplexitätsreduktion und die Frage der Folgeprobleme*. Ms. Berlin.

Heller, H. (1933) Political Power. In: *Encyclopaedia of the Social Sciences*, Vol. 11. New York, 300–5.

Heydte, F. A. F. von der (1952) *Die Geburtsstunde des souveränen Staates*. Regensburg.

Hicks, J. R. (1939) The foundations of welfare economics. *Economic Journal* 49, 696–712.

Hinings, C. R., Hickson, D. J., Pennings, J. M. and Schneck, R. E. (1974) Structural Conditions of Intraorganizational Power. *Administrative Science Quarterly* 19, 22–44.

Hirsch-Weber, W. (1969) *Politik als Interessenkonflikt*. Stuttgart.

Hollander, E. P. (1960) Competence and conformity in the acceptance of influence. *Journal of Abnormal and Social Psychology* 61, 365–9.

Holm, K. (1969) Zum Begriff der Macht. *Kölner Zeitschrift für Soziologie und Sozialpsychologie* 21, 269–88.

Homans, G. C. (1964) Bringing men back in. *American Sociological Review* 29, 809–18.

Hondrich, K. O. (1972) *Demokratisierung und Leistungsgesellschaft*. Stuttgart.

Hovland, C. J., Janis, I. L. and Kelley, H. H. (1953) *Communication and Persuasion: Psychological Studies of Opinion Change*. New Haven.

Husserl, E. (1954) *Die Krisis der europäischen Wissenschaften und die transzendentale Phimomenologie*. Husserliana Vol. VI, The Hague.

Janda, K. F. (1960) Towards the explication of the concept of leadership in terms of the concept of power. *Human Relations* 13, 345–63.

Jessop, R. D. (1969) Exchange and power in structural analysis. *The Sociological Review* 17, 415–37.

Joannes Duns Scotus (1963) *Opera Omnia*, Vol. VI. Civitas Vaticana.

Jones, E. E. et al. (1971) *Attribution: Perceiving the Causes of Behavior.* Morristown, NJ.

Jordan, N. (1965) The asymmetry of liking and disliking: a phenomenon meriting further reflection and research. *Public Opinion Quarterly* 29, 315–22.

Kahn, R. L., Wolfe, D. M., Quinn, R. P. and Snoek, D. J. (1964) *Organizational Stress: Studies in Role Conflict and Ambiguity.* New York.

Kaldor, N. (1939) Welfare propositions in economics and interpersonal comparison of utility. *Economic Journal* 49, 549–52.

Kamano, D. K., Powell, B. J. and Martin, L. K. (1966) Relationships between ratings assigned to supervisors and their ratings of subordinates. *Psychological Reports* 18, 158.

Kanouse, D. E. and Hanson, L. R. Jr. (1971) Negativity in evaluations. In: E. E. Jones et al., *Attribution: Perceiving the Causes of Behavior.* Morristown, NJ, 47–62.

Kaplan, A. (1964) Power in perspective. In: R. L. Kahn and E. Boulding (eds), *Power and Conflict in Organisations.* London, 11–32.

Kawashima, T. (1968) The notion of law, right and social order in Japan. In: C. A. Moore (ed.), *The Status of the Individual in East and West.* Honolulu, 429–47.

Keisner, R. H. (1969) Affective reactions to expectancy disconfirmations under public and private conditions. *Journal of Personality and Social Psychology* 11, 17–24.

Kelley, G. A. (1958) Man's construction of his alternatives. In: Gardner Lindzey (ed.), *Assessment of Human Motives.* New York, 33–64.

Kelley, H. H. (1967) Attribution theory in social psychology. *Nebraska Symposium on Motivation,* 192–238.

Kelsen, H. (1960) Vom Geltungsgrund des Rechts. In: *Festschrift Alfred Verdross.* Vienna, 157–65.

Krause, H. (1952) *Kaiserrecht und Rezeption.* Heidelberg.

Krysmanski, H. J. (1971) *Soziologie des Konflikts.* Reinbek.

Kuhn, T. S. (1967) *Die Struktur wissenschaftlicher Revolutionen.* Frankfurt.

Lammers, C. L. (1967) Power and participation in decision making in formal organizations. *American Journal of Sociology* 73, 204–16.

Lazarus, R. S. (1968) Stress. In: *International Encyclopaedia of the Social Sciences,* Vol. 15. New York, 337–48.

Leach, E. R. (1964) Anthropological aspects of language: animal categories and verbal abuse. In: E. H. Lenneberg (ed.), *New Directions in the Study of Language.* Cambridge, MA, 23–63.

Lefcourt, H. M. (1966) Internal versus external control of reinforcement. *Psychological Bulletin* 65, 206–20.

Lehman, E. A. (1969) Toward a macrosociology of power. *American Sociological Review* 34, 453–65.

Lessnoff, M. H. (1968) Parsons's system problems. *The Sociological Review* 16, 185–215.

Lewis, G. C. (1849) *An Essay on the Influence of Authority in Matters of Opinion.* London.

Likert, R. (1961) *New Patterns of Management.* New York.

Lipp, W. (1972) Anomie, Handlungsmöglichkeit, Opportunismus: Grenzfragen der Systemtheorie. *Zeitschrift für die gesamte Staatswissenschaft* 128, 344–70.

Loh, W. (1972) *Kritik der Theorieproduktion von N. Luhmann und Ansätze für eine kybernetische Alternative.* Frankfurt.

Lovejoy, A. O. (1936) *The Great Chain of Being: A Study of the History of an Idea.* Cambridge, MA.

Luhmann, N. (1964) *Funktionen und Folgenformaler Organisation.* Berlin.

Luhmann, N. (1965) *Grundrechte als Institution.* Berlin.

Luhmann, N. (1969a) *Legitimation durch Verfahren.* Neuwied and Berlin.

Luhmann, N. (1969b) Klassische Theorie der Macht: Kritik ihrer Prämissen. *Zeitschrift für Politik* 16, 149–70.

Luhmann, N. (1970) *Soziologische Aufklärung: Aufsätze zur Theorie sozialer Systeme.* Opladen.

Luhmann, N. (1971a) *Politische Planung: Aufsätze zur Soziologie von Politik und Verwaltung.* Opladen.

Luhmann, N. (1971b) Sinn als Grundbegriff der Soziologie. In: Habermas and Luhmann (1971), 25–100.

Luhmann, N. (1972a) Knappheit, Geld und die bürgerliche Gesellschaft. *Jahrbuch für Sozialwissenschaft* 23, 186–210.

Luhmann, N. (1972b) *Rechtssoziologie.* Reinbek.

Luhmann, N. (1972c) Einfache Sozialsysteme. *Zeitschrift für Soziologie* 1, 51–65.

Luhmann, N. (1972d) Religiöse Dogmatik und gesellschaftliche Evolution. In: K.W. Dahm, N. Luhmann and D. Stoodt, *Religion, System und Sozialisation.* Neuwied and Darmstadt, 15–132.

Luhmann, N. (1973a) Die juristische Rechtsquellenlehre aus soziologischer Sicht. In: *Festschrift Rene König,* Opladen, 387–99.

Luhmann, N. (1973b) Politische Verfassungen im Kontext des Gesellschaftssystems. *Der Staat* 12, 1–22; 165–82.

Luhmann, N. (1973c) Zurechnung von Beförderungen im öffentlichen Dienst. *Zeitschrift für Soziologie* 2, 326–51.

Luhmann, N. (1974a) *Die Funktion des Rechts: Erwartungssicherung oder Verhaltenssteuerung?* In Supplement no. 8 of *Archivs für Rechts- und Sozialphilosophie,* Wiesbaden, 31–45.

Luhmann, N. (1974b) *Rechtssystem und Rechtsdogmatik.* Stuttgart, Berlin, Cologne and Mainz.

Luhmann, N. (1974c) Der politische Code: 'Konservativ' und 'progressiv' in systemtheoretischer Sicht. *Zeitschrift für Politik* 21, 253–71.

Luhmann, N. (1974d) Symbiotische Mechanismen. In: O. Rammstedt (ed.), *Gewaltverhältnisse und die Ohnmacht der Kritik.* Frankfurt am Main, 107–31.

Luhmann, N. (1976) Generalized media and the problem of contingency. In: J. J. Loubser, R. C. Baum, A. Effrat and V. Lidz (eds), *Explorations in General Theory in the Social Sciences,* vol. 2. New York, 507–32.

Luhmann, N. and Mayntz R. (1973) *Personal im Öffentlichen Dienst: Eintritt und Karrieren.* Baden-Baden.

Macaulay J. and Berkowitz, L. (eds) (1970) *Altruism and Helping Behavior: Social Psychological Studies of Some Antecedents and Consequences*. New York and London.

Maciejewski, F. (1972) Sinn, Reflexion und System: Über die vergessene Dialektik bei Niklas Luhmann. *Zeitschrift für Soziologie* 1, 138–55.

MacKay, D. (1969) *Information, Mechanisms and Meaning*. Cambridge, MA.

MacKay, D. M. (1972) Formal analysis of communicative processes. In: R. A. Hinde (ed.), *Non-verbal Communication*. Cambridge, 3–25.

McLeod, J. M. and Chaffee, S. R. (1972) The construction of social reality. In: J. T. Tedeschi, *The Social Influence Processes*. Chicago and New York, 50–99.

Maier, A. (1947) Diskussionen über das aktuell Unendliche in der ersten Hälfte des 14. Jahrhunderts. *Divus Thomas* 25, 147–66; 317–37.

Mannheim, K. (1927) Das konservative Denken: Soziologische Beiträge zum Werden des politisch-historischen Denkens in Deutschland. *Archiv for Sozialwissenschaft und Sozialpolitik* 57, 68–142; 470–95.

March, J. G. (1966) The power of power. In: D. Easton (ed.), *Varieties of Political Theory*. Englewood Cliffs, NJ, 39–70.

March, J. G. and Simon, H. A. (1958) *Organizations*. New York.

Marshall, L. (1961) Sharing, talking, and giving: relief of social tensions among the !Kung Bushmen. *Africa* 31, 231–49.

Maruyama, M. (1963) The second cybernetics: deviation-amplifying mutual causal processes, *General Systems* 8, 233–41.

Maselli, M. D. and Altrocchi, J. (1969) Attribution of intent. *Psychological Bulletin* 71, 445–54.

Massart, A. (1957) L'emploi, en égyptien, de deux termes opposés pour exprimer la totalité. In: *Mélanges bibliques* (Festschrift André Robert). Paris, 38–46.

Mayhew, L. (1971) *Society: Institutions and Activity*. Glenview, IL.

Mayhew, B. H. Jr. and Gray, L. N. (1969) Internal control relations in administrative hierarchies: a critique. *Administrative Science Quarterly* 14, 127–30.

Mayntz, R. (1973) Die Funktionen des Beförderungssystems im Öffentlichen Dienst. *Die Oifentliche Verwaltung* 26, 149–53.

Mayntz, R. and Scharpf, F. W. (eds) (1973) *Planungsorganisation: Die Diskussion um die Reform von Regierung und Verwaltung des Bundes*. Munich.

Mechanic, D. (1962) Sources of power of lower participants in complex organizations. *Administrative Science Quarterly* 7, 349–64.

Melden, A. I. (1961) *Free Action*. London.

Mey, H. (1972) *System und Wandel der gesellschaftlichen Integration*. Ms.

Meyer, W.-U. (1973) *Leistungsmotive und Ursachenerklärung von Erfolg und Mißerfolg*. Stuttgart.

Milgram, S. (1965) Some conditions of obedience and disobedience to authority. *Human Relations* 18, 57–76.

Miller, N., Butler, D. C. and McMartin, J. A. (1969) The ineffectiveness of punishment power in group interaction. *Sociometry* 32, 24–32.

Mitchell, W. C. (1967) *Sociological Analysis and Politics: The Theories of Talcott Parsons*. Englewood Cliffs, NJ.

Montesquieu C.-L. de (1941) *Cahiers 1716–1755*. Ed. Bernard Grasset. Paris.

Moore, S. F. (1972) Legal liability and evolutionary interpretation: some aspects of strict liability, self-help and collective responsibility. In: M. Gluckman (ed.), *The Allocation of Responsibility*. Manchester, 51–107.

Moths, E. and Wulf-Mathles, M. (1973) *Des Bürgers teure Diener*. Karlsruhe.

Mulder, M., Ritsema van Eck, J. R. and de Jong, R. D. (1971) An organization in crisis and non-crisis situations. *Human Relations* 24, 19–41.

Myers, C. A. and Turnbull, J. G. (1956) Line and staff in industrial relations. *Harvard Business Review* 34:4, 113–24.

Nagel, J. H. (1968) Some questions about the concept of power. *Behavioral Science* 13, 129–37.

Naschold, F. (1969) *Organisation und Demokratie: Untersuchungen zum Demokratisierungspotential in komplexen Organisationen*. Stuttgart, Berlin, Cologne and Mainz.

Neuendorff, H. (1973) *Der Begriff des Interesses: Eine Studie zu den Gesellschaftstheorien von Hobbes, Smith und Marx*. Frankfurt.

Oberndörfer, D. (1971) Demokratisierung von Organisationen? In: *Systemtheorie, Systemanalyse und Entwicklungsländerforschung*. Berlin, 577–607.

Offe, C. (1972) *Strukturprobleme des kapitalistischen Staates: Aufsätze zur Politischen Soziologie*. Frankfurt.

Parsons, T. (1951) *The Social System*. Glencoe, IL.

Parsons, T. (1960) Pattern variables revisited. *American Sociological Review* 25, 467–83, reprinted in Parsons (1967), 192–219.

Parsons, T. (1963a) On the concept of political power. *Proceedings of the American Philosophical Society* 107, 232–62, reprinted in Parsons (1967), 297–354.

Parsons, T. (1963b) On the concept of influence. *Public Opinion Quarterly* 21, 37–62.

Parsons, T. (1964a) Some reflections on the place of force in social process. In: H. Eckstein (ed.), *Internal War: Problems and Approaches*. New York and London, 33–70, reprinted in Parsons (1967), 264–96.

Parsons, T. (1964b) Die jüngsten Entwicklungen in der strukturell-funktionalen Theorie. *Kölner Zeitschrift für Soziologie und Sozialpsychologie* 16, 30–49.

Parsons, T. (1966) The political aspect of social structure and process. In: David Easton (ed.), *Varieties of Political Theory*. Englewood Cliffs, NJ, 71–112.

Parsons, T. (1967) *Sociological Theory and Modern Society*. New York.

Parsons, T. (1968) On the concept of value-commitments. *Sociological Inquiry* 38, 135–60.

Parsons, T. (1969) Polity and society. In: *Politics and Social Structure*. New York, 473–522.

Parsons, T. and Shils, E. A. (eds) (1951) *Toward a General Theory of Action*. Cambridge, MA.

Parsons, T., Bales, R. F. and Shils, E. A. (1953) *Working Papers in the Theory of Action*. Glencoe, IL.

Partridge, P. H. (1963) Some notes on the concept of power. *Political Studies* 11, 107–25.

Paterson, T. T. (1955) *Morale in War and Work*. London.

Patterson, G. and Reid, J. B. (1970) Reciprocity and coercion: two facets of social systems. In: C. Neuringer and J. L. Michael (eds), *Behavior Modification in Clinical Psychology*. New York, 133–77.

Peabody, R. L. (1964) *Organizational Authority: Superior-Subordinate Relationships in Three Public Service Organizations.* New York.

Pennings, J. M., Hickson, D. J., Hinings, C. R., Lee, C. A. and Schneck, R. E. (1969) Uncertainty and power in organizations. *Mens en Maatschappij* 25, 418–33.

Pondy, L. (1970) Toward a theory of internal resource-allocation. In: M. N. Zald (ed.), *Power in Organizations.* Nashville, TN, 270–311.

Popitz, H. (1968) *Prozesse der Machtbildung.* Tübingen.

Quaritsch, H. (1970) *Staat und Souveränität.* Frankfurt.

Rabe, H. (1972) Autorität. In: O. Brunner, W. Conze and R. Koselleck (eds), *Geschichtliche Grundbegriffe,* Vol. I. Stuttgart, 382–406.

Rammstedt, O. (1973) *Aspekte zum Gewaltproblem.* Ms. Zentrum für interdisziplinäre Forschung, Bielefeld.

Raven, B. H. (1965) Social influence and power. In: I. D. Steiner and M. Fishbein (eds), *Current Studies in Social Psychology.* New York, 371–82.

Raven, B. H. and Kruglanski, A. W. (1970) Conflict and Power. In: Paul Swingle (ed.), *The Structure of Conflict.* New York and London, 69–109.

Riggs, F. W. (1957) Agraria and industria. In: William J. Siffin (ed.), *Toward the Comparative Study of Public Administration.* Bloomington, IN, 23–116.

Riker, W. H. (1964) Some ambiguities in the notion of power. *American Political Science Review* 58, 341–9.

Ritter, J. (1957) *Hegel und die Französische Revolution.* Opladen.

Roethlisberger, F. J. and Dickson, W. J. (1939) *Management and the Worker.* Cambridge, MA.

Rokumoto, K. (1972, 1973) Problems and methodology of study of civil disputes. *Law in Japan* 5, 97–114; 6, 111–27.

Rose, A. M. (1967) *The Power Structure: Political Process in American Society.* New York.

Rostek, H. (1971) *Der rechtlich unverbindliche Befehl: Ein Beitrag zur Effektivitätskontrolle des Rechts.* Berlin.

Rubington, E. (1965) Organizational strains and key roles. *Administrative Science Quarterly* 9, 350–69.

Rushing, W. A. (1962) Social influence and the social-psychological function of deference: a study of psychiatric nursing. *Social Forces* 41, 142–8.

Sayre, W. S. and Kaufman, H. (1960) *Governing New York City: Politics in the Metropolis.* New York.

Scharpf, F. W. (1971) Planung als politischer Prozess. *Die Verwaltung* 4, 1–30.

Scharpf, F. W. (1973) *Politische Durchsetzbarkeit interner Reformen im Pluralistisch demokratischen Gemeinwesen der Bundesrepublik.* Ms. International Institute of Management, Berlin.

Schelsky, H. (1973) *Systemüberwindung, Demokratisierung und Gewaltenteilung: Grundsatzkonflikte der Bundesrepublik.* Munich.

Schermerhorn, R. A. (1961) *Society and Power.* New York.

Schluchter, W. (1972) *Aspekte bürokratischer Herrschaft: Studien zur Interpretation der fortschreitenden Industriegesellschaft.* Munich.

Schmitt, D. R. and Marwell, G. (1970) Reward and punishment as influence techniques for the achievement of cooperation under inequity. *Human Relations* 23, 37–45.

Schmidt, S. J. (1973) Texttheoretische Aspekte der Negation. *Zeitschrift für germanistische Linguistik* 1, 178–208.

Schmidt, W. H. and Tannenbaum, R. (1960) The management of differences. *Harvard Business Review* 38, 107–15.

Schwartz, M. (1964) The reciprocities multiplier: an empirical evaluation. *Administrative Science Quarterly* 9, 264–77.

Shelley, H. P. (1960) Focused leadership and cohesiveness in small groups. *Sociometry* 23, 209–16.

Sigrist, C. (1967) *Regulierte Anarchie: Untersuchungen zum Fehlen und zur Entstehung politischer Herrschaft in segmentieren Gesellschaften Afrikas.* Olten and Freiburg.

Simon, H. A. (1947) *Administrative Behavior.* New York.

Simon, H. A. (1957) Authority. In: C. M. Arensberg et al. (eds), *Research in Industrial Human Relations,* New York, 103–115.

Simon, H. A. (1969) *The Sciences of the Artificial.* Cambridge, MA.

Smith, C. G. and Ari, O. N. (1964) Organizational control structure and member consensus. *American Journal of Sociology,* 623–8.

Smith, M. G. (1960) *Government in Zazzau 1800–1950.* London.

Sofer, C. (1961) *The Organization From Within: A Comparative Study of Social Institutions Based on a Sociotherapeutic Approach.* London.

Sorel, Georges (1936) *Réflexions sur la Violence.* 8th edition. Paris.

Spaemann, R. (1963) *Reflexion und Spontaneität: Studien über Fénelon.* Stuttgart.

Spaemann, R. (1972) Moral und Gewalt. In: M. Riedel (ed.), *Zur Rehabilitierung der praktischen Philosophie,* Vol. 1. Freiburg, 215–41.

Sprenkel, S. van der (1962) *Legal Institutions in Manchu China: A Sociological Analysis.* London.

Stinchcombe, A. L. (1968) *Constructing Social Theories.* New York.

Strauss, G. (1963) Some notes on power equalization. In: H. J. Leavitt (ed.), *The Social Science of Organizations.* Englewood Cliffs, NJ, 39–84.

Tannenbaum, A. S. (1962) Control in organizations: individual adjustment and organizational performance. *Administrative Science Quarterly* 1, 236–57.

Tedeschi, J. T. (1970) Threats and promises. In: Paul Swingle (ed.), *The Structure of Conflict.* New York and London, 155–91.

Tedeschi, J. T. (ed.) (1972) *The Social Influence Processes.* Chicago and New York.

Tedeschi, J. T., Bonoma, T. V. and Brown, R. C. (1971) A paradigm for the study of coercive power. *Journal of Conflict Resolution* 15, 197–223.

Thibaut, J. (1968) The development of contractual norms in bargaining: replication and variation. *Journal of Conflict Resolution* 12, 102–12.

Thibaut, J. and Faucheux, C. (1965) The development of contractual norms in a bargaining situation under two types of stress. *Journal of Experimental Social Psychology* 1, 89–102.

Thibaut, J. and Gruder, C. L. (1969) Formation of contractual agreements between parties of unequal power. *Journal of Personality and Social Psychology* 11, 59–65.

Thibaut, J. and Kelley, H. H. (1959) *The Social Psychology of Groups.* New York.

Thibaut, J. and Riecken, H. W. (1955) Some determinants and consequences of the perception of social causality. *Journal of Personality* 24, 113–33.

Tierney, B. (1962–3): 'The Prince is not bound by the laws': Accursius and the origins of the modern state. *Comparative Studies in Society and History* 5, 378–400.

Turner, T. S. (1968) Parsons's concept of 'generalized media of social interaction' and its relevance for social anthropology. *Sociological Inquiry* 38, 121–34.

Vandermeersch, L. (1965) *La formation du légisme. Recherche sur la constitution d'une philosophie politique caractéristique de la Chine ancienne.* Paris.

Veit, W., Rabe, H. and Röttgers, K. (1971) Autorität. In: *Historisches Wörterbuch der Philosophie*, Vol. I, Basel and Stuttgart, 724–34.

Vickers, G. (1965) *The Art of Judgment: A Study of Policy Making.* London.

Waiter, E. V. (1964) Power and violence. *American Political Science Review* 58, 350–60.

Walter, B. (1966) Internal control relations in administrative hierarchies. *Administrative Science Quarterly* 11, 179–206.

Watzlawick, P., Beavin, J. H. and Jackson, D. D. (1967) *Pragmatics of Human Communication: A Study of Interactional Patterns, Pathologies, and Paradoxes.* New York.

Webber, R. A. (1970) Perceptions of interactions between superiors and subordinates. *Human Relations* 23, 235–48.

Weber, M. (1948) *Wirtschaft und Gesellschaft.* 3rd edition. Tübingen.

Weinrich, H. (1967) Linguistik des Widerspruchs. In: *To Honor Roman Jakobson: Essays on the Occasion of his Seventieth Birthday*, Vol. 3. The Hague and Paris, 2.212–2.218.

Weltz, F. (1964) *Vorgesetzte zwischen Management und Arbeitern.* Stuttgart.

Wolfe, D. M. (1959) Power and authority in the family. In: D. Cartwright (ed.), *Studies in Social Power.* Ann Arbor, 99–117.

Wrong, D. H. (1968) Some problems in defining social power. *American Journal of Sociology* 73, 673–81.

Yalman, N. (1962) On some binary categories in Sinhalese religious thought. *Transactions of the New York Academy of Sciences*, Ser. 2, 24, 408–20.

Zald, M. N. (ed.) (1970) *Power in Organizations.* Nashville, TN.

Zaleznik, A., Dalton, G. W. and Barnes, L. B. (1970) *Orientation and Conflict in Career.* Boston.

Appendix: Relevant Articles by Luhmann in English

(1974) Sociology of political systems. *German Political Studies* 1, 3–29.

(1976) A general theory of organized social systems. In: G. Hofstede and M. S. Kassem (eds), *European Contributions to Organization Theory*. Assen, 96–113.

(1976) The future cannot begin: temporal structures in modern society. *Social Research* 43:1, 130–52.

(1976) Generalized media and the problem of contingency. In: J. Loubser et al. (eds), *Explorations in General Theory in Social Science: Essays in Honour of Talcott Parsons*. New York, 507–23.

(1977) Differentiation of society. *Canadian Journal of Sociology* 2:2, 29–54.

(1978) Temporalization of complexity. In: R. F. Geyer and J. van der Zouwen (eds), *Sociocybernetics. An actor-oriented social systems approach*, Vol. 2. Leiden, Boston and London, 235–53.

(1981) The improbability of communication. *International Social Science Journal*, 23, 38–45. Reprinted in N. Luhmann, *Essays in Self-Reference*. New York and Oxford, 1990.

(1985) Complexity and meaning. In: *The Science and Praxis of Complexity*. Tokyo, 99–104. Reprinted in N. Luhmann, *Essays in Self-Reference*. New York and Oxford, 1990.

(1988) Familiarity, confidence, trust: problems and alternatives. In: D. Gambetta (ed.), *Trust: Making and Breaking Cooperative Relations*. Oxford, 94–107.